ODDBALL MICHIGAN

ODDBALL MICHIGAN

A Guide to 450 Really
STRANGE PLACES

JEROME POHLEN

CHICAGO
REVIEW
PRESS

Published by Chicago Review Press, Incorporated
814 North Franklin Street
Chicago, Illinois 60610

ISBN 978-1-61374-893-0

The author has made every effort to secure permissions for all the material in this book. If any acknowledgment has inadvertently been omitted, please contact the author.

Cover and interior design: Jonathan Hahn
Map design: Chris Erichsen
Cover photograph: Courtesy Tom Lakenen, Lakenenland
All photographs courtesy of Jerome Pohlen unless otherwise noted.

Library of Congress Cataloging-in-Publication Data
Pohlen, Jerome.
  Oddball Michigan : a guide to 450 really strange places / Jerome Pohlen.
    pages cm. — (Oddball series)
  Includes index.
  ISBN 978-1-61374-893-0 (pbk.)
  1. Michigan—Guidebooks. 2. Curiosities and wonders—Michigan—Guidebooks.
3. Michigan—History, Local—Miscellanea. I. Title.

F564.3.P65 2014
977.4—dc23
                          2013043882

FOR
MARY ANN,
MIKE, AND COLE

Contents

INtRODUCtiON

Si quaeris peninsulam mirum, circumspice.
If you seek a strange peninsula, look about you.
—MICHIGAN'S UNOFFICIAL MOTTO

*M*ichigan's destiny as a weird state was probably determined by none other than Thomas Jefferson while coming up with ways to divide and name the Northwest Territory. For the southern half of the lower peninsula he chose Metropotamia, and for the northern half, Chersonesus; the Upper Peninsula would be called Sylvania. And though mapmakers eventually settled instead on Michigan, derived from the Chippewa word *majigan*, meaning "large clearing," or perhaps *misshikama*, Ojibwe for "big lake," the die was set. Michigan would be unique. Michigan would be different. Michigan would be odd.

How odd? Where else in the United States will you find museums dedicated to pipes, agates, pop bottles, nun dolls, celery, the US Postal Service, and the ice-harvesting industry? Monuments to fluoridation, snurfing, the designer of the Jefferson nickel, and the once-famous Mr. Chicken? Or festivals honoring tulips, Christmas pickles, blueberries, and a 38-acre fungus? Michigan! And where will you find the World's Largest Cherry Pie Tin? A doughnut shop owned by the town's police department? A restaurant known far and wide for its delicious, tender gizzards? Michigan, Michigan, Michigan, home to not one but *two* different three-landing bridges . . . or as they call them, tridges.

The Great Lakes State has also been the location of strange historical events that you're probably already familiar with, but never knew happened here. It's where Harry Houdini perished on Halloween and the Flying Wallendas became the Falling Wallendas. It's where ice skater Nancy Kerrigan got whacked and Jimmy Hoffa got *really* whacked. It's where James Jesse

Strang crowned himself king in 1850, where Paul Bunyan was "born" in 1906, and where Elvis was spotted a decade after his death. *Four times.*

Don't get me wrong, there's plenty to see in the state that isn't weird, hilarious, or borderline disturbing. Every time I see one of those "Pure Michigan" commercials I want to relax on a dune and watch the sun set over Lake Michigan. But I inevitably end up distracted by the big lugnut atop a Lansing smokestack, the Lunkquarium in Edwardsburg, and the Man-Eating Clam in Cheboygan. Because let's face it, you can see a sunset from your backyard, but if you want to see Thomas Edison's last breath, you have to come to Michigan.

While I've tried to give clear directions from major streets and landmarks, you could still make a wrong turn, particularly with those damn "Michigan lefts." Don't panic. Remember these Oddball travel tips:

1. **Stop and ask!** For a lot of communities, their Oddball attraction might be their only claim to fame. Locals are often thrilled that you'd drive out of your way to marvel at their underappreciated shrine. But be careful who you ask; old cranks at the town café are good for information, but teenage clerks at the Gas N Go are not.
2. **Call ahead.** Few Oddball sites keep regular hours, but most will gladly wait around if they know you're coming. Michigan is a seasonal travel state, especially in the Upper Peninsula (UP), and sites can be closed for the winter at a moment's notice. And in the UP, September can be winter. Always call ahead.
3. **Don't give up.** Think of the person who's sitting in a tiny museum dedicated to an obscure topic, and know that they're waiting just for *you*. (Actually, they're waiting for *anyone* . . . so you'll do.)
4. **Don't trespass!** Don't become a Terrible Tourist. Just because somebody built a sculpture garden in their front yard doesn't mean they're looking for chatty visitors.

Do you have an Oddball site of your own? Have I missed anything? Do you know of an Oddball site that should be included in an updated version? Please write and let me know: Chicago Review Press, 814 N. Franklin Street, Chicago, IL 60610.

ODDBALL MICHIGAN

UPPER PENINSULA

Something happens when you drive north across the Mackinac Bridge into Michigan's Upper Peninsula, or UP as it's referred to in shorthand. The trees get a little denser, the service gets a little slower, and the backwoods drawls get a little thicker. It's almost as if you've entered a different state, and certainly a different state of mind.

In fact, the UP might never have been a part of Michigan. Back when Michigan was a territory hoping to become the nation's newest state, there was a border dispute over the so-called Toledo Strip; two early maps drew the southern boundary at different parallels. (Ohio had the better argument—it had been a US state with an established border since 1803.) Between 1835 and 1837, both Ohio and Michigan sent militias to the area to assert their claims. The *Toledo Gazette* sniffed that the Michigan militia was "composed of the lowest and most miserable dregs of the community . . . low drunken frequenters of grog shops, who had been hired at a dollar a day," and events bore that out. The so-called "Toledo War" turned into a series of shoving matches and liquor-fueled brawls, but nobody was ever killed defending Toledo. Which seems right.

Finally, President Andrew Jackson brokered a deal. In exchange for ceding its claims to the Toledo Strip, Michigan was given statehood and three-quarters of the Upper Peninsula, which was then part of the Wisconsin Territory. On January 26, 1837, Michigan became the 26th state in the union.

But not everyone was, or is, happy about the deal. In 1978 a bill was introduced to the Michigan state legislature by Rep. Dominic Jacobetti making the Upper Peninsula its own state: Superior. Perhaps because of concern that Toledo might be forced back upon Michiganders, the bill failed.

Bessemer

Big Skier and Bigger Hill

It's hard to miss the large fiberglass skier in a very unstylish red coat, tan ski pants, and Roy Orbison sunglasses that marks the turnoff to Big Powderhorn Mountain northwest of Bessemer. His skis are barely as long as the bunny hill he stands on—can't somebody find him a more size-appropriate slope?

As a matter of fact, there is one, just up the road from Big Powderhorn Mountain. At 170 meters tall—that's 50 meters *taller* than a regulation Olympic ski jump—Copper Peak holds the record for the world's largest ski flying hill. Some have nicknamed it the "Eiffel Tower of the UP," though it is only half the height of the Paris landmark.

Ski flying competitions are held at Copper Peak in the winter, but unless you're an idiot with a death wish, you should only ascend the tower during the summer. To get to the top, ride the chairlift 36 stories from the base of the landing hill to the base of the tower, then take the elevator another 18 stories to the upper platform. If you want to go even higher—and at this point, why stop?—climb the steps alongside the jump for another eight

He's almost as big as the mountains in these parts.

stories to the tippy, tippy, tippy top. From here, you'll be able to see the far shore of Lake Superior 85 miles away. The ground below looks just as far.

Big Powderhorn Mountain, N11375 Powderhorn Rd., Bessemer, MI 49911
Phone: (800) 501-7669 or (906) 932-4838
Hours: Always visible
Cost: Free
Website: www.bigpowderhorn.net
Directions: Where Rte. 2 meets Powderhorn Rd.

Copper Peak, Black River Rd., PO Box 159, Ironwood, MI 49938
Phone: (906) 932-3500
Hours: June–August, Wednesday–Sunday 10 AM–4:30 PM
Cost: Adults $15, Kids (14 and under) $7
Website: www.copperpeak.org
Directions: Take Powderhorn Rd. north to Black River Rd., then continue north on Black River Harbor Pkwy.; Copper Peak is hard to miss.

Bete Grise
Singing Sands Beach

Ah, to be serenaded at the beach . . . or better yet, to be serenaded *by* the beach! If you're willing to make the trip to this secluded stretch of sand along the shore of Bete Grise Bay, the earth will sing you the lullaby of "Gitche Gumee." All you have to do is place your palm on the sand, push down, and rotate.

Now some will say this is just a natural, explainable phenomenon unique to the geologic composition of the sand in this area, but those are the same folks who would call a sunset a refraction of solar light through the earth's atmosphere. Exactly: unsentimental nerds. One thing they can't seem to explain is why, if you take home a jar of this stuff, it will no longer make the same sound.

Bete Grise Beach, Bete Grise Rd., Bete Grise, MI 49950
No phone
Hours: Daylight hours
Cost: Free
Website: www.betegrisepreserve.org/Stewards_of_Bete_Grise_Preserve/Home.html
Directions: South of Rte. 41, follow Lac La Belle Rd./Bete Gris Rd. to its southeastern terminus.

Big Bay
Anatomy of a Murder

On July 31, 1952, Lieutenant Coleman Peterson walked into the Lumberjack Tavern in Big Bay and shot the owner, Mike Chenoweth, six times. Peterson claimed Chenoweth had raped his wife after he had given her a ride to the couple's trailer park in Michigamme. Tried for murder, Peterson was found not guilty by reason of temporary insanity. The defense attorney at the trial, John Voelker, fictionalized the story as *Anatomy of a Murder* under the pen name Robert Traver.

The book soon caught the attention of director Otto Preminger, who filmed his 1959 noir classic of the same name in and around the UP. It starred Jimmy Stewart as the defense lawyer, Ben Gazzara as the murderer, Lee Remick as the murderer's wife, and George C. Scott as the assistant state's attorney general. Stop by the **Ishpeming Public Library** (317 N. Main St., (906) 486-4381, www.uproc.lib.mi.us/ish/) and you can pick up a list of shooting locations, from both the actual murder and the movie re-creation. The library itself doubled as the film's law library. Trial and jailhouse scenes were shot at the **Marquette County Courthouse** (234 W. Baraga Ave., (906) 228-9691, www.co.marquette.mi.us/courthouse_complex.htm) in Marquette. Barney Quill, the unfortunate bartender in the film, was killed in the **Thunder Bay Inn** (400 Bensinger St., (906) 345-9220, http://thunderbayinn.net) in Big Bay, though the exterior shown was of the Tripoli Bar (closed) in Ishpeming. Depending how deep you want to go in your investigation, you can also visit the train depot, lunch counter, trailer park, and more from this famous case/film.

Of course, most people just go to the original Lumberjack Tavern where they've painted the movie poster's chalk outline on the floor, and where they will gladly point you to the bullet holes from Peterson's very real gun. Just don't make any passes at anyone's spouse.

202 Bensinger St., Big Bay, MI 49808
Phone: (906) 345-9912
Hours: Daily noon–2 AM
Cost: Free
Website: www.lumberjacktavern.com
Directions: Just before the Dump Rd. intersection at Bensinger St., at the bay.

Calumet

International Frisbee Hall of Fame

The International Frisbee Hall of Fame is not an entirely accurate name for this establishment—it should be called the International *Guts* Frisbee Hall of Fame. And what is "Guts Frisbee"? Essentially dodgeball played with a Frisbee.

The game was invented by brothers Bob and John "Boots" Healy on July 4, 1958, while at a picnic in nearby Eagle Harbor. The rules are simple: two teams of five players stand 15 yards apart and one player chucks a Frisbee as hard as he or she can at the opposing team. If the throw is catchable, but not caught, the thrower's team earns a point. If it is caught (with one hand), no point is scored. The catcher then heaves it back at the original team, and play continues until one team scores 21 points. Pretty simple. And often painful.

Guts Frisbee calls itself "The Original Extreme Sport," though it has hardly caught on at national levels. If you want to honor great players, you have to come to the Colosseum in Calumet, which looks more like an old fieldhouse, not the shrine at Cooperstown.

The Colosseum, 110 Red Jacket Rd., Calumet, MI 49913
Phone: (906) 337-2507
Hours: Call ahead
Cost: Free
Website: www.usgpa.com and www.gutsfrisbee.com
Directions: Two blocks west of Rte. 41 (Calumet Ave.) on Red Jacket Rd.

Italian Hall Stampede

Like so many labor struggles in Michigan history, the 1913–14 Copper Country strike was marred by violence, but this time it was mostly children who died. The Western Federation of Miners (WFM) organized the strike, which started in July 1913 and affected most of the mines in the region. The miners were asking for better wages and improved safety measures—in 1911 alone, 63 men had been killed in mining accidents in Copper Country. The walkout tore the community apart, with some residents joining the pro-business Citizens Alliance.

Five months into the strike, union families were struggling, so in an effort to cheer up their children, a holiday celebration was organized for Christmas Eve at Calumet's Italian Hall. Estimates say 175 adults and 500 kids crammed into the second-floor auditorium. During the event, a man in a black trenchcoat with a hat pulled low over his eyes (and, some said, a Citizens Alliance lapel pin) walked in and yelled, "Fire!" The crowd rushed down a flight of stairs toward the only exit and piled up against the doors, which opened inward. The stampede killed 73, and 59 of the dead were children. There was no fire.

The instigator was never found. The tragedy ultimately broke the will of the strikers, who returned to the mines in April, having gained few concessions. Woody Guthrie wrote a song about the events titled "1913 Massacre," one of the few memorials to the dead. In 1984 the crumbling Italian Hall was razed, though some thoughtful citizens saved the building's archway. It was later rebuilt in a park at the site. You can learn more about the strike and stampede at the nearby national park museum, where some of the hall's wooden folding chairs are on display.

Italian Hall Memorial Park, 401 Seventh St., Calumet, MI 49913
No phone
Hours: Always visible
Cost: Free
Directions: One block west of Sixth St. on Elm St.

Keweenaw National Historical Park Headquarters, Calumet Unit, 98 Fifth St., Calumet, MI 49913
Phone: (906) 337-3168
Hours: June–September, Monday–Saturday 9 AM–5 PM; October–May, hours vary (call ahead)
Cost: Free
Website: www.nps.gov/kewe/
Directions: Where Red Jacket Rd. turns to become Fifth St.

Caspian
Monigal Logging Miniatures

William Monigal was injured in a logging accident in 1931, but rather than begrudge his chosen profession, he decided to create a $1/_{12}$-scale model of a lumbering operation, from forest to finished two-by-fours. It took him about eight years to carve the 2,000 miniatures and tiny buildings used in

Giant not to scale.
Photo by author, courtesy Iron
County Historical Museum

the snow-covered diorama. One can assume the whole operation is faithfully portrayed, with the exception of the Paul Bunyan figure standing in the center of camp. There are also no maimed loggers, like Mr. Monigal.

The diorama is just a *tiny* portion of what you'll find at this sprawling museum complex. You'll feel like a rat in a maze as you wind from room to room through narrow passageways and cluttered display cases filled with old typewriters, artillery for World War I, Victorian women's hats, local artwork, unrecognizable tools and utensils, old-fashioned diving suits, and a totem of a large monkey in a bellman's hat holding a banana. Did anyone in Caspian ever throw anything out?

Nope! Outside, the larger complex covers 10 *acres* and has two art galleries and 26 relocated buildings—a pioneer school, a tavern, an old homestead, a sleigh shed, a sauna, and the old St. Mary's Church. Be sure to wear comfortable shoes if you plan to see it all.

Iron County Historical Museum, 100 Brady Ave., PO Box 272, Caspian, MI 49915

Phone: (906) 265-2617

Hours: May–August, Monday–Saturday 10 AM–4 PM; September, Monday–Saturday noon–4 PM; October–April, by appointment only

Cost: Adults $8, Seniors (65+) $7, Kids (5–18) $3

Website: www.ironcountyhistoricalmuseum.org

Directions: East off Rte. 424 on Spring Valley Ave., two blocks to Brady Ave., then north one block.

Crystal Falls
Humungus Fungus

It's 1,500 years old, weighs 111 tons, and covers 38 acres. And it's *ALIVE*!! Yet this single *Armillaria bulbosa* fungus is difficult to identify because most of it is below the soil's surface. Occasionally it sprouts up button mushrooms here and there to take a look around, but when these "fruiting bodies" die back, the Humungus Fungus (the local spelling) stays hidden for another season. At its current growth rate, it could expand as far as Milwaukee . . . it'll just take 1.6 million years. You'd move that slowly, too, if you were born in 514 AD.

For many years biologists thought this thing was the world's largest living organism, but then a much larger fungus was discovered in Washington state. The exact location of the Michigan fungus is a tightly guarded secret, but if you find yourself in the woods south of town, surrounded by mushrooms, you just might be standing on it.

If you're interested, Crystal Falls does hold a Humungus Fungus Fest (www.humungusfungusfest.com) each August. Organizers cook a 10-foot-diameter pizza covered in mushrooms, which seems a rather cruel way to honor their most famous citizen.

Rte. 2, Crystal Falls, MI 49920
No phone
Hours: Visible in summer
Cost: Free
Website: www.crystalfalls.org/humongou.htm
Directions: "South of town near the Wisconsin border."

Daggett
Udder-Flashing Cow

Flying along US Highway 41 south of Daggett you might be shocked when you spot a cow with cherry-red lipstick raising her blue dress to flash her udder at passing vehicles. Whatever you do, don't throw any beads—it just encourages that sort of unseemly behavior.

The painted fiberglass statue is just part of what's going on at Tom Wangerin Excavating. There's also a statue of a giant hotdog squirting ketchup

Don't throw beads—it just encourages her.

on his head, two bright purple grain silos, and a miniature Little Cedar River Railroad that loops an artificial pond. None of it is open to the public but instead serves as a jovial advertisement for Tom's excavation business.

Tom Wangerin Excavating, N9273 US Hwy. 41, Daggett, MI 49821

Phone: (906) 753-4415

Hours: Always visible; view from road

Cost: Free

Website: www.wangerinexcavating.com

Directions: On Rte. 41 at the south end of town.

Gladstone
Pet Caskets

As a pet owner, it never hurts to plan ahead. Understanding that Fluffy burns up seven years of life for every one of yours, you should probably expect her to head for that big doghouse in the sky before you do. Shouldn't she go out in style?

As the Hoegh Pet Casket Company reminds us, "People bury people because they have to. People bury pets because they want to." And if *you* want to, Hoegh offers a modest selection of coffins for your pet burial needs—seven sizes in a variety of colors, even camo, all tastefully displayed in the company's Gladstone showroom. And out back in the model cemetery you can see how Hoegh's photo-metal headstones withstand the elements . . . better than Fluffy, apparently! (The minicaskets can also be used for amputated limbs.)

If they can't sell you a coffin on compassion alone, the folks here want to remind you of two important points, one legal and one theological: "Burying pets in the backyard is against the law," and "If Christ had a dog, he would have followed Him to the cross." Think about it.

311 Delta Ave., PO Box 311, Gladstone, MI 48837
Phone: (906) 428-2151
Hours: Monday–Friday 8:30 AM–3 PM
Cost: Free
Website: www.hoeghpetcaskets.com
Directions: Railway Ave. east to Superior Ave., east to Delta Ave.

Grand Marais
Gitche Gumee Agate and History Museum

If you like rocks—I mean *really* like rocks—you need to make the trek to this small museum. Where a big-city natural history museum might have a larger collection with more impressive specimens, the Gitche Gumee Agate and History Museum captures the love of geology as told by three generations of rock hounds.

Axel Niemi founded the place in his home in 1954, where he would sing and tell stories about his rock finds for visitors. In 1990 Niemi sold the place to Ronald Marshall, who years earlier Niemi had taught to play cribbage. And finally, in 1998, Marshall sold it to Karen Ann Brzys. The pair had shared a bond after Brzys wrote a poem about the museum titled "Perspective."

Brzys refurbished the building and combined her many years' worth of rocks and minerals to make the impressive collection you see today. Browse the display cases, ask as many questions as you have, or better yet, bring your own rock finds and Brzys will help you identify them.

E21739 Brazel St., PO Box 308, Grand Marais, MI 49839

Phone: (906) 494-3000 or (906) 494-2590

Hours: May–June & September, Sunday–Friday 2–5 PM, Saturday noon–5 PM; July, Monday–Saturday Noon–7 PM, Sunday 2–5 PM

Cost: Adults $1, Kids (17 and under) Free

Website: http://agatelady.com

Directions: One block north of Carlson St., two blocks west of M-77.

Teenie Weenie Pickle Barrel Cottage

Starting in 1914 and continuing until the mid-1960s, a comic strip called "The Teenie Weenies" graced the funny pages of newspapers nationwide. It was about a family of tiny people who lived beneath a rose bush, inside a pickle barrel. The Teenie Weenies were also the spokescartoons for the Monarch Pickle Company of Chicago. Evidently, somebody felt that the pickles resembled Teenie Weenies, or vice versa.

The popular strip was drawn by William Donahey. In 1926, Monarch built Donahey a summer cottage on Sable Lake near Grand Marais as a gesture of appreciation. The building, designed by the Pioneer Cooperage Company, had three rooms: a ground floor living area, a second-story bedroom, and a kitchen (a smaller barrel) attached at the rear. When Donahey was given the keys to his big barrel bungalow, the entire town joined in the media hoopla. Local children dressed up as little people for the big celebration, making Donahey feel like Dorothy dropping in from Kansas, minus the dead witch.

Well, it didn't last forever. Donahey must have felt there was no place like home, clicked his heels, and stopped going to Grand Marais after 1937. The cottage was then dragged into town to be used as an ice cream stand,

The people were Teenie Weenies, but the barrel was full-size.

and then a souvenir hut. After falling into disrepair, it was converted into a senior citizens lodge/tourist information center in 1970. The local historical society returned it to its former glory in 2005, and it is now a museum surrounded by a beautiful iris garden (https://sites.google.com /site/picklebarrelhouseirisgarden/).

Grand Marais Historical Society, Pickle Barrel House Museum, Lake Ave. & Randolph St., Grand Marais, MI 49883

Phone: (906) 494-2404

Hours: July–August, daily 1–4 PM; June and September, Saturday–Sunday 1–4 PM; or by appointment

Cost: Free

Website: http://historicalsociety.grandmaraismichigan.com/

Directions: On M-77 (Lake Ave.) one block south of Carlson St. (County Rd. 58).

Hancock
Big Louie

Louis "Big Louie" Moilanen was just four years old when his family immigrated to the United States from Finland. Like most strapping farm boys, he grew taller as he grew older, but unlike most boys, he didn't stop growing until he was 8 feet, 3 inches tall. At the time, he was the tallest person in the world.

As a young man, Moilanen worked in the Franklin Copper Mine before signing with the Ringling Brothers Circus as the Copper Country Giant. He toured for two years before returning to his hometown of Hancock to work as a bartender. Moilanen would also become the town's justice of the peace, since nobody wanted to mess with a bona fide giant.

Moilanen died of tubercular meningitis on September 16, 1913, at the age of 27. His 560-pound body was laid to rest in the Waasa Cemetery north of town. And he would be all but forgotten today were it not for a new monument outside the Finnish American Heritage Center. They've erected an 8-foot, 3-inch tall block of black granite outside the building with a plaque that bears Big Louie's likeness. Stand beside it and see how you would have measured up.

Finnish American Heritage Center, 435 Quincy St., Hancock, MI 49930
Phone: (906) 487-7302
Hours: Monday–Friday 8 AM–4:30 PM
Cost: Free
Website: www.finlandia.edu/FAHC.html
Directions: On Rte. 41 (Quincy St.) at Montezuma St.

Waasa Cemetery, Waasa Rd., Hancock, MI 49930
No phone
Hours: Daylight hours
Cost: Free
Directions: Between Salo and Pontiac Rds. on County Rd. H-14 (Waasa Rd.).

Ironwood
World's Largest Hiawatha

Years ago, the Ironwood Chamber of Commerce was looking for a way to draw more tourists to the area and thought a tribute to Hiawatha might

Very High-a-watha.

work. After all, folks loved Henry Wadsworth Longfellow's epic poem, *The Song of Hiawatha*, or at the least the folks who knew nothing about Native American history or culture. Hiawatha was actually a co-founder of the Iroquois Confederacy and a member of the Onondaga tribe of present-day upstate New York, not the Ojibwe people of this region. No matter, this was 1964, and an Indian was an Indian was an Indian.

The Chamber ordered a 52-foot, 9-ton, fiberglass statue and erected it on a hill overlooking Ironwood. To further confuse the issue, Hiawatha is dressed in neither the traditional garb of the Chippewa nor of the Onondaga, but that of a Plains Indian with a large feather headdress. He cradles a peace pipe in his left hand, raised to the elbow of his right arm. The sculptor claimed this was a traditional sign of peace, but with very little imagination he could be preparing to grasp his biceps and raise his right forearm—the Italian *gesto dell'ombrello* or the French *bras d'honneur*—to give a bold FU to the city. You can make up your own mind which.

Hiawatha Park, Houk St. and Burma Rd., Ironwood, MI 49938
Phone: (906) 932-1122
Hours: Always visible
Cost: Free
Website: www.cityofironwood.org/?111490000000
Directions: Seven blocks south of Aurora St. at the end of Burma Rd.

If you insist on perpetuating Longfellow's phony poetic tale, you can also visit Upper Tahquamenon Falls (mentioned in the poem) in Michigan's UP. At 200 feet wide and 50 feet tall, it is the second largest waterfall east of the Mississippi River, behind only Niagara Falls. During the spring snowmelt, about 50,000 gallons of tea-brown water rolls over the precipice each second.

Tahquamenon Falls State Park, Upper Falls, 41382 W. M-123, Paradise, MI 49768
Phone: (906) 492-3415
Hours: Always open
Cost: State Recreation Passport (In-state); $8.40/car (Out-of-state)
Website: www.michigan.gov/tahquamenonfalls
Directions: At the west end of Tahquamenon Falls State Park on M-123.

World's Largest Stormy Kromer Cap

Yoopers are nothing if not resourceful. But stylish? Not so much. Take the example of railroad engineer George "Stormy" Kromer. This Kaukauna native kept losing baseball caps whenever he stuck his head out the window of his locomotive to see where he was going. Not to mention, it was

Calling all Fudds!

cold. So in 1903 he asked his wife Ida to sew ear flaps onto a cap, shorten the brim, and add a string to tighten it around the band. The Stormy Kromer was born! (The couple first called it the Blizzard, but eventually it was renamed for the guy who came up with the idea.)

For years, Stormy Kromers could be seen on everyone from Elmer Fudd to Ed Gein, but the company almost went out of business in 2001. Businessman Bob Jacquart came to the brand's rescue, which is why they're still manufactured in the USA—Ironwood, to be more specific. You can take a factory tour every weekday at 1:30 PM. And a block away, check out the large fiberglass version of the famous red cap with the flaps.

Cap Site, Hobby Wheel, 1435 E. Cloverland Dr., Ironwood, MI 49938

Stormy Kromer Mercantile, 1238 Wall St., Ironwood, MI 49938

Phone: (888) 455-2253

Hours: Always visible; Store, Monday–Friday 8 AM–5 PM, Saturday 9 AM–noon; Tours, Monday–Friday 1:30 PM

Cost: Free

Website: www.stormykromer.com

Directions: The cap is in front of Hobby Wheel on Rte. 2 (Cloverland Dr.); the store is one block southwest of the cap.

Ishpeming
Big Gus and Big Ernie

Let's say you have an enormous tree you'd like cut down, but you don't have a lot of time—what would you do? Hire Big Gus for the job! Big Gus isn't a lumberman, he's the World's Largest Working Chainsaw. Built in 1990 by Jim "Hoolie" DeClaire of Moran Iron Works (see page 84), this megamachine is 22 feet and 11 inches long, 6 feet high, and is powered by a GMC V-8, 305 cc, water-cooled engine with a three-speed transmission. It weighs almost four tons, so it's not practical for most situations. Or any. But it sure *looks* cool!

Big Ernie, on the other hand, is much easier to move around—it's mounted on the back of an old flatbed truck. Big Ernie is said to be the World's Largest Working Rifle. Just jam a large projectile into the 35-foot-muzzle and let the propane and 12-volt igniter system do the rest.

These two deadly contraptions are just the beginning of what you'll find at Da Yoopers Tourist Trap, da wackiest souvenir stand in da UP. Visitors can also visit Camp Buck-n-Brew, where deer knock back cold ones and hunters are strung up their ankles; a double-decker outhouse;

A Texas-sized chainsaw, but no massacre.

and another privy called "Da 2-Holer Outhouse" where you can stick your head through the upper seat for a gag (and we do mean gag) photo.

Da Yooper Tourist Trap, 490 N. Steel St., Ishpeming, MI 49849
Phone: (800) 628-9978 or (906) 485-5595
Hours: May–October, Monday–Friday 9 AM–9 PM, Saturday 9 AM–8 PM, Sunday 9 AM–6 PM
Cost: Free
Website: http://dayoopers.com
Directions: At the intersection of Rte. 41 and County Hwy. 587.

US Ski & Snowboard Hall of Fame and Museum

When you think American skiing you probably think of Colorado or Utah, not northern Michigan. Yet it was here in 1887 that the sport was introduced to the New World by Norwegian immigrants—Carl Tellefsen and the Den Nordiske Ski Klub (Nordic Ski Club). In 1905, they formed the National Ski Association, which has been the governing body ever since.

In 1954 the organization opened the US Ski & Snowboard Hall of Fame and Museum with artifacts from the sport's history and its inductees. You'll see a diorama of two Norwegian "Birchleg" soldiers carrying the infant Prince Haakon to safety in 1206 (on skis, of course); a replica of a 4,000-year-old ski and pole pulled out of a Swedish bog, and the first snow-grooming machine from Sun Valley, California. There's also an exhibit on the 10th Mountain Division—the skiing soldiers of World War II. Downhill skiing, cross-country skiing, snowboarding (see page 294), ski jumping, and all those goofy ski-and-shoot Olympic competitions are represented as well.

610 Palms Ave., PO Box 191, Ishpeming, MI 49849
Phone: (906) 485-6323
Hours: Monday–Saturday 10 AM–5 PM
Cost: Free (donations are welcome)
Website: www.skihall.com
Directions: On US Hwy. 41W (Palms Ave.) at Second St.

Kearsarge

USS Kearsarge

In all of history, there have been five ships named the USS *Kearsarge*. The first was a steam sloop of war that sank the Confederate CSS *Alabama* on

Not exactly seaworthy.

June 19, 1864, and continued in service until 1894, when it struck a reef off Nicaragua. The second, commissioned in 1900, was a battleship that served through World War I, before being converted into a crane ship in 1939. The third *Kearsarge* was an Essex-class aircraft carrier that went into service in 1946, participated in the Korean and Vietnam Wars, and retrieved astronauts Wally Schirra, and later Gordon Cooper, from their Mercury capsules after splashdown. The fourth *Kearsarge*, an amphibious assault ship, was commissioned in 1989 and is currently sailing the high seas. In 1995 it rescued Captain Scott O'Grady after he was shot down in Bosnia.

But what about the fifth *Kearsarge*? It's made of stone and mortar, and never sailed anywhere. This rock replica of an 1862 ship was built by a crew from FDR's Works Progress Administration in 1933–34, mostly to keep unemployed miners busy. Officially named the Stone Boat, most people call it the USS *Kearsarge* after the town in which you can find it today. Plans are underway to make the surrounding park into a veterans memorial.

58874 US Hwy. 41, Kearsarge, MI 49942

No phone

Hours: Always visible

Cost: Free

Directions: Where Smith Ave. intersects with County Rd. (Rte. 41).

L'Anse
Jumbo Cinnamon Rolls

Do you like cinnamon rolls? I mean, do your *realllly* like cinnamon rolls? Because if you order one of the Hilltop Family Restaurant's hassock-sized creations, you're going to be eating it for a while. Each iced roll weighs more than a pound and is stuffed with chopped apple slices. If a blizzard is on the way, toss a few of these in your car's trunk for traction, or to feed you until the rescue crew arrives. This 1950s recipe comes from the owner's aunt who, we assume, was the mess cook at Paul Bunyan's logging camp.

The portions of everything else at the Hilltop Family Restaurant are more reasonable—standard American fare. If you're stopping by for dinner, be aware that this establishment is not located at the top of a hill, despite its name.

Hilltop Family Restaurant, 18047 US Hwy. 41, L'Anse, MI 49946
Phone: (906) 524-7858
Hours: November–May, Sunday–Thursday 7 AM–7 PM, Friday–Saturday 7 AM–8 PM;
   June–October, daily 7 AM–8 PM
Cost: Sweet rolls, $3.99; Meals, $7–15
Website: www.sweetroll.com
Directions: Just north of Dynamite Hill Rd. on Rte. 41.

Shrine of the Snowshoe Priest

When it comes to Catholic missionaries in the upper Midwest, nobody can fill the snowshoes of Father Frederic Baraga. Baraga came to the Upper Peninsula from Slovenia in 1831 and taught himself several native dialects. Over the next 23 years he would hike the region, through 700 miles of snow each winter if necessary, and establish five missions in the UP: Grand River, La Pointe, L'Anse, Sault Ste. Marie, and Aubre Croche. Later he became the bishop of Sault Ste. Marie, and after that, Marquette.

Today Baraga is honored with a strange shrine bursting with not-so-subtle symbolism in a cliff overlooking Keewenaw Bay. Five tepees, each representing a different mission, shoot five arching wooden "laser beams" that support a puffy stainless steel cloud. A 35-foot-tall bronze Baraga

Up, up and away!

stands on the cloud, a 7-foot cross in one hand and two 26-foot snowshoes in the other.

In 1973, Baraga was nominated for beatification, but so far the Vatican has only approved him as "venerated." Should you wish, you can venerate him here or at two other UP locations: **St. Peter Cathedral** (311 Baraga Ave., (906) 226-6548, www.stpetercathedral.org) in Marquette, where he is buried; or **St. Mary's Pro-Cathedral** (320 E. Portage Ave., (906) 632-3381, http://home.catholicweb.com/Holy_Name_of_Mary/index.cfm) in Sault Ste. Marie, where a small museum of his personal effects can be found.

Bishop Baraga Shrine, 17570 US Hwy. 41, L'Anse, MI 49801

Phone: (906) 524-7021

Hours: Always visible

Cost: Free

Website: www.exploringthenorth.com/bishopb/shrine.html

Directions: West of town on Rte. 41, turn south at the tepees.

Laurium and Calumet
George Gipp Memorial, Home, and Grave

Contrary to what you may have learned from watching *Knute Rockne All American*, George Gipp might have been *somewhat* responsible for his own early demise, and not from some noble, Reaganesque behavior. While a student at Notre Dame, Gipp had been out late at a poker game (or was carousing), staggered home in a snowstorm, and passed out drunk on the back steps of Washington Hall. He came down with pneumonia and strep throat, from which he died on December 14, 1920.

The Gipper hailed from Laurium, Michigan, born here on February 18, 1895. His family's home still stands, just a few blocks from where WPA crews erected a stone memorial in 1935 (which was restored in 1999). Gipp attended Calumet High School, then went off to South Bend on a *baseball* scholarship before Knute Rockne recognized his football talents. Gipp's body was interred in Calumet's Lake View Cemetery, Section 20, Plot 70, but was exhumed in 2007 to obtain DNA to see if he fathered a love child, Bette Bright Weeks. He didn't, which supports the poker theory.

Birthplace, 432 Hecla St., Laurium, MI 49913

Calumet High School, 57070 Mine St., Calumet, MI 49913

Memorial, Tamarack St. & Lake Linden Ave., Laurium, MI 49913

Grave, Lake View Cemetery, 24090 Veterans Memorial Hwy., Calumet, MI 49913

Phone: (906) 337-2510

Hours: Always visible

Cost: Free

Website: www.laurium.net and www.cmgww.com/football/gipp/

Directions: Birthplace, one block east of M-26 (Lake Linden Ave.); High School, just west of US 41, north of Red Jacket Rd.; Memorial, on M-26 two blocks southeast of Hecla St.; Grave, east of Calumet on M-203 (Pine St./Veterans Memorial Hwy.).

Mackinac Island
Dr. Beaumont Museum

On June 6, 1822, a Canadian trapper named Alexis St. Martin was in the American Fur Company store on Mackinac Island when a musket being cleaned by two other men accidentally discharged, blowing a fist-sized hole in his abdomen. It turned out to be a stroke of good luck for everyone, except of course for the Canadian voyageur. Dr. William Beaumont, Fort Mackinac's surgeon, tended to the trapper's wound, and although St. Martin recovered, the hole in his stomach never healed over. Instead, it formed a gastric fistula—a permanent hole in his gut.

Beaumont seized on St. Martin's misfortune to poke around in the man's stomach, first in 1825 and then 250 more times before 1833. (St. Martin was tricked into this arrangement because Beaumont convinced the illiterate man to sign a contract making him Beaumont's personal servant for $40/month.) Beaumont would place pieces of food on string, push them through the hole in St. Martin's side, and pull them out later for analysis. Through this work he was able to learn how quickly certain foods were digested. Beaumont published his findings in an 1833 book titled *Experiments and Observations on the Gastric Juice and the Physiology of Digestion*.

In appreciation for the doctor's contribution to medical science, as well as "The Man with the Hole in His Stomach," the Michigan State Medical Society paid to have the American Fur Company Store rebuilt in 1954 as a museum. The docents no longer leave loaded muskets lying around.

Fort & Market Sts., Mackinac Island, MI 49757
Phone: (231) 436-4100
Hours: June–August, daily 11 AM–6 PM
Cost: Downtown pass only, Adults $5, Kids $5; Fort pass, Adults $12, Kids (5–17) $7
Website: www.mackinacparks.com/history/index.aspx?l=0,1,4,32,40,195,1032
Directions: Across from Bark Chapel, west of the park below Fort Mackinac.

The Haunted Theatre

The proprietors of this eerie establishment claim the old Orpheum Theatre was built on an ancient Indian burial ground, but let's face it, so is most of this town. No, the real haunts in this place all arrived in 1974 when it was converted from a spooky, decrepit theater into a spooky, decrepit walk-through attraction.

Rather than go the traditional Phantom of the Opera route, most of the creepy characters you'll meet here are nonhuman. Sure, they start with rotting corpses in the theater's old fold-down seats, but soon you're passing an enormous mutant housefly in a baby's bassinet, a half-rat, half-boy

Was *Reds* really that long? Photo by author, courtesy the Haunted Theatre

eating spiders, an alien predator in a laboratory, a Sasquatchy goatman, a fluorescent heron pulling a skeleton from Davy Jones's Locker, and finally, Beelzebub reading from the *Book of the Damned* in an underground lair. Fun for the whole family!

7396 Main St., PO Box 251, Mackinac Island, MI 49757

Phone: (231) 597-8154

Hours: May–Labor Day 11 AM–8 PM; Labor Day–October, Saturday–Sunday 11 AM–8 PM

Cost: Adults $7, Kids $7

Website: www.hauntedtheatremackinacisland.com

Directions: Between Hoban and Astor Sts., across from the ferry docks.

The Original Mackinac Island Butterfly House & Insect World

Who doesn't love butterflies? Somehow they get a pass from the "insects are icky" crowd, even though, if you ignore their beautiful wings, they *are* kinda icky with their buggy eyes, spindly black legs, and long, coiled proboscises. Try not to think about that as you walk through the 1,800-square-foot habitat where hundreds of these things swarm all about you.

OK, maybe that's an exaggeration—mostly they just sit on flowers and suck nectar while you take pictures . . . but you never know when they might attack.

Around since 1991, the Original Mackinac Island Butterfly House is the first live exhibit of its kind in Michigan, and the third oldest in the United States. Each guest is handed a handy chart before entering the greenhouse area to help identify the species inside—Monarchs, Red Postmans, Common Lacewings, Zebra Longwings, Bamboo Pages, Orange Emigrants—from five different continents.

When you exit the habitat, you enter Insect World, and finally you start getting the creepy crawlies. Most of the insects here are dead and tastefully mounted with pins on corkboard, but they do have live specimens, as well as a turtle and toad habitat.

6750 McGulpin St., Mackinac Island, MI 49757

Phone: (906) 847-3972

Hours: June–August, daily 10 AM–7 PM; September–May, daily 10 AM–6 PM

Cost: Adults $9, Kids (4–11) $4.50

Website: www.originalbutterflyhouse.com

Directions: Three blocks east of the park below Fort Mackinac, two blocks north of the lake, at Truscott St.

World's Longest Front Porch

From the day the Grand Hotel opened on July 10, 1887, owner W. Stewart Woodfill bragged that he'd built the longest front porch in the world—880 feet! But in time, people grew suspicious and brought out a tape measure, and discovered Woodfill was nearly a football field short of his claim. Nonetheless, it still holds the record at 660 feet, though you won't be able to verify it yourself without booking a room or paying a hefty porch strolling fee. This is the Grand, after all, and they're not interested in entertaining the tourist riffraff from the fudgaterias along the docks.

This Greek Revival structure has hosted many events and celebrities over the years. Thomas Edison first unveiled the phonograph to the public here. Esther Williams shot *This Time for Keeps* (1947) in and around the pool, which is today named in her honor. Presidents Truman, Kennedy, Ford, Bush (41), and Clinton have stayed here, and some of its 385 rooms, each one unique, were designed by first ladies Johnson, Ford, Carter, Reagan, and both Bushes.

The hotel's snootiness kicks into high gear at 6:30 PM, when all guests are expected to adhere to the formal dress code: jackets and ties for the gentlemen, dresses or suits for the ladies. Thus straitjacketed, you're free to play croquet on the lawn, peruse the original bird lithographs at the Audubon Wine Bar, or indulge in the hotel's signature dessert, Grand Pecan Balls, ice cream rolled in pecans and smothered in chocolate syrup. Don't drip on your ascot!

It's all vaguely reminiscent of *The Shining*, down to the Indian burial ground that was unearthed while the Grand was being built. It doesn't help that the carriages that convey its geriatric guests from the docks to the hotel look like glass-windowed hearses, their drivers in spooky black top hats.

Grand Hotel, 286 Grand Ave., PO Box 286, Mackinac Island, MI 49757

Phone: (800) 33-GRAND or (906) 847-3331

Hours: May–October, daily

Cost: $10/porch stroll; Rooms, check website

Website: www.grandhotel.com

Directions: Huron St. west from the ferry dock, then north on Grand Ave.

Manistique
Siphon Bridge

Though it was originally named the Trunk Line Bridge when it was built in 1918, most people today refer to it as the Siphon Bridge. The 296-foot-long structure was a joint venture between the Manistique Pulp & Paper Company and the state highway department. As the Manistique River flows through town and into Lake Michigan, it is forced through a concrete flume that passes beneath the bridge, yet the dry roadway sits four feet *below* the waterline when the river is running high.

Scientifically speaking, calling this the Siphon Bridge is a bit of a stretch. What makes a siphon special is that water can be made to go *higher* than its intake level, like a hose inserted into a car's gas tank, if the tube's exit point is lower than its intake. In Manistique, the water is just pushed under the bridge by the flow of the water, and blocked from crossing the roadway by a very tall wall. Some siphon.

Siphon Bridge, M-94 (old Rte. 2/River St.), Manistique, MI 49854

No phone

Hours: Always open

Cost: Free

Directions: Downtown, where River St. crosses the river.

Marquette
Lakenenland

Lakenenland is one of those oddball attractions that's worth driving out of your way to see, which is good, because you'll be driving *waaaaay* out of your way to get to it. This unique drive-thru sculpture park is the creation of Tom Lakenen. After giving up drinking, he decided to do something

Randolph, the Big-Eared Sort-of Reindeer. Photo by author, courtesy Tom Lakenen

more productive with his time. Using metal scraps from his job as a construction worker, he began welding bizarre animals and unique commentaries on issues of the day. He originally placed the pieces on his home's front lawn, but local zoning killjoys forced him to remove the art. Undeterred, Lakenen moved them to new property adjoining Lake Superior, and in 2003 Lakenenland was born.

Here, a dirt road winds through a pine forest filled with more than 80 colorful creations. Among them, a flying saucer with aliens, a skeleton jumping a motorcycle through a flaming ring, mermaids on a sunny beach, fanged creatures in cages, a fat corporate pig pooping on an Average American Worker, oversized insects, and more than a few dancing wolves.

Lakenen has recently added two fishing ponds, a bandshell, and a nature walk through a cedar bog. The park is wide open and free, day or night—snowmobilers are even welcome in the winter.

2800 M-28 East, Marquette, MI 49855
Phone: (906) 249-1132
Hours: Always open
Cost: Free ("Donations accepted but not expected")
Website: http://lakenenland.com/
Directions: Nine miles east of the M-28/US Rte. 41 intersection in Harvey, at Shot Point Rd.

Yooper Dome, the World's Largest Wooden Dome

It looks like a giant, tan igloo, but it's not made of snow—it's made to *withstand* snow, 60 pounds per square inch, to be exact, as well as 80 mph winds. The Superior Dome, which most people call the Yooper Dome, was built on the campus of Northern Michigan University in 1991. The football team plays its games here in front of up to 16,000 fans, which is about three-quarters of the population of Marquette.

More specs: the Yooper Dome is 536 feet in diameter, stands 14 stories tall, and covers 5.1 acres. Yes, there are four other dome structures in the world that are larger, but they're all built with, get this, *steel*. Wimps. The Yooper's geodesic frame was made with 781 all-natural Douglas fir beams, no more, no less.

Superior Dome, Northern Michigan University, 1401 Presque Isle Ave., Marquette, MI 49855
Phone: (906) 227-2850

Hours: Always visible; check website for event schedule

Cost: Free

Website: www.nmu.edu/sportsusoec/node/302

Directions: Between Presque Isle Ave. and Lakeshore Blvd., south of Wright St.

Mohawk
Snow Thermometer Park

It's not exactly news to anyone who's been to Michigan's Upper Peninsula between September and May: it snows a lot in the UP, especially on the Keweenaw Peninsula, which juts out into the middle of Lake Superior. On average, locals have to shovel 187 inches of the stuff each year—about 15½ feet. Since 1910, the *lowest* snowfall was in the winter of 1930–31, a mere 81.3 inches. But in 1978–79? Just over 390 inches—that's 32½ feet!

How do yoopers keep track of these statistics? With the Snow Thermometer, of course. Despite its name, this towering sign doesn't measure temperature but the cumulative depth of the white stuff. Built to scale, you can get an accurate feel for just how deep 32½ feet really is, or keep track of this winter's total. If you don't want to slog through the drifts, you can always check out the total via the Snow Thermometer's website while wearing your jammies and slippers.

US Hwy. 41, Mohawk, MI 49913

Phone: (906) 337-1610

Hours: Always visible

Cost: Free

Website: www.pasty.com/snow/index.html

Directions: Four miles north of town on the road to Phoenix.

Munising
Dogpatch Restaurant

Though L'il Abner and his hillbilly friends hail from Dogpatch, *Arkansas*, apparently they've got franchises in other states. Since 1966 this establishment has been serving "legendary vittles" to Yooper Yokums, and the restaurant lays on the hokey shtick pretty thick—you almost need to be a comic strip scholar to decipher the menu. For breakfast: "Bufford Haw-

A hillbilly RV.

gington Porksides, Delishus Pork luv Sausages (four of 'em) from the wildly romantic boar, carefully rolled 'n nurtured to perfection, with two hen aigs, Idaho taters, toast."

Dogpatch certainly looks the part, a ramshackle mountain cabin with painted characters from the Sunday funnies on every wall, and a moonshine-running pickup parked out front. Thankfully, it isn't to distract from a bad menu, because the vittles here are mighty fine.

325 E. Superior St., Munising, MI 49862

Phone: (906) 387-9948

Hours: Breakfast, daily 7–11 AM; Lunch, 11 AM–5 PM; Dinner, 5–10 PM

Cost: Meals, $7–15

Website: www.dogpatchrestaurant.com

Directions: Where M-28 (Munising Ave.) turns south and becomes Cedar St.

Newberry

Oswald's Bear Ranch

"Bear Ranch" sounds like a tourist attraction where you saddle up a grizzly and go in search of salmon, but Oswald's Bear Ranch isn't that dangerous. In fact, it's a rescue operation for orphaned black bear cubs run by Dean and Jewel Oswald. The couple also takes in and rehabilitates injured bears before releasing them back into the wild. The rescued cubs, however, spend the remainder of their lives in one of the facility's four habitats, only because they're unable to learn the hunting skills they would need to survive on their own.

The ranch's entry fee, while steep, goes to the year-round care of these beautiful creatures. If Oswald's has any new young cubs when you visit, you're welcome to hold them for an adorable, cross-species photo (for an additional fee).

13814 County Rd. 407, Newberry, MI 49868

Phone: (906) 293-3147

Hours: June–September, daily 9:30 AM–5 PM

Cost: $20/carload, $10 if you're alone

Website: www.oswaldsbearranch.com

Directions: Four miles north of town on M-123, turn west on Deer Park Rd., then four more miles to the McMillan Ave. intersection.

NEWBERRY

⇒ Newberry claims to be the official "Moose Capital of Michigan."

Norway

Viking Ships

Ask any Norwegian American who "discovered" America and you're likely to hear the name Leif Erikson, not Christopher Columbus. They believe Erikson landed in present-day Newfoundland in 1001 AD, almost 500 years before that syphilitic Italian came up just short in the Bahamas. But they're not biased.

While you might expect to find this town filled with Oles and Ingas, the population isn't exceptionally Norwegian American. Instead, it was named after the nearby Norway Mine. But in an effort to confuse tourists, local boosters have erected three Viking ships, one along each main highway as it enters this UP Valhalla. They're small ships—not much larger than canoes—but they have tall masts with sails/banners announcing the town's name. Downtown, next to City Hall, there's another ship, this one painted into a mural of the westward voyage on the back wall of the city bandshell.

Western Ship, Rte. 2 & Ninth Ave., Norway, MI 49870

Southern Ship, Rte. 8 & Stadium Rd., Norway, MI 49870

Eastern Ship, Rte. 2 & Eighth Ave., Norway, MI 49870

City Bandshell, 900 N. Main St., Norway, MI 49870

Phone: (906) 563-9961

Hours: Always visible

Cost: Free

Website: www.norwaymi.com

Directions: At each of the town's main entrances from the east, west, and south.

Paradise

The Wreck of the *Edmund Fitzgerald*

You might have known about the wreck of the *Edmund Fitzgerald* without having heard the 1970s ballad by Gordon Lightfoot ("The Wreck of the *Edmund Fitzgerald*"), but I doubt it. On November 10, 1975, the 729-foot ore freighter was 17 miles north-northwest of Whitefish Point and was sailing through 35-foot swells. At 7:10 PM it vanished with all 29 crew members aboard.

Some say the ship was doomed from the beginning; it took three hits to break the champagne bottle when it was christened in 1958, a sign of bad luck, then the ship rolled back against the dock on launching and gave a bystander a heart attack. But superstition aside, what ultimately caused the ship to sink? People debate that to this day—structural failure, rogue wave, flooded cargo holds, or some combination of factors? Divers later found the wreckage beneath 530 feet of water, snapped in half like a cheap pencil. In 1995 they retrieved its 200-pound bronze bell, which today is the centerpiece of the Great Lakes Shipwreck Historical Museum on Whitefish Point. Each year on November 10 it is rung 29 times. (The museum also has unused flares and a life ring from the freighter.)

The waters around the point are known as the "Graveyard of the Great Lakes," having claimed 320 lives in 150 wrecks over the years. Thirteen sinkings are highlighted at the dark and funereal museum, each with retrieved artifacts, including the first documented commercial sinking, the 1816 *Invincible* disaster.

Great Lakes Shipwreck Historical Museum, 18335 N. Whitefish Point Rd., Paradise, MI 49768

Phone: (888) 492-3747

Hours: May–October, 10 AM–6 PM

Cost: Adults $13, Kids (6–17 and under) $9

Website: www.shipwreckmuseum.com

Directions: At the northern end of Whitefish Point Rd.

THE ANCHOR'S AWAY . . . IN DETROIT

Though the Great Lakes Shipwreck Historical Museum has the bell from the *Edmund Fitzgerald*, other remnants of the doomed ship can be found elsewhere around Michigan. The freighter's **bow anchor** is at the Dossin Great Lakes Museum in Detroit (100 Strand Dr., Belle Isle, (313) 833-5538, http://detroithistorical.org). Two of its **lifeboats** are in the hull of the Museum Ship *Valley Camp* in Sault Ste. Marie (501 E. Water St., (888) 744-7867 or (906) 632-3658, www.thevalleycamp.com). And for Gordon Lightfoot fans, the **Mariners' Church** mentioned in the song is in Detroit (170 E. Jefferson Ave., (313) 259-2206, http://marinerschurchofdetroit.org/). This Anglican parish was also the site of rocker Patti Smith's marriage to MC5 guitarist Fred "Sonic" Smith on March 1, 1980. (Fred died of a heart attack in 1994 at age 44; his funeral was held at this same church.)

Paulding

The Paulding Light

Is it the lantern of a headless brakeman from the Choate Branch Railroad, still looking for his noggin? Perhaps the spirit of a long-dead Native American whose grave has been disturbed? Burning swamp gas? A piezoelectric rock outcropping? Or perhaps something less remarkable?

The Paulding Light, sometimes called the Dog Meadow Light, was first spotted in 1966, and unlike many so-called paranormal phenomena, this mysterious light can be seen on every day with clear weather. On any given evening you'll find spook hunters out on the road with their cameras, hoping to solve the mystery. The glowing white orb, sometimes a different shape or color, can be seen along the power line right-of-way on Old Route 45, south of town. The light appears just above the tree line at the north end of the road . . . which just happens to align with a stretch of the *new* Route 45 that many automobiles with headlights traverse. You figure it out.

Robins Pond Rd./Old Rte. 45, Paulding, MI 49969

No phone

Hours: After dark

Cost: Free

Directions: Head north on Old Rte. 45 from current Rte. 45 north of Watersmeet; it follows the power lines.

Ramsay
Keystone Bridge

It's an impressive structure, even today. Built in 1891 by the Chicago and North Western Railroad at a cost of $48,322, the 57-foot-tall Keystone

Still standing.

Bridge was built entirely without mortar. Wooden forms held the thick limestone blocks in place until the final keystone was inserted at the peak. Pull out the forms and gravity should hold them all together, right? Right?

Well it did, and has. Trains no longer cross the Black River over this 45-foot-long span, but pedestrians and snowmobiles still do. The bridge is located at the north end of a city park that also has a World War II–era M3A1 Stuart light tank. Though pointed at the bridge, the tank no longer has a gun, so there no risk of an accident.

Bessemer Township Memorial Park, Ramsay Rd., Ramsay, MI 49959

No phone

Hours: Always visible

Cost: Free

Directions: South of Main St. on Ramsay Rd.; best viewed from the Main St. bridge on the north side of the Keystone Bridge.

Rapid River
Adhoc Workshop

Ritch Branstrom doesn't like to see garbage lying around, which is why he picks the stuff up and uses it to make art—"found object sculpture" he calls it. His most popular (and downright affordable) works are known as Beercan Fish, nine-inch metal guppies made from old shotgun casings, bottle caps, and empty beer cans, all of which are in plentiful supply in the UP. The fish are for sale in his sporadically open Adhoc Workshop. If you want to visit, your best strategy is to call ahead and make an appointment.

Branstrom also does larger pieces built from car parts, driftwood, and rusty machinery. You can find a nine-foot-tall robin, its red breast the hood of a long-gone VW Beetle, outside a former gallery in the lower-peninsula town of Harbor Springs (6915 S. M-119).

Main St. & Rte. 2, Rapid River, MI 49878

Phone: (906) 399-1572

Hours: Display window, always visible; Store, "by appointment or chance"

Cost: Free

Website: www.adhocworkshop.com

Directions: Just south of Rte. 2 on Main St., next to Jack's Restaurant.

St. Ignace
Curio Fair

Curio Fair would be like any other tacky souvenir shop in the UP, its walls papered in birch bark, its shelves stocked with bows and rubber-tipped arrows, but when Clarence Eby built the store in 1956 he added an eight-story lookout tower reminiscent of a lighthouse. This coincided with the construction of the Mackinac Bridge (see page 78), which is why he also installed a coin-operated telescope on the upper deck.

You can still climb the 100 steps to the top, but be sure to bring a Sharpie with you because the modern tradition is to immortalize your ascent by writing your name(s) somewhere on the plywood walls, floors, ceilings, or steps. But just write them once—after all these years, there's not a lot of room left for everyone still to come.

1119 US Hwy. 2 W, St. Ignace, MI 49781

Phone: (906) 643-8626

Hours: May–October, daily 10 AM–6 PM

Cost: Free; Tower, $1/person

Directions: West of I-75 on Rte. 2, just west of Pointe LaBarbe Rd.

Deer Ranch

As you approach the Deer Ranch your first reaction might be, "Oh, my God! A giant deer has escaped its pen! Run for your lives!!!" But soon you'll realize that the 14-foot-tall buck you spotted vaulting over a log isn't moving, it's just hanging in midair. And it's fiberglass.

Big Bambi.

Don't worry, there are plenty of real deer inside, and they're all under lock and key. Deer Ranch has been entertaining Michigan tourists since 1950, and has dozens of whitetail deer, from fawns to does to bucks. They've even got albino deer—good camouflage in the winter, but in the warmer seasons, not so much. They're better off behind a fence.

Deer Ranch also has a nice gift shop that sells, among other things, genuine deerskin moccasins. Hey, where's Bambi? You just might be wearing him!

W1540 US Hwy. 2, St. Ignace, MI 49781

Phone: (906) 643-7760

Hours: June–August, daily 9 AM–8 PM; May & September–October, daily 9 AM–5 PM

Cost: Adults $5, Kids (5 and under) free

Website: http://deerranch.com

Directions: Four miles west of I-75, just east of the southeastern end of Gros Cap Rd.

MORE JUMPING BUCKS

If you're more interested in the big fiberglass deer outside Deer Ranch than the living creatures inside, you don't have to go all the way to St. Ignace to see one. There's another roadside jumping buck west of Ludington at **Grassa's Farm Market** (2442 W. US 10, (231) 843-8020), high atop its sign. It was even made with the same mold. So was the deer along the highway at the north end of **Wallace** (US Rte. 41). And the jumping buck at the **Jerome Country Market** (8985 E. Chicago Rd./US 12, (517) 688-4041, www.jeromecountrymarketllc.com) in Jerome looks might familiar, too. That Irish Hills establishment also has a half-dozen fake gutted bucks hanging from a log frame, as well as stuffed dead specimens inside the store as part of its Timberland Taxidermy store.

Indian Village

The classic neon signs—a large tepee and an American Indian in a breech-cloth firing an arrow—pull you in from your crawl along the main drag in St. Ignace. A hand-painted sign then promises a museum, which turns out to be more of a diorama in the back corner. On the left, a re-creation of Fort De Buade as it appeared in St. Ignace in 1689. On the right, an Ojibwe village with birch bark wigwams and a Christian mission built from logs. The mural backdrop looks oddly out of scale; a colossal canoe dwarfs the village below, and a bear appears poised to crush the fort with a few swipes of its mighty paws.

Other than the museum, Indian Village offers the traditional tourist trap fare—cedar jewelry boxes, dreamcatchers, and T-shirts with wolves on them. Outside, a family of four can pose behind a plywood cutout, putting their faces on the bodies of Indians from 1950s TV westerns.

499 N. State St., St. Ignace, MI 49781

Phone: (906) 643-8980

Hours: May–October, 8:30 AM–8 PM

Cost: Free

Directions: At Marquette St., two blocks south of the Star Line Ferry docks.

Mystery Spot

As the story goes, back in 1953 three surveyors named Clarence, Fred, and McCray were crossing the UP and "taking measurements" (who knows why?) and they discovered a spot near St. Ignace, about 300 feet in diameter, where their tripod went all screwy. The bubble on the level looked correct, yet the plumb bob swung to the east. After many tries and no logical explanation, they just pronounced it a mystery spot, and so the Mystery Spot was born.

Your teenage guide takes you on a tour through a wacky shack built on the land. Chairs and their occupants hang off walls, balancing in mid-air. Two people of the same height appear to grow and shrink before your very eyes. Water and balls run uphill. There's no attempt to explain any of it, just take it for what it's worth. "Even a blind person could be affected," they say, as if mysterious electro-magneto-gravitational forces should affect the blind any differently.

In what seems like an attempt to frustrate even Tiger Woods, the Mystery Spot has also built an 18-hole miniature golf course on the land. How is anyone supposed to putt around here? And they've also erected two ziplines . . . though riders on both definitely go downhill, unlike the water. I guess the magical effects come and go . . .

150 Martin Lake Rd., St. Ignace, MI 49781

Phone: (906) 643-8322

Hours: May, daily 9 AM–8 PM; June–August, daily 8 AM–9 PM; September–October, daily 9 AM–7 PM

Cost: Adults $7, Kids (5–11) $5 (zip line, maze, and mini golf cost extra)

Website: www.mysteryspotstignace.com

Directions: Five miles west of I-75 on Rte. 2, at Gros Cap Rd.

The Newberry Tablet

What exactly did two workers find on the McGruer farm near Newberry in 1897? After felling a tree, they discovered a large flat stone tangled in its roots; it had obviously been there a long time. They also found three small statues—a male, a female, and a child.

What became known as the Newberry Tablet was covered in scratches that were later determined to be from the Bronze Age Hittite-Minoan culture, on the island of Crete, which thrived 2,000 years ago. Odder still, the tablet described how birds feed on grain that was scattered before them. Why would Cretans traveling thousands of miles from home, presumably looking for copper, bother to write about such an arcane topic? Why not describe their journey, or directions to the nearest copper outcropping? Eventually the Smithsonian weighed in, and dismissed the Newberry Tablet as a hoax. The artifacts were returned to McGruer, who unceremoniously dumped them in his barn where, over the years, they were knocked around and broken.

ST. IGNACE

➡ Fr. Jacques Marquette is buried in **Marquette Mission Park** (566 N. State St.) in St. Ignace. The explorer died on May 18, 1675, on the shore of Lake Michigan near Buttersville, where a 45-foot cross stands over his original burial site.

But then the Smithsonian backed off its assessment—it no longer claims the tablet to be a fake, but doesn't go so far as to say it proves Hittites visited the New World. It's old, probably genuine, and, well, that's about it. Today you can see hunks of the shattered tablet and the two adult statues' heads in a small storefront museum in this dinky little town. You'll just have to make up your own mind as to their significance.

Fort de Buade Museum, 334 N. State St., St. Ignace, MI 48781

Phone: (906) 643-6627

Hours: May–September, Tuesday–Thursday 10 AM–6 PM, Friday 10 AM–9 PM, Saturday 10 AM–6 PM

Cost: Donations accepted

Website: http://fortdebuade.com/

Directions: North of Central Hill St. on I-75 Business (State St.).

Paul and Babe

The folks at Castle Rock try to sell you on the beautiful view from atop their 200-foot-tall platform on the lake bluffs—Pontiac's Lookout, they called it—but most oddball travelers will be more interested in the huge

He's a lumberjack, and he's OK.

cement replicas of Paul Bunyan and Babe, located at the base just north of the gift shop. The pair, built in 1957, is surrounded by a camera-unfriendly chain link fence installed to discourage climbers. Paul sits, as if on a toilet, and Babe stands faithfully alongside, his tongue hanging out.

Castle Rock has been around as a tourist attraction since 1930, back when climbing it cost 10¢—STOP AND CLIMB. STILL ONLY A DIME, the signs bragged. Today it costs ten times that much, yet still a bargain at less than a penny for each of its 170 steps.

Castle Rock, N2690 Castle Rock Rd., PO Box 185, St. Ignace, MI 49781

Phone: (906) 643-8268

Hours: May–mid-October, daily 9 AM–9 PM

Cost: $1/person

Website: www.castlerockmi.com

Directions: Four miles north of the Mackinac Bridge; on the west side of I-75 at Exit 348.

Point LaBarbe Inn

There was a time when travelers didn't expect a free continental breakfast with their stay, or chocolate chip cookies at check-in, or high-speed Wi-Fi. *Why would they ask for Wi-Fi?* you point out, *The Internet hadn't even been invented yet.*

Fine, Mr. or Ms. Smartypants. The point is, most travelers were happy with a clean room and a strong deadbolt. And if the rooms in the establishment happened to look like giant tepees or frontier forts, even better. The cabins at the Point LaBarbe Inn are just that: green stockade enclosures lined up facing the highway, waiting for an Indian attack. Some have lookout towers (which you can't climb) while others look like Wild West storefronts or churches. Bring along a trapper costume and you'll look right at home.

And by the way, they *do* have Wi-Fi.

1374 W. US 2, St. Ignace, MI 49781

Phone: (906) 643-8566

Hours: May–October, daily

Cost: $42–79/night

Website: www.ptelabarbeinn.com

Directions: Southeast of the intersection of Point LaBarbe Rd. on Rte. 2.

Sault Ste. Marie
Antlers Bar

Do you like stuffed animals? Not teddy bears or velveteen rabbits, but honest-to-Mother-Nature animals that have been stuffed and mounted? Then you might appreciate the Antlers Bar, where every square inch of the walls and rafters are covered in critters and half-critters.

This establishment opened years ago as an ice cream parlor and saloon named the Bucket-of-Blood. During Prohibition the owners claimed to be selling only ice cream, but revenuers got suspicious of the profits the store was raking in. Who would buy so much ice cream from a place called Bucket-of-Blood? Eventually a pair of Detroit cops, Harold and Walter Kinney, bought the place and changed its name to the Antlers Bar. The pair also started buying up every piece of taxidermy they could find: two bear cubs, a two-headed calf, a pride of lions, a polar bear, a mighty anaconda wrapped around a tree, a fur-bearing trout, and the heads of every horned creature known to humankind.

Two heads are not necessarily better than one.

Despite its name, the Antlers Bar is more than a drinking establishment. Its menu includes Wild Game Lasagna, Soo Stew Canoes, and a Paul Bunyan Burger that has two half-pound beef patties. Bring your lumberjack appetite.

804 E. Portage Ave., PO Box 1939, Sault Ste. Marie, MI 49783
Phone: (906) 253-1728
Hours: Daily 11 AM–11 PM
Cost: Free; Meals $7–15
Website: www.saultantlers.com
Directions: Six blocks east of Ashmun St. (I-75 Business Spur) along the river.

Cairnscape

Most people would be upset if a road crew dumped a pickup truck–sized boulder on their front lawn, but Kevin Milligan isn't like most people. Back in 1983, workers on Seymour Road pushed a massive rock onto his land and he said, essentially, "Thank you very much."

Soon Milligan had amassed even more boulders, which he piled into crude cairns, and then filled the holes between the boulders with upside-down dead trees, their roots jutting into the sky. He then named his art project Cairnscape. There's no sign to mark the park, but it's hard to miss along Seymour Street.

What will this modern-day Bedrock look like when he's finished? I'm not sure even Milligan knows.

2296 Seymour St., Sault Ste. Marie, MI 49783
Private phone
Hours: Daylight hours
Cost: Free
Directions: East of I-75 Business on Marquette Ave., then south on Seymour St.

Vulcan

Big John

Big John is big, but then again, everything around here is. This 40-foot major miner wears a hard hat that lights up at night, and stands outside the Iron Mountain Iron Mine, a hole from which 20 million tons of iron

Jumbo John.

ore have been extracted over the years. Today, the mine is open for tours. Hop aboard the mine train and it'll take you 2,600 feet into the mountain, down, down, down, until you're 40 feet below the surface. To get a sense of how big this hole is, another Big John has been erected in the underground chamber, off in the distance, and he looks *tiny*.

No, this is not an attraction for claustrophobics. You might just want to stay behind at the surface, contemplating the mine's Redwood-tall Ax-and-Shovel-Tree. Seventy or so sharp mining tools are embedded into a wooden pole, dangling high above your easy-to-split-open skull.

Come to think of it, maybe you should just wait in the car.

Iron Mountain Iron Mine, W4852 US Hwy. 2, PO Box 177, Vulcan, MI 49801

Phone: (906) 563-8077

Hours: June–October, daily 9 AM–5 PM

Cost: Adults $12, Kids (6–12) $7.50

Website: www.ironmountainironmine.com

Directions: On Williams St. (Rte. 2) north of Main St.

Wetmore
Edith Ann-dirondack Chairs

Adirondack chairs are fairly big to start with, but blow them up to three or four times their size and you'll look like Edith Ann while sitting on them. The two chairs outside the AmericInn are meant to be sat upon, for there are steps attached to get you up into the seats. Perfect for gag photos of you and Buster the dog. And that'th the truth—pffthhhhh!!

AmericInn, E9926 State Hwy. M-28, Wetmore, MI 49895

Phone: (800) 634-3444 or (906) 387-2000

Hours: Always visible

Cost: Free

Website: www.americinn.com/Hotels/MI/Munising

Directions: Just east of Connors Rd. on M-28.

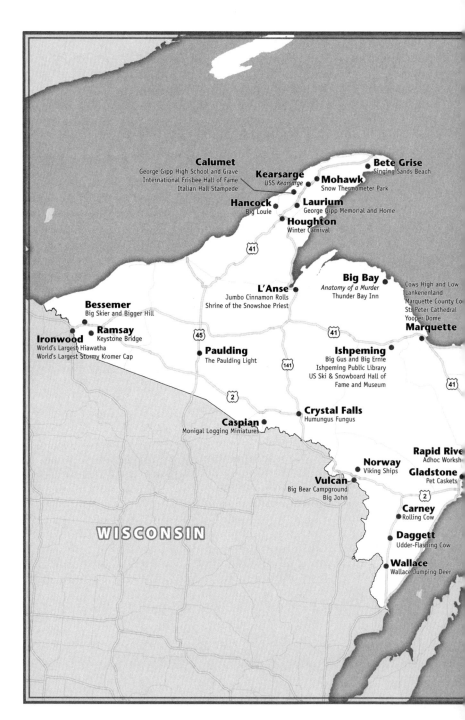

Calumet
George Gipp High School and Grave
International Frisbee Hall of Fame
Italian Hall Stampede

Kearsarge
USS *Kearsarge*

Bete Grise
Singing Sands Beach

Mohawk
Snow Thermometer Park

Hancock
Big Louie

Laurium
George Gipp Memorial and Home

Houghton
Winter Carnival

Big Bay
Anatomy of a Murder
Thunder Bay Inn

L'Anse
Jumbo Cinnamon Rolls
Shrine of the Snowshoe Priest

Cows High and Low
Lankenenland
Marquette County Co
St. Peter Cathedral
Yooper Dome

Marquette

Bessemer
Big Skier and Bigger Hill

Ramsay
Keystone Bridge

Ironwood
World's Largest Hiawatha
World's Largest Stormy Kromer Cap

Paulding
The Paulding Light

Ishpeming
Big Gus and Big Ernie
Ishpeming Public Library
US Ski & Snowboard Hall of
Fame and Museum

Crystal Falls
Humungus Fungus

Caspian
Monigal Logging Miniatures

Rapid Rive
Adhoc Worksh

Norway
Viking Ships

Gladstone
Pet Caskets

Vulcan
Big Bear Campground
Big John

Carney
Rolling Cow

WISCONSIN

Daggett
Udder-Flashing Cow

Wallace
Wallace Jumping Deer

Christmas
Christmas Town

Grand Marais
Gitchie Gumee Agate and History Museum
Teenie Weenie Pickle Barrel Cottage

Paradise
Tahquamenon Falls State Park
Wreck of the *Edmund Fitzgerald*

Munising
Dogpatch Restaurant

Newberry
Oswald's Bear Ranch

Sault Ste. Marie
Antlers Bar
Cairnscape
Karl's Cuisine Café and Winery
Soo Locks Visitors Center & Tower of History
Museum Ship *Valley Camp*
St. Mary's Pro-Cathedral

Wetmore
Edith Ann-dirondack Chairs

Soo Junction
Toonerville Trolley

Manistique
Big Meese
Hometown Bunyan
Siphon Bridge

St. Ignace
Curio Fair
Deer Ranch
Indian Village
Marquette Mission Park
Mystery Spot
The Newberry Tablet
Paul and Babe
Point LaBarbe Inn
Star-Spangled Moose

Mackinac Island
Dr. Beaumont Museum
The Haunted Theatre
Original Mackinac Island Butterfly House
& Insect World
World's Longest Front Porch

Lake Superior

CANADA

Lake Huron

Lake Michigan

2

NORTHERN MICHIGAN

When most people refer to "northern" Michigan they're not really referring to the northernmost part of the state, but rather the northernmost part of the southern peninsula. It's northern*ish*.

People from the Upper Peninsula—the UP, or the Yoop—sometimes call citizens of northern Michigan trolls, because they live "below the bridge." And strangely enough, there are other reasons to call people in these parts trolls. As the following pages will demonstrate, in northern Michigan you can find hobbit houses, dragons and dinosaurs, Easter Island heads, frolicking leprechauns, oversized mythical loggers, concrete cavemen, and 1,000-pound pumpkins carved to look like ogres. But there are surprisingly few goats.

So yeah, maybe they *are* trolls . . . what's it to ya?

Acme

FUDGE!!

With so many fudge outlets in northern Michigan, how does one decide where to shop? How about a place with an enormous wedge of boxed fudge

That's a lot of fudge to pack.

on the roof? Doug Murdick opened his first store in Traverse City (116 E. Front St.) in 1964, and a year later built this place in Acme, just northeast of town along the bay. And its big brown wedge has been there from the beginning.

Just how did Murdick accomplish this fabulous, fudgy feat? The same way he makes all his confections: it was cooked in a copper kettle, poured onto a marble slab, "then worked with *Paul Bunyan size tools*, loaved, and sliced."

Doug Murdick's Fudge, 4500 US Rte. 31, Acme, MI 49685

Phone: (800) 2-FUDGE-2 or (231) 938-2330

Hours: Always visible; Store, May–October, daily 9 AM–7 PM; July–August, daily 9 AM–9 PM

Cost: Free; Fudge, $6.99/half pound

Website: www.murdicksfudge.com

Directions: On Munson Ave. (Rte. 31/M-72) north of Holiday Rd.

Music House Museum

Have you ever wanted to listen to George Gershwin play "Rhapsody in Blue" live, on a real piano, but you can't because he's . . . you know . . . *dead*? Do not fret, just head over to the Music House Museum where a Weber Duo-Art Grand Piano bangs out the tune exactly as Gershwin did years ago. His performance was recorded onto a paper roll that was punched with holes, the same roll that drives this live re-recital. And boy could George wail on those keys!

The Weber is just one of the 15 or so mechanical music machines you'll hear on the hour-and-a-half tour. So screw those iPods—nothing beats music played by genuine instruments. These devices use metal drums and discs, motors and bellows, and perforated cards and paper to produce their loud and happy tunes. Most of them sound like merry-go-round calliopes, oversized music boxes, or upright pianos from Old West saloons, and can be quite intoxicating. Crank an organ grinder while your tour guide uses a monkey puppet to pass a tin cup. Enjoy the Mills Violano Virtuoso that uses vibrating wheels in place of fingers and a bow to play a mounted violin. Drop 5¢ into the 1917 Cremona nickelodeon to hear "Jingle Bells." And for the grand finale, sit back as the two-story 1922 Amaryllis Mortier Dance Organ, direct from the Victoria Palace Ballroom in Belgium, belts

An iPod from 1917. Photo by author, courtesy Music House Museum

out one of 2,200 different tunes with its 97-piece mechanical orchestra, shaking the rafters of this converted dairy barn.

7377 US 31 North, PO Box 297, Acme, MI 49610

Phone: (231) 938-9300

Hours: May–October, Monday–Saturday 10 AM–4 PM, Sunday noon–4 PM; November–December, Saturday 10 AM–4 PM

Cost: Adults $11, Kids (6–15) $4

Website: www.musichouse.org

Directions: North of Brackett Rd. on Rte. 31.

Alpena
Big Patriotic Heads

Let's face it—when it comes to patriotic imagery, bigger is better. Or at least easier to see. Mount Rushmore. The Statue of Liberty. Sarah Palin's hair. Big, big, big. So when Tom Moran made two busts for the Besser Museum for Northeast Michigan, he made them each 12 feet tall.

OK, so Moran makes *all* of his busts this large (see page 84), but that doesn't detract from the pieces here. His first commission was made in 2000, the head of a bald eagle with a brass beak and shingle-sized feathers made of stainless steel. It was followed in 2007 by a somewhat spooky head of an unknown soldier in a khaki green army helmet, his face painted in camouflage, with beady gold eyes, *and no mouth*. Both sit out by the highway, so you can see them any time, day or night, perhaps even from outer space.

Besser Museum for Northeast Michigan, 491 Johnson St., Alpena, MI 49707

Phone: (989) 356-2202

Hours: Always visible; Museum, Monday–Saturday 10 AM–5 PM

Cost: Free; Museum, Adults $5, Seniors (60+) $3, Kids (5–18) $3

Website: www.bessermuseum.org

Directions: East of Rte. 23, just west of Alpena Community College.

Atlanta

Elk Under Glass

For thousands of years, elk thrived in what is today Michigan and the eastern United States. But with unrestrained logging and hunting in the 1800s, settlers killed off every last one. The last live Eastern elk was spotted in Pennsylvania in 1877, right down the barrel of a gun. But then in 1917 seven Rocky Mountain elk were introduced into Pigeon River country, the area around present-day Atlanta. And were they frisky! By the middle of the century they'd humped up a bunch of offspring, the largest wild elk herd east of the Mississippi River.

In the 1970s, oil and gas exploration put Michigan's elk population again at risk, so local conservationists and hunters banded together to prevent the destruction of their habitat, and won! To commemorate its standing as the "Elk Capital of Michigan," Atlanta mounted a stuffed elk in a glass case outside the town's post office. If you push a red button at the base of the display, the elk bellows out a loud mating call for all its still-living relatives. So watch your back.

US Post Office, 12606 State St., Atlanta, MI 49709

Phone: (989) 785-4415

Hours: Always visible

Cost: Free
Website: http://atlantamichiganchamber.com/
Directions: One block east of the M-32/33 intersection.

Baldwin
Shrine of the Pines

Raymond W. "Bud" Overholzer must have been the most patient man on the planet. Not one for power tools or store-bought anything, he built a 2,500-square-foot "cabin" along the Pere Marquette River, then filled it with 200 unique pieces of furniture. It took him 22 years, and once you see inside, you'll understand why.

Each item in this hunting lodge home was hand carved by Overholzer, and all joints were made without nails, screws, or metal of any kind—he even made his own sandpaper and wood glue. Everything has a gnarled, organic, backwoods feel. The dining room table was crafted out of a 700-pound white pine stump, which he whittled down to 300 pounds and added 60 hardwood inlays. (Henry Ford reportedly offered $50,000 for it, but Overholzer declined.) A 12-rifle gun rack turns on 39 wooden roller bearings, and a rocking chair he built is so well balanced that it will cycle back and forth 55 times when given a single starting push.

Overholzer was just as patient in his personal life. He waited years for his true love to marry him. When they first met she was 23 years his senior, and needed some convincing. She was also his third-grade teacher at the time.

Shrine of the Pines, 8962 S. M-37, PO Box 548, Baldwin, MI 49304
Phone: (231) 745-7892
Hours: May–October, Monday–Saturday 10 AM–6 PM, Sunday 1:30–5:30 PM
Cost: Adults $5, Seniors (65+) $4, Kids (6–17) $2.50
Website: www.shrineofthepines.com
Directions: Two miles south of town on Michigan Ave. (M-37).

Bear Lake
Kampvilla Dinosaur

Anyone deathly afraid of bears or other wild creatures probably shouldn't go camping, unless they park their Winnebago or pitch their tent at

Bears beware.

Kampvilla RV Park. Since 1985, this outdoor establishment has had the king of all scarecrows . . . or should that be scarebears? That's when the owners purchased a 30-foot-long concrete dinosaur from Gordon Clute of Tawas City and placed it at the park's entrance. The bright yellow statue has red eyes that light up at night to frighten away any nocturnal beasties. Has Kampvilla lost a patron since? Nope!

Kampvilla RV Park, 16632 Pleasanton Hwy., Bear Lake, MI 49614

Phone: (800) 968-0027

Hours: Always visible

Cost: Free

Website: www.facebook.com/KampvillaRVPark

Directions: Between Lumley Rd. and Glovers Lake Rd. on Rte. 31 (Pleasanton Hwy.).

Beaver Island
The Kingdom of Zion

The United States might have overthrown the British monarchy in 1776, but that didn't stop James Jesse Strang from giving it a second shot. Strang crowned himself King James during a ceremony on Beaver Island on July 8,

1850, while dressed in a red Shakespearean robe and tin crown that he'd purchased from an actor.

Strang wasn't born of a royal family, but he *was* a saint, the Latter Day kind. He had converted to Mormonism in 1844, shortly before Joseph Smith was murdered in Carthage, Illinois. In the power vacuum after Smith's death, Strang produced a letter signed by Smith (of dubious origin) proclaiming that he was to be new head of the church. Brigham Young called Strang's bluff and led most of Smith's flock west, to Utah Territory.

But Strang had his followers, too, who lived for a time in a colony called Voree near Burlington, Wisconsin. Then Strang found his own tablets on a hillside, supposedly written by Rajah Manchou, that said the group should head *east* to a remote island in Lake Michigan. The so-called Kingdom of Zion was established in 1847 and would grow to 5,000 followers, who called themselves Strangites.

Strang had secretly longed to be king from an early age. At ten years old he wrote in his journal, "I have spent the day trying to contrive some plan of obtaining in marriage the heir to the English crown." When that didn't pan out, he crowned himself anyway and made his own rules. It's good to be king! Polygamy was accepted practice on Beaver Island, mostly for him (Strang had five wives), and his subjects were forced to adhere to increasingly bizarre proclamations. Ordering all women to wear bloomers so angered some husbands that they hatched a plot to kill him.

On June 16, 1856, church members Thomas Bedford and Alexander Wentworth jumped and pistol-whipped Strang, then shot him three times. Remarkably, he survived long enough to return to Wisconsin, where he died on July 9. Most of his followers then fled or were driven from the island, and angry non-Strangites burned the sect's temple and homes to the ground. What little evidence left of the Strangites is now on display in the Mormon Print Shop Museum.

Old Mormon Print Shop Museum, St. James Harbor, PO Box 263, Beaver Island, MI 49782

Phone: (616) 448-2254

Hours: June–August, Monday–Saturday 11 AM–5 PM, Sunday noon–3 PM

Cost: Free

Website: www.beaverisland.net/beaver-island-history/Museums/index.htm

Directions: Off Charlevoix; ferry takes three hours, one-way.

Beaverton

Big Dragon

Knights and damsels beware—an enormous rusty dragon guards the entrance to the Lyle Industries plant southwest of Beaverton. The 50-foot winged lizard seems particularly protective of this establishment, which is understandable; its employees manufactured the giant beast. The dragon stands on two clawed feet, its mouth open in a frozen roar, baring its fangs at all who trespass.

Don't worry, you won't be bitten, though tetanus is a possibility.

Lyle Industries, 4144 W. Lyle Rd., Beaverton, MI 48612

Private phone

Hours: Always visible

Cost: Free

Website: www.lyleindustries.com

Directions: South on Rte. 18 to Lyle Rd., then west two miles.

Have you had your tetanus shot?

Beulah

Beulah's Sculpture Gardens

Who'd have thought little ol' Beulah, barely a speck on the map, would have *two* sculpture gardens for travelers to enjoy? Neither collection is located in town, and both are on private property, but they can each be comfortably appreciated from the road.

The first sculpture garden, found north of town on the west side of Route 31, was made by Don Crossman for his grandkids. Crossman welded cans, pipes, and old car parts to empty (we hope) propane tanks to create a small cast of wacky characters—Goofy and Pluto, an alligator and a fat dog, Uncle Sam and a risen-from-the-dead Jesus. All face the highway, arranged like a police lineup. Nothing's for sale, so don't ask. Just enjoy.

8775 US Hwy. 31, Beulah, MI 49617

Private phone

Hours: Always visible; view from road

Cost: Free

Directions: Where Michigan Ave. (Rte. 31) bends east, north of town and north of Worden Rd.

The second sculpture park is the work of Dewey Blocksma, a former ER doctor who called it quits at the age of 36—too many stabbings and gunshots for him. Instead, he put his talented hands to work creating bizarre creatures from cast-off junk—tennis rackets, Jell-O molds, bike wheels, wash basins, and yes, propane tanks.

Many of Blocksma's brightly painted pieces are whirligigs, so if a breeze is blowing across Crystal Lake—his home is just north of the northeast shore—stop by for a look. If you really like his creations, Blocksma *does*

BIG RAPIDS
⇒ Kids cannot play marbles "for keeps" in Big Rapids.

BOYNE CITY
⇒ When he was young, Ernest Hemingway and a few of his drunken pals shot out every streetlight in Boyne City.

---

sell them through the Tamarack Gallery in Omena, at the northwestern end of Grand Traverse Bay.

2579 Warren Rd., Beulah, MI 48617
Private phone
Hours: Always visible; view from street
Cost: Free
Directions: Between Crystal Dr. and Platte Rd., on the east side of the road.

Tamarack Gallery, 5039 N. West Bay Shore Dr., PO Box 1, Omena, MI 49674
Phone: (231) 386-5529
Hours: January–May, Thursday–Saturday 10 AM–5 PM, Sunday noon–5 PM; June–August, Monday–Saturday 10 AM–5 PM, Sunday noon–5 PM; September–December, Wednesday–Saturday 10 AM–5 PM, Sunday noon–5 PM
Cost: Free
Website: www.tamarackartgallery.com
Directions: On M-22 (Bay Shore Dr.) north of Omena Pt. Rd.

Cadillac
Cadillac Sound Garden

Anyone expecting state-of-the-art musical instruments at the Cadillac Sound Garden might be disappointed at first, but pick up a log mallet and start banging and you just might have some fun. This small park on the north side of Lake Cadillac looks like a prop from an episode of *The Flintstones*, perhaps when Fred and Barney took Wilma and Betty to see Frank Sinrocka at Rock-a-Fella Center. But it's real.

Built by music teacher Frank Youngman and a group of helpers called the Log-Rhythmics, the garden's instruments are made from painted logs arranged in oversized xylophones and long wooden gongs. There's also a series of hanging bells made from rusty truck wheels and brake drums. Just whack away and see what music you can make—the perfect stop for any parents with ADHD children. Or ADHD adults.

Cadillac Sound Garden, 340 Chestnut St., Cadillac, MI 49601
No phone
Hours: Daylight hours
Cost: Free
Website: www.facebook.com/pages/Cadillac-Sound-Garden/398853993497201
Directions: On the northeast shore of Lake Cadillac, west of Lake St. and the Consumers Energy building, at the Clam River Bridge.

Charlevoix
Mushroom Buildings

As you drive around the west side of Charlevoix you might get the feeling you've stepped into a Peter Jackson movie. Dozens of stone homes look as if they've been built by or for hobbits, their walls wavy and uneven, their roofs lumpy blankets of cedar shingles. These buildings, 26 in all, were built by self-trained organic architect Earl Young, who used only materials he scrounged from around town.

Young built his first structure in 1921 at 304 Park Avenue, and it's still standing. If the doors and roofline look a little shorter than standard size, it's because Young chose to make many of his buildings match his diminutive stature. He later built a home at 306 Park Avenue and moved in with his family, where they lived for many years. If you want to see all of Young's creations, pick up a map at the Chamber of Commerce (408 Bridge St., (231) 547-2101).

To get an even closer look at his handiwork, there are two Young buildings open to the general public: the Weathervane Restaurant and the Lodge of Charlevoix. Inside the Weathervane, Young placed a nine-ton limestone boulder over the fireplace, a rock he'd saved for 26 years because he thought it looked like the lower peninsula of Michigan. He also claimed the veins in the boulder replicated Michigan's interstates, but that's a bit of a stretch. Nearby, the Lodge at Charlevoix, while certainly impressive, does not have quite the elfin feel of most of his buildings, though it makes up for it with *Mad Men* retro flare.

Stafford's Weathervane Restaurant, 106 Pine River Ln., Charlevoix, MI 49720
Phone: (231) 547-4311
Hours: Always visible; Restaurant, daily 11 AM–2:30 PM and 4:30–9:30 PM
Cost: Meals, $9–30
Website: www.staffords.com/weathervane
Directions: West of Rte. 31 (Michigan Ave./Bridge St.) just north of the river.

The Lodge of Charlevoix, 120 Michigan Ave., Charlevoix, MI 49720
Phone: (888) 547-6565 or (231) 547-6565
Hours: Always open
Cost: Rooms, $59–184/night
Website: www.thelodge-charlevoix.com
Directions: Two blocks north of the bridge on Rte. 31 (Michigan Ave./Bridge St.).

World's Largest Cherry Pie Oven

Will you be having a large gathering for the Fourth of July this year? Try this 7-ton cherry pie recipe: 850 pounds flour, 325 pounds water, 110 pounds milk, 375 pounds shortening, 55 pounds baking powder, and 15 pounds salt. That's just for the crust. To make the filling, mix 4,950 pounds Michigan cherries (pitted), 2,850 pounds water, 3,850 pounds cherry juice, 540 pounds sugar, 260 pounds butter, 120 pounds lemon juice, 90 pounds tapioca, 90 pounds salt, and a pinch of cinnamon. Press half the crust into a 14-foot, 4-inch pan, add the filling, and roll the remainder of the crust over the top. Use a helicopter to spread the egg wash and sugar topping. Bake for five hours. Serves thousands.

That's precisely what the folks of Charlevoix did to celebrate this nation's Bicentennial, led by David R. Phillips. The Medusa Cement Corporation built the 18-foot-wide oven; Will-Flow made the custom pie tin.

Only the oven is a current record-holder.

Charlevoix held the record for the world's largest pie until they were outbaked by Traverse City (see page 96) in 1987, which itself was bested five years later. But unlike those other two cities, Charlevoix kept its ginormous tin *and* oven, which you can still see in a small park next to the town's south-side fire station. (The monument and park were refurbished by a local Boy Scout troop in 2008–09.) Since Traverse City kept its pan, Charlevoix has to be content with having the World's Largest Cherry Pie Oven, but only the World's *Second* Largest (Extant) Cherry Pie Pan. They've placed a replica slice of pie into the pan, but I wouldn't try eating it—concrete is murder on dental work.

Fire Department #2, 6591 S. US Hwy. 31, Charlevoix, MI 49720

No phone

Hours: Always visible

Cost: Free

Directions: West of Old Norwood Rd. on Bridge St (Rte. 31), on the southwest side of town.

Cheboygan
Sea Shell City

Beware the Man-Eating Clam! So scream the billboards up and down I-75. No, it's not native to Michigan, but neither are any of the tropical shells found in this enormous beach-themed gift shop in the middle of northern nowhere.

As you look around Sea Shell City, you quickly realize that *none* of this stuff looks like it belongs in the Great Lake State—the shell lamps, the children's pirate costumes, the sea foam green toothpick holders would all look more at home in Florida, the Bahamas, or a Cheeseburger in Paradise souvenir hut.

CADILLAC
➡ Cadillac calls itself "Chestnut Town, USA."

CHEBOYGAN
➡ By law, Cheboygan men may not swear in front of their wives.

Oh, don't worry about it—you should be much more concerned about that Man-Eating Clam! Scan the aisles, search the shelves. Wait—there it is, all 505 pound of it, over by the men's bathroom! Move closer . . . closer . . . cloooooser . . . to read the nearby sign. It says the colossal clam is from the Philippines . . . and it's quite dead. And it only eats *algae.*

Blimey, ye be hornswaggled!

7075 Levering Rd., Cheboygan, MI 49721

Phone: (877) 435-5248 or (231) 627-2066

Hours: Daily 9 AM–5 PM

Cost: Free

Website: http://seashellcitymi.com

Directions: East of I-75 at the Levering Rd. exit.

Clare
Cops & Doughnuts

Certainly every police officer alive knows the profession's doughnut-loving stereotype—at this point, why fight it? That must have been the thinking of the nine cops who bought the Clare City Bakery in 2009. The store had been a cornerstone of the community since 1896, and the law enforcement establishment had become quite fond of its chocolate-iced and glazed products. So when they learned that it would be shutting its doors forever, the entire department rallied and saved the institution.

Today the place is thriving, taking up three storefronts on the town's main drag—one for the bakery, one for the customers to sit and eat, and the third filled with merchandise bearing the store's signature logo: a pink strawberry doughnut ringing a police badge, like a fat hula hoop. Good-natured officers from around the nation flock to Clare to buy T-shirts and mugs and embroidered patches. The doughnuts are tasty, too.

521 N. McEwan St., Clare, MI 48617

Phone: (989) 386-2241

Hours: Always open

Cost: $1–3

Website: www.copsdoughnuts.com

Directions: Just south of Main/Fifth St. (M-115) on Rte. 127 (McEwan St.).

MICHIGAN LAWS

If you go to Cops & Doughnuts you're going to run into the police, so be sure you're not breaking any of these Michigan laws.

⇒ You may not varnish vegetables before selling them.

⇒ You cannot lift your skirt more than six inches when dodging a mud puddle.

⇒ If you step into the path of a moving vehicle, you are breaking the law by creating a hazard.

⇒ It is illegal to put a skunk in your boss's desk.

⇒ Husbands cannot use cattle, horses, or mules to hunt waterfowl in their wives' hair.

⇒ Speaking of which, a wife's hair is her husband's property.

⇒ If you kiss your wife on Sunday, the courts may punish whoever is at fault.

⇒ Couples cannot have sex before marriage or they risk drawing a $5,000 fine. If a person has sex with a corpse, however, the fine is only $2,500.

⇒ Finally, once married, if you do not live with your spouse in Michigan you may be imprisoned.

Leprechauns at the Tap Room

Some folks—most folks, actually—go their entire lives without seeing a leprechaun. If you're one of those people, stop by the restaurant at the Doherty Hotel and get your fill . . . they've got dozens of the itty-bitty Irish imps!

Back in 1932, in exchange for room and board, Saginaw artist Jay McHugh spent six months painting a 75-foot mural that wraps around

The life of a leprechaun isn't always a pot of gold. Photo by author, courtesy Doherty Hotel

the upper wall of the hotel's bar and lounge. It depicts an elaborate booze-making operation and little person picnic. Some of the leprechauns seem to be enjoying themselves, namely the drunk picnickers with steins in their hands, but most of the rest frown as they lug barrels, stoke fires, and generally break their backs for their elfin customers.

Doherty Hotel, 604 N. McEwan St., Clare, MI 48617

Phone: (800) 525-4115

Hours: Always open, check at front desk

Cost: Free

Website: http://dohertyhotel.com

Directions: On the northeast corner of Fifth St. (M-115) and McEwan St. (Rte. 127).

Cross Village
Legs Inn

Polish immigrant Stanley Smolak moved to northern Michigan in 1921, and by the end of the decade was building a trading post to sell handiwork made by the local Ottawa tribe. The curio shop did quite well, and the Ottawa appreciated his efforts so much they made him an honorary tribal member: Chief White Cloud. Over the years Smolak expanded and decorated his establishment with totem poles, hand-carved furniture, and surreal creatures made from twisted roots and branches. And he used a pile of cast-iron stove legs to decorate the building's roofline, giving the shop its new name: Legs Inn.

The Smolak family still owns Legs Inn, which looks pretty much the way it did when Stanley passed away in 1968. In addition to the gift shop, they serve authentic Polish food—pierogi, golabki, nalesniki, kabanosy, and zurek soup—which you're not likely to find (or even hear uttered) anywhere else in these parts. Legs Inn has an outdoor deck when the weather is nice, live entertainment inside the lounge, and even cabins should you want to stay awhile.

6425 N. Lake Shore Dr., PO Box 157, Cross Village, MI 49723
Phone: (231) 526-2281
Hours: May–October, Sunday–Thursday noon–8 PM, Friday–Saturday noon–9 PM
Cost: Free; Meals $15–20
Website: www.legsinn.com
Directions: On M-119 (Lake Shore Dr.) in the middle of town.

Elk Rapids
Big Swan

What, you were expecting a Big *Elk* in Elk Rapids? How predictable! No, the front entrance to the Elk Rapids Chamber of Commerce is graced with a beautiful 15-foot *swan*. Back in 1966 it was used to carry Miss Elk Rapids in the annual Cherry Festival parade.

What, you think she should have ridden in a Big Red Cherry? How inappropriate!

This old bird was made with a wooden frame, chicken wire, and a stucco coating. A few years ago it looked pretty sad, but the chamber paid for repairs and a fresh coat of white paint. These days it looks almost seaworthy.

Elk Rapids Chamber of Commerce, 305 US 31 North, PO Box 854, Elk Rapids, MI 49629
Phone: (231) 264-8202
Hours: Always visible
Cost: Free
Website: www.elkrapidschamber.org
Directions: South of the bridge on Rte. 31, between First St. and River St.

Elmira
Potato Burgers

It sounds like a nightmare from the test kitchens at Hamburger Helper, but it's actually quite good. Ellen Czyloski invented the Potato Burger back when this place was known as the Elmira Inn. The recipe is simple: mix shredded potatoes with ground beef, press into a thick patty, dip in beer batter, and deep fry. Charge up the defibrillator and you're ready to eat.

Though the bar has since changed names and ownership, they wouldn't think of dropping this signature item from the menu. Your cardiologist might have a thing or two to say about this delicacy, but the locals stand by it. And by stand, I mean sit, bloated, in their chairs.

Railside Bar & Grill, 8805 M32 West., Elmira, MI 49730

Phone: (231) 546-3248

Hours: Sunday–Thursday noon–9 PM, Friday–Saturday noon–10:30 PM

Cost: $8.99

Website: www.therailsidebar.com

Directions: On M-32 (Underwood Ave.) at Division Rd., north of the tracks.

Frankfort
Pumpkin Ed

Here's an oddball site to put on your calendar, because it only exists for a couple weeks each year. Ed Moody has been carving pumpkins for Halloween since he was six years old, first with the standard jab-a-knife-three-times-to-make-an-eye technique, but later graduating to full-fledged sculpture as he started sharing his talents with his young kids.

Not satisfied to work on regularly sized pumpkins, these days Moody buys freaky Dills Atlantic Giants that weigh 1,000 pounds or more—typically 25 each season—and creates a sculpture park around his house for the Frankfort Fall Festival. The largest, roundest pumpkin he carves into a Cinderella carriage that's big enough for little princesses and princes to sit in for adorable photo ops and unrealistic life expectations. Most of the other pumpkins are sculpted into jumbo jack-o-lanterns with the twisted faces of ogres, giants, and trolls.

Lately, Moody has been taking his show on the road, creating pumpkin displays for every children's hospital in the nation. Money he raises from donations and the sale of seeds go to this worthwhile effort.

722 Leelanau Ave., Frankfort, MI 49635

Private phone

Hours: October, check website

Cost: Free

Website: http://pumpkined.com

Directions: Just east of M-22 (Seventh St.) five blocks north of Betsie Lake.

Gaylord
Big Buck Brewery's Big Beer Bottle

How big would a Big Buck Brewery beer bottle be if the Big Buck Brewery built a big beer bottle? 'Bout 30 feet, apparently.

Big Buck Brewery is a typical craft ale bar and Northwoods steakhouse. The on-site brewery stores its grain in this large silo disguised as a giant bottle, which also attracts customers from the nearby freeway.

550 S. Wisconsin Ave., Gaylord, MI 49735

Phone: (989) 732-5781

Hours: Always visible; Bar, May–October, Monday–Thursday 11 AM–10 PM, Friday–Saturday 11 AM–11 PM, Sunday 11 AM–9 PM; November–April, Monday–Thursday 11 AM–9 PM, Friday–Saturday 11 AM–10 PM, Sunday 11 AM–8 PM

Cost: Free; Meals $10–20

Website: www.bigbuck.com

Directions: Between Fourth St. and Eighth St., just east of I-75, two blocks south of Main St. (M-22).

Call of the Wild

Let's face it: most natural history museums are considerably less vivacious than experiencing wildlife in the great outdoors. Maybe it's that the animals are dead and stuffed. And silent. But at the privately owned Call of the Wild North American Wildlife Museum, the dioramas are sometimes animated and often wired for sound. Just pick up one of the cow horn–shaped phones on the walls, press a button, and listen to the bugle of an elk or the howl of a wolf. Or marvel at the Four Seasons Display, which changes from summer to fall to winter to spring, right before your eyes. Then watch a barn owl's head turn around at regular intervals, just like in *The Exorcist*.

A Michigan white-tailed deer in its natural habitat: the headlights.
Photo by author, courtesy Call of the Wild

Call of the Wild's other, more static wildlife displays are not as elaborate or refined as you'd find in larger institutions, but they're generally more entertaining. Fawns frolic with friendly coyotes in a forest, four baby raccoons scurry up a dead tree, a polar bear and cub growl at you from an icy lair, and a deer stares bleary-eyed, trapped in the headlights of an oncoming car.

Yet strangest of all, the museum has two human dioramas featuring trapper Joseph Baily. In the first, his face comes alive as he sits by a campfire and talks about life in the Northwoods. It's tough, he admits, but it's better than living in Detroit. (Some attitudes never change.) Later on, you find Baily in another diorama, settled down and married to an American Indian woman. Their backs are to you as they gaze into the cabin fireplace and reminisce about the old days—like Grandma at Thanksgiving, but without her box of wine.

850 S. Wisconsin Ave., Gaylord, MI 49735

Phone: (800) 835-4347 or (989) 732-4336

Hours: June–August, daily 9 AM–9 PM; September–May, Monday–Saturday 9:30 AM–6 PM, Sunday 11 AM–5 PM

Cost: Adults $7, Seniors (62+) $6.50, Kids (5–13) $4.50

Website: http://gocallofthewild.com

Directions: Exit I-75 at Main St. (M-32), east two blocks, then south on Wisconsin Ave. for two blocks.

Glen Arbor
Cherry Republic

Like the Vatican or Monte Carlo or the Neverland Ranch, the Cherry Republic is a country within a country, a micronation unto itself. Border security is rather lax, but customs asks that you declare all bananas on entry. Once cleared, it's time to shop—salsa, pie filling, cookies, jams, wines, candies, sodas, chocolates, soap, granola, all infused with the region's favorite fruit. (About 80 percent of America's red tart cherries come from northern Michigan.) If you're hungry, step next door where the Grand Café of the Republic serves cherry hot dogs, cherry hamburgers, cherry pie, and 14 types of cherry ice cream.

Cherry Republic's founder and pitted potentate, Bob Sutherland, seems bent on world domination, opening an Embassy in Traverse City (154 E. Front St., (231) 932-9205) and two Outposts, one in Charlevoix (411 Bridge St., (231) 437-3600) and another in Ann Arbor (223 S. Main St., (734) 585-5231). The republic's motto is "Life, Liberty, Beaches, and Pie," so if he ever does take over, who would complain?

Cherry Republic Headquarters, 6026 Lake St., Glen Arbor, MI 49636

Phone: (800) 206-6949

Hours: Daily 9 AM–9 PM

Cost: Free

Website: www.cherryrepublic.com

Directions: One block east of M-22 (Ray St.) at State St.

Grayling
Bottle-Cap Museum

Dang lawyers! If you're a bottle cap buff, don't come to the Bottle-Cap Museum expecting to see caps from every soda ever produced. No, the only caps you'll see are still on bottles of Coca-Cola. Why? Because this is actually a museum of Coca-Cola merchandise and memorabilia. The

Whatever you do, don't use the C-C words.

owners of this 1950s diner have more than 10,000 red-and-white items on display, all bearing the brand's signature signature. They've got trays and toys, bells and bottles, cans and cups. They've got pedal cars, coolers, signs, dolls, clocks, banks, mugs, ashtrays, and lots of commemorative plates. There's even a city-sized Coca-Cola Christmas village above the antique soda fountain.

So why is it called the Bottle-Cap Museum? Apparently a lawyer advised not using the brand's name because the Coca-Cola Corporation might look on it as an unauthorized endorsement of a charming establishment that clearly loves its product. Horror!

Gimme a break. Screw those Atlanta lawyers—I'm gonna call it what it really is: the Coca-Cola Museum, the Coca-Cola Museum, THE COCA-COLA MUSEUM! Sue me.

Dawson & Stevens Classic 50's Diner, 231 Michigan Ave., Grayling, MI 49738

Phone: (989) 348-2111

Hours: Monday–Thursday 7 AM–7 PM, Friday–Saturday 7 AM–8 PM, Sunday 7 AM–6 PM

Cost: Free; Meals, $5–10

Website: www.bottlecapmuseum.com

Directions: On Michigan Ave., one block northeast of M-72/I-75 Bus. (James St.).

Honor
Cherry Bowl Drive-In Theatre

There aren't many places like the Cherry Bowl Drive-In Theatre any more. Blame DVDs, Netflix, or the Internet. Blame light pollution from the cities. Blame them no good kids with their cell phones and saggy pants. Damn kids! Personally, I think it's that too few people today have experienced how much fun you can have at a drive-in (nudge-nudge), probably because there are so few fun drive-ins left to visit, like this one in Honor.

The Cherry Bowl has been around since 1953, opening with *The Greatest Show on Earth*, Cecil B. DeMille's epic of the Ringling Brothers Circus, starring Charlton Heston, Dorothy Lamour, Betty Hutton, and Jimmy Stewart. Sure, it was hokey, but that's what going to a drive-in is all about. The Cherry Bowl still has old-style in-window speakers, a playground just below the big screen, miniature golf, and a refreshment stand filled with classic movie memorabilia. Outside the fence, directing theatergoers in from the highway, you'll see a Pepto-Bismol pink VW Beetle, a giant chicken and hot dog, and a fiberglass steer pulling an Amish buggy. It's hard to miss. Check the website for upcoming car cruise nites, pony rides, and roaming movie characters like sword-swinging pirates and a downsized Godzilla.

Or you could just sit at home on your couch.

9812 Honor Hwy., Honor, MI 49640

Phone: (231) 325-3413

Hours: Check website for show times

Cost: Double-feature, Adults $8.50, Kids (12 and under) free

Website: www.cherrybowldrivein.com

Directions: West of town on Rte. 31 (Honor Hwy.), just west of Marshall Rd. (Co. Hwy. 679).

DRIVE ON TO DRIVE-INS

Honor is a long way from, well, just about everywhere except Traverse City, so if you're looking for a drive-in theater a little closer to home, check out the following:

Ford Wyoming Drive-In

10400 Ford Rd., Dearborn, (313) 846-6910, www.fordwyomingdrivein.com

This mega-drive-in claims to be the Largest Drive-in Theater in the World, and at one time had nine different screens. However, today it's been scaled back to five, and the largest title is in doubt. The Ford Wyoming opened in 1950 with one screen for 750 cars, but now can accommodate up to 3,000 vehicles.

Capri Drive-In Theater

119 W. Chicago Rd., Coldwater, (517) 278-5628, www.capridrive-in.com

Open since 1964, the Capri is still a family-run operation, well maintained and operated. It offers double features on each of its two screens every night in the summer.

Hi-Way Drive-In

E. Sanilac Rd./M-46, Carsonville, (810) 657-MOVI, www.thehiwaydrivein.com

The Hi-Way is Michigan's oldest drive-in, having opened for business in 1948. It offers nightly double features on its single screen.

US 23 Drive-In

5200 Fenton Rd., Flint, (810) 238-0751, www.us23driveintheater.com

The US 23 has three screens for moviegoers, each running a nightly double feature. Under a list of customer "Dont's," the drive-in says, "Consumption of alcoholic beverages in discouraged." But it doesn't say *banned*.

Indian River

Big Jesus and the Nun Doll Museum

When the Franciscan Friars first erected a 55-foot-tall, 22-foot-wide redwood megacross in 1954, it looked a bit barren. But five years later, a 31-foot-tall bronze Jesus was installed on the structure, and hung with giant nails by, one presumes, a Roman Paul Bunyan. The seven-ton sculpture was created by artist Marshall Fredericks, and for more than 30 years held the title of world's largest crucifix.

But then a parish in Bardstown, Kentucky, built an even larger crucifix, its cross topping out at 60 feet, and the Cross in the Woods dropped to the silver medal platform. Nevertheless, this Michigan shrine is still a wonderful place to visit. In addition to its large outdoor chapel nestled in a moss-carpeted forest, it has shrines to Our Lady of the Highway, St. Peregrine (the Patron Saint of Cancer Patients), and Kateri "Lily of the Mohawks" Tekakwitha, surrounded by dozens of adoring bronze turtles.

Sister Barbara's dream house. Photo by author, courtesy of Cross in the Woods National Shrine

As beautiful as it is outside, don't leave before checking out the well-stocked gift shop and the Nun Doll Museum in the basement. Sally Rogalski began creating nun dolls as a child after her mother was nursed back to health by the Daughters of Charity. By the time she was an adult, along with help from her husband, Wally, she had created 525 different dolls, ranging in size from Barbies to mannequins, to model 217 different religious orders' habits. Rogalski also created dioramas of nuns at work—Teacher, Missionary to Foreign Lands, and Home Maker for the Community—as well as a few dozen priest dolls to remind the sisters who are the fathers.

Cross in the Woods National Shrine, 7078 M-68, Indian River, MI 49749

Phone: Shrine, (231) 238-8973; Gift Shop, (231) 238-8722

Hours: Daily, sunrise–sunset

Cost: Free

Website: www.crossinthewoods.com

Directions: One mile west of I-75 on Sturgeon St. (M-68).

Kaleva
Big Grasshopper

"Heinäsirkka, Heinäsirkka, mene täälä hiiteen!" St. Uhro commanded, banging his pitchfork on the earth. "Grasshopper, grasshopper, go to hell!" And with this mighty proclamation, all the pests that had infested Finland fled the country, never to return, saving the country's grape harvest. Which is why, on March 16, contemporary Finns celebrate St. Urho's holy fumigation by drinking red wine and grape juice while dressed in purple and green clothing. Or at least they have since the 1950s, when this preposterous fake holiday was concocted to upstage St. Patrick's Day.

To keep this loony legend alive, students from Brethren High School Service Learning and Manistee Intermediate School, under the direction of Andy Priest, created a quarter-ton grasshopper statue to be placed on the Kaleva Centennial Walkway. The enormous metal insect was welded together from old car parts donated by Bill's Auto Body in Wellston and A&L's Auto Parts of Kaleva. It's 18 feet long, 10 feet tall, and isn't going anywhere, St. Uhro or not.

Kaleva Centennial Walkway, Walta and Sampo Aves., Kaleva, MI 49645

Phone: (231) 362-3480

Hours: Always visible

Cost: Free

Website: www.kalevami.com

Directions: Four blocks north of 9 Mile Rd., one block west of Aura St., at Sampo Ave.

Bottle House

Many years ago, Finnish immigrant John Jacob Makinen Sr. decided to put the modified adage "people who live in glass houses should always wear clothes" to the test. As the owner of the Northwestern Bottling Works and a bit of a cheapskate, he decided to construct his Kaleva home from his plant's irregular and slightly damaged leftovers—about 60,000 soft drink bottles, give or take a few. The nine-room house was completed in 1941, though Makinen died just before he could move in. His surviving family lived there until 1980.

One way to save on bricks.

Only the ground floor walls of the Bottle House were made from glass, most of it clear. Makinen inlaid diamond-shaped patterns into the surface using green and brown bottles, and spelled out "Happy Home" with additional colored bottles on either side of the front door. However, it's no longer a home; the local historical society later purchased the structure and turned it into a museum that you can visit today.

Kaleva Historical Museum, 14551 Wuoski Ave., PO Box 252, Kaleva, MI 49645

Phone: (231) 362-2080

Hours: June–August, Saturday–Sunday noon–4 PM; September–October, Saturday noon–4 PM

Cost: Free

Website: www.kalevami.com/The_Bottle_House_Museum.html

Directions: Downtown between Osmo and Kauko Sts.

Kalkaska
National Trout Memorial

Take off your fishing cap when you approach the National Trout Memorial—these finned friends give their lives so that you have something to do with your weekends, your summer vacations, and your "sick" days. Show some respect, or at the very least be impressed by its size—it's a 204-incher!

Leo Nelson, with the help of engineer Ben Robinson, created this 600-pound fishy fountain back in 1966. Kalkaska was chosen for this honor because it has hosted a National Trout Festival (www.nationaltroutfestival.com) every April since 1935, and it still does. The trout depicted is a brook trout, the Michigan State Fish. The garden surrounding the memorial also has statues of an American robin, the Michigan State Bird, and a wolverine, which is *not* the State Mammal, just the state's nickname.

Kalkaska Museum, 335 S. Cedar St., Kalkaska, MI 49646

Phone: (231) 258-9719

Hours: Always visible; Museum, June–August, Wednesday–Saturday 1–4 PM

Cost: Free

Website: www.kalkaskacounty.net/kalkhistory.asp

Directions: On Rte. 131/M-72 (Cedar St.) between Third and Fourth Sts.

KALKASKA

➡ Kalkaska Sand is the official Michigan State Soil.

Kewadin
Michigan Cairn

All hail Hugh J. Gray, Dean of Michigan's Tourist Activity! Come, intrepid vacationers, to see the mighty pyramid constructed in this bureaucrat's honor!

All right, so this 1938 monument may be shaped like a pyramid, but it's no Giza. In fact, it's only 12 feet tall. Nevertheless, it has something the Egyptians pyramids lack: an engraved stone from each of Michigan's 83 counties. Look—there's a limestone slab from Mackinac, a granite boulder from Leelanau, and from Shiawassee . . . is that schist?

The bronze plaque on the Michigan Cairn says this monument stands astride the 45th parallel, halfway from the equator to the North Pole, or if you're Canadian, the other way around. However, anyone with a GPS or a detailed map will tell you it's a few miles short—it should have been located farther north. Hugh Gray might have been Dean of Michigan Tourism, but he wasn't Dean of the Geography Department.

5899 Cairn Hwy., Kewadin, MI 49648

No phone

Hours: Always visible

Cost: Free

Directions: East of Rte. 31 on Winters Rd., then north on Cairn Hwy.

Mackinaw City
Keyhole Bar & Grill

Have you ever misplaced your keys, and perhaps wondered whether they ran away to live among their own kind, were snatched by key gnomes, or crawled off to die in a key graveyard?

Wow, you have some imagination. Well, if there were such a place, it would probably look like the Keyhole Bar & Grill. Every spare inch of this establishment

More motel keys than the stage of a Tom Jones concert.

has been adorned with old keys and fobs, about 23,000 at last count, which was some time ago. Most were donated by customers, from hotels they'd visited, cars they'd wrecked, or apartments of exes who have since gotten restraining orders. Have a seat at one of the keyhole-shaped tables; hundreds of loose keys are encased in the clear Lucite tabletops. Then order something from the menu of seafood and specialty subs called the Yale, the Master, and the Dexter. Yeah, the theme gets a little repetitive, but that's the idea.

323 E. Central Ave., Mackinaw City, MI 49701

Phone: (231) 436-7911

Hours: Monday–Saturday, 11 AM–11 PM, Sunday, noon–11 PM

Cost: Free; Meals, $10–20

Website: www.facebook.com/goodtimesgoodfood

Directions: Three blocks east of I-75 on Central Ave.

The Mighty Mac

For many years—decades even—a bridge connecting Michigan's upper and lower peninsulas was just talk, talk, talk. First proposed in 1884, the state didn't break ground until 70 years later, on May 7, 1954. Granted, this was no small undertaking. As eventually designed by D. B. Steinman, the Mackinac Bridge required 466,300 cubic yards of concrete, 4,851,700 steel rivets, and 42,000 *miles* of steel wire to build. Most of that wire was woven into the thick, main suspension cables between the towers, each two feet in diameter with 12,580 wires per cable.

The Mackinac Bridge finally opened for business on November 1, 1957. Half a century later, it still holds the record for the longest suspension bridge between two towers in North America—7,400 feet—8,614 if you include the anchorages. Including approaches, it is five miles (and 44 feet) long. The top of the towers are 552 feet above the water; the deck is 200 feet high.

If the thought of driving over such a structure makes you a little queasy, the bridge offers a free service: they'll drive your car across while you're curled up in a fetal position in the backseat. If, on the other hand, you're really, really into big bridges, you have one chance each year to see it up close: the annual Bridge Walk. On Labor Day, half the lanes are shut down for pedestrian traffic only. The walk is traditionally led by the governor, starting from the north end. Free shuttles will bring you back to your car when you're done.

N 415 I-75, St. Ignace, MI 49781

Phone: (906) 643-7600

Hours: Always open

Cost: $4/car

Website: www.mackinacbridge.org

Directions: I-75 between Mackinaw City and St. Ignace.

Of course, a structure like the Mackinac Bridge doesn't go up by itself—somebody has to build it. You can learn all about who they were at the Mackinac Bridge Museum, located in a Mackinaw City pizzeria. Here you'll learn that five ironworkers lost their lives during its construction. (One more died in 1997 while repainting it.) The museum is filled with hard hats and harder stories, as well as tools, rivets, and foot-long bolts that divers have recovered from the lake bottom. Don't worry, the thing isn't falling apart—they were all dropped during construction. Or so we're told.

Mama Mia's Mackinaw City, 231 E. Central Ave., Mackinaw City, MI 49701

Phone: (231) 436-5534

Hours: Daily 8 AM–midnight

Cost: Museum, Free; Pizza, $4–8

Website: www.facebook.com/MamaMiasMackinaw

Directions: Two blocks east of I-75 on Central Ave., on the north side of the street.

Manistee
Death Site of the World's Tallest Man

Robert Pershing Wadlow was the tallest man ever known, topping out at 8 feet, 11.1 inches before he died in Michigan at the young age of 22. He will probably hold that record forever, because today there are ways to treat the pituitary gland problem that caused his giantism.

Back in the late 1930s, after Wadlow graduated from high school, there weren't many employment opportunities for people of his stature; he was already more than eight feet tall. For a while, Wadlow toured with the Ringling Brothers Circus, but later he signed on as spokesman for the International Shoe Company. During one of his promotional tours, Wadlow made an appearance at the Manistee National Forest Festival. While walking in the parade, a misadjusted leg brace rubbed his ankle and caused a blister to become infected. He was taken to the Coral Gables Hotel at the west end of River Street, where doctors monitored his condition. In the years before antibiotics, his chances weren't good. He died in his sleep on July 15, 1940, from a fever brought on by the infection.

Today Manistee remembers its sad place in history at a shoe store near the river. Inside they have a full-sized stature of Wadlow, along with one of his size 37½ AA shoes. The Coral Gables Hotel burned down years ago.

Snyder's Shoe Store, 397 River St., Manistee, MI 49660

Phone: (231) 723-3383

Hours: Monday–Wednesday 9 AM–6 PM, Thursday–Saturday 9 AM–8 PM

Cost: Free

Website: http://snydershoes.com/

Directions: Just east of the Maple St. bridge on the south side of the river.

Mio
Genevieve's Giant Chair

VERY UNSTABLE reads the sign on the giant chair, warning passersby not to climb up to its seat. Anyone looking at it, however, should be able to figure this out, as the highback looks seriously askew, arching backward in a slow roll to the ground. Fortunately, it's not falling toward Genevieve's Flowers & Gifts, located in a prefab building just feet away.

The massive chair was built in 2004 by artist James Jennings. Debbie Bellow, owner of Genevieve's, wanted something to attract potential customers who raced past her store on Miller Road, and this was as good an idea as any. The chair was created from hand-carved cedar logs and stands 25 feet tall. Now 24. Soon to be 23. Then 2.

Genevieve's Flowers & Gifts, 1520 Caldwell Rd., Mio, MI 48647

Phone: (989) 848-2994

Hours: Always visible; Store, Monday–Friday 9 AM–5:30 PM, Saturday 9 AM–noon

Cost: Free

Website: www.facebook.com/mio.genevieves.flowers

Directions: Just east of the intersection with Miller Rd. (M-72/33).

Perma Log

One of the enduring mysteries of the 80-ton heads on Easter Island, known as *moai*, was how they were transported from the quarry where they were carved to their final locations, sometimes as far as 15 miles away. Were they rolled on logs? "Walked" using a combination of levers and ropes? Or ordered on a truck from Perma Log?

The last theory seems unlikely, since the big heads for sale at Perma Log are made of hollow stucco, not chiseled basalt or tuff. Still, these Michigan *moai* don't look half bad from the highway, or in your backyard. Perma Log also makes concrete "log" cabins, the company's specialty, as well as Hobbit huts, ramshackle cartoon outhouses, and Stonehenge replicas. You can see them all at their manufacturing facility south of Mio.

Perma Log, 2218 S. Mt. Tom Rd., PO Box 472, Mio, MI 48647

Phone: (989) 826-3161

Hours: Always visible

Cost: Free

Website: www.permalogco.com

Directions: South of town on M-33 (Mt. Tom Rd.).

One in every size.

Pink Elephant

LOVELY TO LOOK AT / DELIGHTFUL TO HOLD / *PLEASE* DON'T CLIMB ON ME / I AM VERY OLD. So says the poetic warning sign in front of the pink elephant at the Mio Pizza Shop. And it's true—this poor pachyderm has made the rounds. It started life in front of the Pink Elephant Party Store, logically enough, which later became a restaurant called Tomasino's. When that establishment burned to the ground, the statue was moved to a new location on the town's main drag. That store later went bankrupt, and the future looked grim for the pink elephant, its trunk raised high into the air as if in a final salute. But the Mio Pizza Shop finally took the colorful creature in and gave it a nice retirement, with a note to its customers to go easy on the old statue. We should all be so lucky.

Mio Pizza Shop, 421 S. Morenci Ave., Mio, MI 48647

Phone: (989) 826-5746

Hours: Always visible

Cost: Free

Website: www.miopizzashop.com

Directions: On M-33 (Morenci Ave.) at 11th St.

Shrine Central

If there's one problem with the world's Catholic shrines, it's that they're scattered everywhere. What's a believer on a budget to do? Answer: come to Mio, where they've all been re-created in one megashrine.

Construction on Our Lady of the Woods Shrine began in 1953. The central structure looks like a *Price Is Right* showcase carousel with unique shrines built into concave walls that face outward. They've got most of the major Marian shrines—Our Lady of Fatima, Our Lady of Lourdes, Our Lady of Guadalupe, the Black Madonna, Our Lady of La Salette, and Our Lady of Częstochowa—as well as re-creations of Michelangelo's *Pietà* and a less-than-Michelangelo *Holy Family*. And, for good measure, they've included a niche for St. Hubert, Patron Saint of Hunters; and a Sainte-Anne de Beaupré shrine, for any visiting Canadians.

Our Lady of the Woods Shrine, 100 Deyarmond St., PO Box 189, Mio, MI 48647

Phone: (989) 826-5509

Hours: Daylight hours; Store, June–August, Friday 2–4 PM, Saturday noon–6 PM, Sunday 10 AM–
noon; September–May, Sunday after mass

Cost: Free

Website: www.ourladyofthewoodsshrine.org

Directions: One block west of the intersection of Rtes. M-33 and M-72.

THE ARCHANGEL GROTTO, A SMALLER, SELECTIVE SHRINE

According to Roman Catholic tradition, the faith of those who built this rural shrine, there are only three archangels: Gabriel, Michael, and Raphael. (Ringo came later.) Each has been rendered as a nine-foot statue and given a place of honor in his own alcove at the **Marian Center** (2680 Maxwell Rd., (231) 347-6279, http://mariancenter.org) east of Petoskey. Gabriel kneels, his trumpet nowhere to be seen. Raphael wears a fetching, front-gathered robe. And Michael? He's dressed like a Roman and grasps an impressive sword in his upraised hand, ready to do battle for the God of Love.

Northport
Pop Bottle Collection

Kilcherman's Christmas Cove Farm has been around for 40 years, long enough that the owners have been able to plant 240 varieties of apple trees from around the world, including "antiques" like the Kandil Sinap, the Saint Edmunds Pippin, the Sheepnose, the Zabergau Reinette, and the Esopus Spitzenburg, Thomas Jefferson's favorite. Now *that's* an apple!

OLD MISSION
➡ The **Old Mission Point Lighthouse** (M-37, (231) 223-7324, www.missionpointlighthouse.com) is said to be exactly halfway between the equator and the North Pole.

All that would be reason enough to visit the orchard, but Kilcherman's has something else: the world's largest collection of empty glass pop bottles. (No, they don't call it soda here.) All 10,000 or so are lined up in alphabetical order on the shelves. This makes it easier to demonstrate that they aren't counting any duplicates among their grand total.

Kilcherman's Christmas Cove Farm, 11573 N. Kilcherman Rd., Northport, MI 49670

Phone: (231) 386-5637

Hours: September 15–November, daily 10 AM–5 PM

Cost: Free

Website: www.christmascovefarm.com

Directions: Just north of Woolsey Lake Rd. (Rte. 640) at the intersection with Mill St.

Onaway
Big Busts

Tom Moran likes busts. BIG busts.

No, not bosoms, you filthy-minded reader—busts, as in sculptures of subjects' shoulders and heads. But Moran doesn't make busts that you'd place on your grand piano, unless that piano was mighty grand. Just look at the field east of Moran Iron Works. On a recent visit, you'd see a gold, 15-foot-tall replica of Gerald Ford's noggin. Farther away, you'd find a supersized silver likeness of George Washington, which Moran made in 1998, and a green replica of the Statue of Liberty's head, the only one of the three that is smaller than its inspiration.

There's really no guarantee what you'll find in Moran's Field—these things are huge, but made to move. Miss Liberty been towed through many Fourth of July parades, and Gerald Ford once stood outside a brewery in Grand Rapids. You just might see a new creation, or one of Moran's earlier works, back for a hometown visit.

Other giant sculptures made by Moran can be found scattered around northern Michigan. Two huge heads, one of a soldier and the other of an eagle, are located in Alpena (see page 51). Big Gus, the chainsaw, and Big Ernie, the musket, stand outside Da Yopper Tourist Trap in Ishpeming (see page 17). An enormous water pump, a giant Abe Lincoln head, a large Liberty Bell . . . he's done more than a dozen works, and they're often

Ford's real head had more dents. Photo by author, courtesy Moran Iron Works

changing locations. Your best bet is to go to the artist's webpage and map out an up-to-date tour.

Moran's Field, Moran Iron Works, 11739 M-33/68, Onaway, MI 49765

Phone: (989) 733-2011

Hours: Always visible

Cost: Free

Website: www.moraniron.com/community/artwork

Directions: West of County Line Rd. on the west side of town.

Oscoda
Paul Bunyan's Birthplace

Where was Paul Bunyan born? Nobody has yet produced his birth certificate, and some say he came from French-speaking Canada during the 1837 Papineau Rebellion. However, the first time he was ever mentioned in print was in an August 10, 1906, article in the *Oscoda Press* by "reporter"

James MacGillivray. The story did not suggest Bunyan to be unusually sized (or Canadian), nor did it mention his sidekick Babe, but he *was* a superhuman lumberman. Some believe the character was based on local logger Fabian Fournier.

MacGillivray's story got picked up, ripped off, and expanded upon by other writers, most notably by ad man William Laughead, who made the mythical character the spokesgiant for the Red River Lumber Company. That's when the tall tales really took off.

Oscoda celebrates its place in non-history with an annual Paul Bunyan Festival each September. Events center around the not-especially-large statue of Bunyan holding a tree over his shoulder in the center of town. It originally appeared in 1971 on a Hudson's float in a Detroit parade; locals purchased the papier-mâché statue (hmmmm . . . maybe he *is* French-Canadian) for $50 and covered it in the weather-resistant fiberglass you see today.

Paul Bunyan Park/Furtaw Field, 4986 N. State St., Oscoda, MI 48750
Phone: (800) 235-4625 or (989) 739-7322
Hours: Always visible
Cost: Free
Website: http://oscodachamber.com
Directions: On Rte. 23 (State St.) opposite Ottawa Dr.

A BUNCH OF BUNYANS

Legend has it there is only one Paul Bunyan, but the evidence along Michigan's highways says otherwise. There are statues of Paul and Babe in St. Ignace (see page 40), just as there are in Ossineke (see page 89). The big guy also stands, hands on hips, atop the famous Paul Bunyan Trophy, given since 1953 to the winner of the annual University of Michigan–Michigan State football game. That Paul is only three feet tall, though he is mounted atop a taller pedestal. Here are a few more:

Hometown Bunyan

Schoolcraft County Chamber of Commerce, 1000 W. Lakeshore Dr., Manistique, (888) 819-7420 or (906) 341-5010, www.schoolcraftcountychamber.org

Manistique claims to be the "Mythical Home of Paul Bunyan," so to celebrate this . . . um, *fact* . . . it has erected a 15-foot likeness swinging a double-headed ax in front of the town's chamber of commerce. Babe is nowhere to be seen.

Recycled Paul Bunyan

Alpena Community College, 665 Johnson St., Alpena, (888) 468-6222 or (989) 356-9021

This 28-foot-tall metallic Paul Bunyan has been around. Artist Betty Conn built him out of old Kaiser auto parts in the 1960s for William Woelk, owner of the Paul Bunyan Gas Station in Gaylord. In the 1970s he was relocated to advertise an Indian museum in Grayling, and later a real estate office in the same town. But since 1988 he's been the mascot for the community college in Alpena. You can find him in the parking lot near the gymnasium, his foot propped on a pile of logs, an ax over his shoulder.

Flat Paul Bunyan

Paul Bunyan Antique Mall, 9175 S. M-37, Baldwin, (231) 745-2637

Poor Paul Bunyan! Did Babe drag a logging skid over him? This 20-foot-tall bearded lumberman sign outside an antique mall south of Baldwin looks rather flat. Plywood flat. He also appears to be wearing a red yarmulke.

Beat-Up Bunyan on a Buckboard

6760 S. US Hwy. 31, Charlevoix

The Paul Bunyan found outside the now-closed "Smith's Little Acres" attraction has seen better days. He sits on a logging sled pulled by Babe, who is draped in a tattered plastic tarp . . . blue, of course.

Ossineke
Dinosaur Gardens Prehistoric Zoo

Imagine if Jim and Tammy Faye Bakker had built a dinosaur park instead of Heritage, USA—that park would be Dinosaur Gardens. Started in the late 1930s by Paul N. Domke Sr., a devout Lutheran and amateur sculptor, this 40-acre roadside attraction mixes paleontology and theology for what is a truly bizarre and charming travel destination.

There's certainly no bait-and-switch for you science lovers; a statue of Jesus, not T. rex, holds a globe in one hand and welcomes you to the park with his other. Nevertheless, Domke still does manage to surprise its fore-warned visitors. Take, for example, the 30-ton, 85-foot brontosaurus just inside the front gate. A stairway leads up and into its ribcage, where you'll discover a shrine to Jesus Christ, "The Greatest Heart." Farther along the trail, ugly cavemen with spears and topless cavewomen do battle with mastodons, each playing their God-ordained gender roles. A large python squeezes the life out of another unfortunate human in another action-packed concrete tableau.

Don't expect a biology lesson.

If there is anything unfortunate about Domke's park it's that it could have been so much more—he even planned to make an adjoining utopian village, but it never happened. He did, however, contribute to the local cultural landscape by creating the Paul Bunyan statue on the west side of town (see below).

11160 US Hwy. 23 South, Ossineke, MI 49766

Phone: (877) 823-2408 or (989) 471-5477

Hours: May, daily 9 AM–4 PM; June–August, daily 9 AM–6 PM; September, Saturday–Sunday 9 AM–4 PM

Cost: Adults $6, Kids (12 and under) $4

Website: www.dinosaurgardensllc.com

Directions: On Rte. 23 north of Ossineke Rd.

Paul and Babe

According to lumberjack lore, Paul Bunyan came before Babe. After Paul found the blue ox, he dug the Great Lakes so that Babe would have a watering hole. But in Ossineke, Babe definitely came before Paul, even if he wasn't Babe to begin with.

Babe's a little gun-shy.

Walter Hayden crafted a 10-foot horny bull outside a local bar in 1938. Originally, it was white, and could just as easily be called a steer—it's kinda hard to tell. Then in the 1950s, the bar painted the statue blue and hired Paul Domke, from Dinosaur Gardens Prehistoric Zoo (see page 88), to create a Paul Bunyan to stand by the ox's side. Domke's 25-foot logger looked a bit French; he wore a beret and had his flannel shirt open to expose his hairy pecs. He also had a speaker built into his front chest pocket.

Unfortunately for Babe, the bar turned out to be a dangerous establishment. The ox's balls were shot off by a gun that was used a week later in a local murder. To keep the pair safe, the 11-ton Monsieur Le Bunyan and his 10-ton castrated sidekick were moved to a new location on the west side of town. Though Bunyan's speaker no longer works, the two are otherwise in good shape, having been repainted in 2007.

Rte. 23 & Nicholson Hill Rd., Ossineke MI 49766
No phone
Hours: Always visible
Cost: Free
Directions: West of town on Nicholson Hill Rd. at Rte. 23.

Paris
Eiffel Tower

La Tour Eiffel? Oui—you read that right. Back in 1980, the welding shop at Chippewa Hills High School took a pile of leftover bunk beds from an abandoned WPA camp and welded them into a 20-foot replica of the French landmark. The project was funded by the Mecosta County Council for the Arts. Sure, this Paris attraction is not as big as the original, but there are barely 3,000 people in the surrounding township. It's plenty big for them.

Today the tower stands in a grove of trees just down the hill from the old fish

C'est magnifique!

hatchery ladder on the north side of Paris Park. If you want to spend a romantic getaway in the Township of Very Few Lights, there's also a campground. But bring your bug spray.

Paris Park, 22090 Northland Dr., Paris, MI 49338

Phone: (231) 796-3420

Hours: Always visible

Cost: Free

Directions: One block north of 22 Mile Rd. on Northland Dr.

Petoskey
Skin Diver's Church

Jesus was said to walk on water, but in Little Traverse Bay he's 68 feet *below* the surface. What's going on here?

The Skin Diver's Church is not a typical Christian sanctuary, just a simple marble crucifix on the lake bottom. The sculpture was originally purchased by a Rapson farm family for their son's grave, but it arrived damaged from Italy. In 1962 their insurance company sold it at a loss for $50 to the Michigan Skindiving Council. The group then submerged it in Lake Michigan to honor member Charles Raymond, who had recently died in an accident beneath Torch Lake.

You're not a skin diver, you say? How would you ever visit this "church"? Every February the club chops a hole in the ice off Petoskey, scrapes off the zebra mussels, and illuminates the crucifix with underwater lamps. Walk out onto the lake, peer down into the depths, and ask, "Who's walking on water now?"

Bayfront Park, 101 E. Lake St., Petoskey, MI 49770

Phone: (231) 347-4150

Hours: Check website for dates

Cost: Free

Website: www.petoskey.com

Directions: Where the Bear River meets the lake, north of Rte. 31 (Bay View Rd.).

SCOTTVILLE

➡ The **Scottville Clown Band** (www.scottvilleclownband.com) has had more than 200 pancake-faced members since its inception in 1903.

Suttons Bay
Pear and Its Spirit

It ain't easy to make a ship in a bottle, but at least you can insert it in pieces. How would you get a single, oversized item like a billiard ball or a pear into a thin-necked bottle? Well I don't know about the billiard ball, but a pear is relatively easy: grow it in there.

That's just what the folks at Black Star Farms do. Clear bottles are placed over budding Bartlett pears while they are still on the tree, and (if everything goes as planned) the fruit grows to maturity. Pull the bottle off at harvest time, gently wash and rinse the pear inside, then fill it to the top with 80-proof Spirit of Pear brandy. If the fruit remains submerged, it calcifies without spoiling. You can continue to top off the brandy and keep this pricy souvenir for years of drunken conversation starters.

Black Star Farms, 10844 E. Revold Rd., Suttons Bay, MI 49682
Phone: (231) 944-1271
Hours: May–November, Monday–Saturday 10 AM–6 PM, Sunday 11 AM–5 PM
Cost: $74.50/bottle
Website: www.blackstarfarms.com
Directions: West of West-Bay Shore Dr. (M-22), south of Send Rd.

Tawas City
Gordon Clute's Statues

Paris had Auguste Rodin. Florence had Michelangelo. Tawas City had Gordon Clute. But unlike *The Thinker* or *David*, Clute's sculptural creations were designed to be played on, in, or around.

Gordon Clute started making his concrete cartoon characters for his front lawn. As more people came to appreciate them, he got commissions from public parks and beaches. Most of his early pieces can be found in Gateway Park at the lakefront—a camel, a goldfish, a buffalo, a dinosaur, a kangaroo, a horse, and a very large seagull. All are painted bright, bold colors, and many are outfitted with slides or contain large, smooth holes for kids to crawl through. A lonely hippo can be found farther north, across from the county jail, along the beach.

Another place to find Clute's work is outside the town's library. Here you'll find a sculpture garden straight out of popular children's television

Jonathan Livingston Seagullslide.

shows: Barney, Snoopy, Big Bird, Elmo, SpongeBob SquarePants, Tweety Bird, Donald Duck, Goofy, Dora the Explorer, Winnie the Pooh, Eeyore, Tigger, and Pikachu.

A few more Clute statues can be found at the south end of town— a steer in front of **Freel's Market** (1139 W. Lake St./US 23), a polar bear outside the **North Star Motel** (1119 W. Lake St./US 23), and an Indian on horseback at the **Tawas Indian Museum & Gift Shop** (1702 S. US 23). A giant yellow dinosaur was moved to a Bear Lake campground years ago (see page 53).

Gateway Park, 815 W. Lake St., Tawas City, MI 48763

Phone: (989) 362-8688

Hours: Always visible

Cost: Free

Website: www.tawascity.org/places/parks/gateway-park

Directions: On Rte. 23 at the south end of town, north of Ninth Ave., along the lake.

Tawas City Public Library, 208 North St. W., Tawas City, MI 48763
Phone: (989) 362-6557
Hours: Always visible
Cost: Free
Website: www.tawascity.org/places/library
Directions: At Second Ave.

Traverse City
Randolph the Moose

If you want your luck to change, then pucker up, losers. For more than 100 years, Randolph the Moose has been passing out good fortune to anyone in Traverse City willing to give him a kiss. You might wonder just how lucky this creature could be, seeing that years ago he was shot, beheaded, skinned, and stuffed, but folks at Sleder's Tavern swear by him.

Perhaps luckiest of all is the establishment itself. Vencel Sleder built this bar in 1882, and it has been in business ever since—the oldest continuously operating tavern in the state. It even survived Prohibition by giving away free "root beer," a mixture of bourbon and rye, to law enforcement officials. That's marketing! Today, Sleder's serves both booze and food—burgers, salads, lake fish, steak, and Mexican dishes. Their root beer, however, has less kick than in the olden days.

Sleder's Family Tavern, 717 Randolph St., Traverse City, MI 49684
Phone: (231) 947-9213
Hours: Monday–Thursday & Saturday 11 AM–10 PM, Friday 11 AM–midnight, Sunday noon–9 PM
Cost: Free; Meals, $7–18
Website: www.sleders.com
Directions: One block west of Division St. (Rte. 37), two blocks south of Bay St.

TRAVERSE CITY
➡ Actor David Wayne was born Wayne James McMeekan in Traverse City on January 30, 1914.

VANDERBILT
➡ Vanderbilt recorded the state's lowest temperature, –51° F, on February 9, 1934.

MORE MICHIGAN MEESE

For those who'd rather not kiss a dead moose, there are three meese in the Upper Peninsula you can pucker up for, and they're all fiberglass. Just wipe them down with a little hand sanitizer and you're ready to go. Two are in the town of Manistique; one is outside the **Bob's Big Boy Restaurant** (607 E. Lakeshore Dr., (906) 341-6941) and is dressed/painted with a white T-shirt and red-and-white checkered overalls, and another is outside the **Hotel Peninsula Pointe** (905 E. Lakeshore Dr., (906) 341-3777), draped/painted in a pink robe with gold fringe. At the other end of the UP, a star-spangled moose statue stands outside of the **St. Ignace Happy Car Wash** (149 W. US Hwy. 2, (906) 643-7627)—its head is blue and covered in stars, its rump covered in red and white stripes.

Traverse Colantha Walker, Champion Dairy Cow

Traverse Colantha Walker sure knew how to deliver. During her nine-lactation lifetime at the Northern Michigan Asylum's dairy farm, Walker produced 200,114.9 pounds of milk and 7,525.8 pounds of butterfat, enough to keep Paula Deen busy in the kitchen for three and a half weeks.

When this mighty mooer died on January 8, 1932, she was laid to rest on the hospital's grounds beneath a large granite headstone detailing her udderly amazing accomplishments. Today, the surrounding Northern Michigan Asylum's buildings are being transformed into an impressive multiuse campus, but developers assure everyone that the monument to Traverse Colantha Walker will remain a part of the site's history—they even throw a Dairy Festival each June in her honor.

S. Red Dr., Traverse City, MI 49684

No phone

Hours: Daylight

Cost: Free

Website: www.thevillagetc.com/colantha.html

Directions: North from Silver Lake Rd. on Franke Rd./Silver Dr., then left (west) at the first road, one block to Red Dr.; at that intersection.

World's Largest Cherry Pie Pan

The good folks of Traverse City sure do like their cherries. Every July since 1925 the town has hosted the National Cherry Festival (www.cherryfestival.org) to celebrate the local orchards that made Traverse City the "Cherry Capital of the World." They have pie-eating contests and pit spits, and a whole lot of events that have nothing to do with the fruit, but are fun anyway—beer tents and movies, bingo and bands, and even an acrobatic air show.

But all of that fun is nothing compared to what happened at the 1987 celebration. On July 25, Chef Pierre Bakeries dragged out a custom-made 17-foot, 6-inch diameter pan and baked a 28,350-pound cherry pie. Organizers even arranged for *Guinness Book of World Records* auditors to be on hand to certify that he had indeed baked the world's largest cherry pie.

Attendees gobbled up the award-winner and left nothing but the pan, which was later mounted in its own park just outside the Sara Lee factory, the new owners of Chef Pierre. Sadly, a Canadian town that shall not be named baked a 39,683-pound pie—what they would call an 18,000-kilogram

The pie might now be in second place, but the pan still holds the gold.

tarte—in 1992. The Canucks threw away their pie tin when they were done, which means at least Traverse City still holds the record for the World's Largest Cherry Pie *Pan.*

Sara Lee Bakery Group, 3424 Cass Rd., Traverse City, MI 49684
Phone: (231) 922-3296
Hours: Always visible
Cost: Free
Directions: Two blocks north of Airport Rd. on Cass Rd.

West Branch
Lumber Jack

One of the strangest features of the Bunyanesque mascot outside Lumber Jack Food & Spirits is that the statue is dressed in actual clothes— they're not painted on or part of the sculpture. If he were normal-sized, the outfit could have been purchased off a rack, but Lumber Jack is 25 feet tall. Where would you buy a flannel work shirt for him? Men's Wearhouse for Warehouse-Sized Men? Nope, they're custom made.

His laundry bill must be outrageous.

Unlike many roadside giants, Lumber Jack sits on the ground, resting as he leans his enormous hands on a six-foot spoon. The restaurant replaced his damaged head in 2008, and he looks quite happy about it, judging from his faraway smile.

Lumber Jack Food & Spirits, 2980 Cook Rd., West Branch, MI 48661
Phone: (989) 343-0892
Hours: Always visible; Restaurant, daily 6 AM–10 PM
Cost: Free
Website: www.visitthelumberjack.com
Directions: North of I-75 one block on County Rd. 23 (Cook Rd.).

Mackinaw City
The Bear Company
Icebreaker *Mackinaw*
Keyhole Bar & Grill
Mackinac Bridge Museum
The Mighty Mac

Beaver Island
The Kingdom of Zion

Cross Village
Legs Inn

(31)

Lake
Michigan

Harbor Springs
Junk Robin

Charlevoix
Beat-Up Bunyan on a Buckboard
Cherry Republic Outpost
Mushroom Buildings
World's Largest Cherry Pie Oven

Petoskey
Archangel Grotto
Skin Diver's Church

Indian Rive
Big Jesus and the N
Doll Musel

(31)

(131)

Northport
Pop Bottle Collection

Omena
Tamarack Gallery

Elmira
Potato Burgers

Gaylord
Big Buck Brewery's Big Beer Bottle
Call of the Wild
Gaylord Ice Tree
Turkey Cone?

Suttons Bay
Pear and Its Spirit

Glen Arbor (22)
Cherry Republic

Kewedin
Michigan Cairn

Honor
Cherry Bowl Drive-In Theatre

(72)

Elk Rapids
Big Swan

Acme
FUDGE!!!
Music House Museum

Traverse City
The Bear Company
Cherry Republic Embassy
Randolph the Moose
Traverse Colantha Walker, Champion Dairy Cow
World's Largest Cherry Pie Pan

Kalkaska
National Trout Memorial

Grayling
Bottle-Cap Museum

Beulah
Beulah's Sculpture Gardens

Frankfort
Pumpkin Ed

(31)

(131)

(22) (31)

(27)

Bear Lake
Kampvilla Dinosaur

(42)

Kaleva
Big Grasshopper
Bottle House

(37)

(55)

Manistee
Death Site of the World's
Largest Man
SS *City of Milwaukee*
USCGC *Acacia*

(55)

Cadillac
Cadillac Sound Garden

(115)

Ludington
Grassa's Farm Market
Jumping Deer

(131)

Custer (10)
Steer Face

Baldwin
Flat Paul Bunyan
Shrine of the Pines

(27)

(10)

Clare
Big Clucker
Cops & Doughnuts
Leprechauns at the Tap Room

(31)

(37)

(66)

Paris
Eiffel Tower

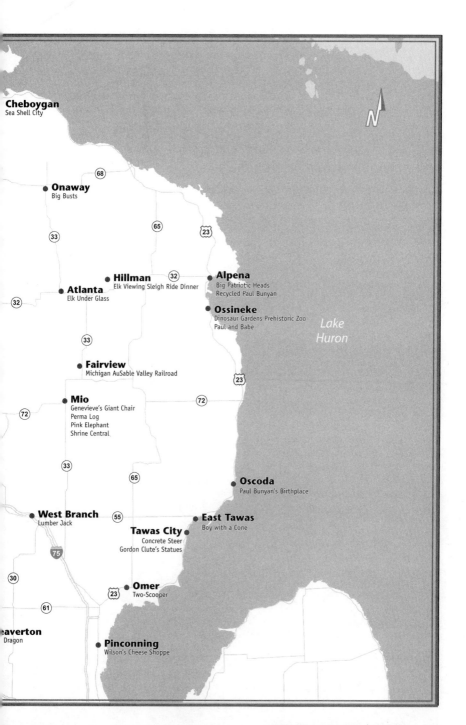

Cheboygan
Sea Shell City

(68)

● **Onaway**
Big Busts

(33)

(65)

(23)

● **Hillman** (32)   ● **Alpena**
Elk Viewing Sleigh Ride Dinner   Big Patriotic Heads
● **Atlanta**   Recycled Paul Bunyan
Elk Under Glass
(32)   ● **Ossineke**
Dinosaur Gardens Prehistoric Zoo
Paul and Babe

*Lake
Huron*

(33)

● **Fairview**
Michigan AuSable Valley Railroad

(23)

● **Mio**   (72)
Genevieve's Giant Chair
(72)   Perma Log
Pink Elephant
Shrine Central

(33)

(65)

● **Oscoda**
Paul Bunyan's Birthplace

● **West Branch** (55)   ● **East Tawas**
Lumber Jack   Boy with a Cone
● **Tawas City**
Concrete Steer
Gordon Clute's Statues

(75)

(30)

● **Omer**
(23) Two-Scooper
(61)

●averton
Dragon   ● **Pinconning**
Wilson's Cheese Shoppe

3

WESTERN MICHIGAN

*T*o browse the travel brochures, you'd think that western Michigan had nothing to offer but wide-open golf courses and beautiful beaches. And that is partially true—why else would Elvis choose to live out his post-"death" years in the region? Yet there's so much more than sand and sunsets over Lake Michigan. Weird stuff. Things you wouldn't expect.

You want to visit a town inhabited by skeletons? A two-headed lamb or a half-sized version of Stonehenge? What about history—care to see the Watergate burglars' break-in tools, paintings by Sitting Bull, or the birthplace of celery? They're all here!

Ada

Amway World Headquarters and Welcome Center

Have you ever thought about becoming your own boss? Retiring when you're still young enough to enjoy it? Living your dreams? Has anyone ever told you about the financial opportunity that is multilevel marketing? If so, you probably have a neighbor or relative that has given you the Amway pitch . . . *multiple* times. But if not, stop on by the Amway Welcome Center at the company's Ada headquarters where you can take it in at your own pace without all the familial guilt.

Amway—short for The American Way—was started by friends Richard DeVos and Jay Van Andel in 1959. What began as a soap-selling operation expanded to include all sorts of products—nutritional supplements, cosmetics, water purifiers, light bulbs, protein powders, baby wipes, and on, and on. Here, at the Amway Welcome Center, samples of each product hum by on a never-ending conveyor that weaves from room to room. Punch your personal data into the interactive displays, which will calculate your "life-age," show you how to rejuvenate your skin (not surprisingly, with Amway products), and teach you about the Ten Pillars of Economic

Wisdom, brought down from the mount by DeVos and Van Andel all those years ago. And contemplate your financial future as you gaze into the tumbling waters of the Freedom/Family/Hope/Reward Fountain.

You know, maybe I *do* want to retire at 45 . . .

7575 E. Fulton St., Ada, MI 49355

Phone: (616) 787-6701

Hours: Monday–Friday 8:30 AM–noon and 1–5 PM

Cost: Free

Website: www.amway.com/about-amway/our-company/experience-amway

Directions: On M-21 (Fulton St.) southwest of the river.

Bangor

Bangor Viking

He stands on the far side of Viking Stadium in a too-short tunic and a silly horned helmet, stripped of his shield and sword. As this town's high school's mascot, he doesn't look like he'd instill fear in his opponents—he was more threatening when he was a roadside advertisement for the Viking Carpet Company. But if large Norwegians are your thing, here he is.

Bangor High School, 801 W. Arlington St., Bangor, MI 49013

Phone: (269) 427-6844

Hours: Always visible

Cost: Free

Website: www.bangorvikings.org

Directions: Take Alexander St. south to Arlington St., then one block west, on the southwest side of town.

Benton Harbor and Watervliet

Eden Springs, the House of David Amusement Park

You really have to hand it to the followers of the House of David. Historically, most kooky religious groups find remote locations to set up their compounds, far from the prying eyes of local busybodies and federal authorities. Not the House of David. They built one of the most popular amusement parks in the Midwest, fielded a minor league baseball team whose players all had long beards and longer hair, and comported themselves in a manner that said, "Yeah, we're different—what's it to you?"

The House of David was established by Benjamin Franklin Purnell and his wife, Mary. Purnell believed himself to be the Seventh Messenger as described in the prophecy of Joanna Southcott, a religious leader from the late 1700s/early 1800s. Purnell started his ministry in Fostoria, Ohio, but the citizens ran him out of town after he continued preaching a sermon instead of rushing to the aid of his daughter Hettie, who was barely clinging to life after being mortally burned in a fireworks plant explosion.

Later, in Michigan, Purnell convinced several wealthy patrons to bankroll a colony in Benton Harbor for his 1,000 followers. Centered around Eastman Springs, a mineral water outflow that Purnell renamed Eden Springs, the House of David constructed an elaborate roadside attraction to bring money, attention, and followers to the church. The amusement park had a zoo, eight miniature steam trains, an Indian Artifact Museum, pony rides, Midget Autos, ice cream parlors, bowling alleys (where the automatic pinsetter was invented), billiard halls, fountains made from petrified wood, and a silent movie theater, all centered around an enormous beer garden (tourists particularly loved that).

Followers of Purnell were vegetarians and did not believe in cutting their hair or beards because it made them more Jesus-like. They fielded a minor league baseball team that in 1933 signed the first woman to play pro, Jackie Mitchell, who once struck out both Babe Ruth and Lou Gehrig *in the same inning*. Satchel Paige also played briefly for the team, wearing a fake red beard so as to not look out of place.

But everything at House of David wasn't entirely wonderful. Followers who bucked Purnell's authority—even children—were labeled "scorpions" and banished to the colony's lumbering operation on High Island at the far northern end of Lake Michigan. Purnell was accused of statutory rape in 1923, but died in 1927 before the drawn-out court battle ever went before a jury. His body was then embalmed and placed in a sealed coffin at Diamond House.

The colony soldiered on for many years, finally closing in 1974. The faithful split into two factions: the Israelite House of David (www.israelitehouseofdavid.com) and Mary's City of David (www.maryscityofdavid

House of David members lobby the White House to keep their beards after being drafted into the army, 1920. Library of Congress Prints and Photographs Division (LC-DIG-npcc-01485)

.org). Burglars broke into Diamond House in the late 1980s, smashed open Purnell's glass coffin, and stole the ruby locket from around his neck.

Efforts are underway today to restore some of the House of David's buildings and trains, as well as its beer garden. You can see artifacts from the colony at the Mary's City of David Museum, which offers tours of the surviving buildings during the summer, and the House of David Museum in nearby Watervliet. Also, in the summer, the House of David Echoes team plays old-timey baseball without gloves at Eastman Field.

Mary's City of David Museum (and Tours), 1385 E. Britain Ave., PO Box 187, Benton Harbor, MI 49022

Phone: (269) 925-1601

Hours: June–September, Saturday–Sunday 1–5 PM; Walking tours begin 1:30 PM

Cost: Museum, $1/person (ages 10 and up); Tour, $4/person (ages 10 and up)

Website: www.maryscityofdavid.org

Directions: Two blocks east of M-139 on Britain Ave.

House of David Museum, 349 Main St., Watervliet, MI 49098

Phone: (616) 463-8888 or (616) 849-0432

Hours: By appointment

Cost: Donations accepted

Website: http://hodmuseum.tripod.com

Directions: Two blocks south of Red Arrow Hwy. on Main St. (M-140).

Skellville

"Everybody's gotta go there sometime!" the owner said when I asked him if I could step out back to see Skellville. I assumed he was talking in general terms, little s skellville, the boneyard, boot hill, marble town, but I went anyway. The front of this garden decoration business looked odd enough, with concrete statues that went beyond the traditional gnomes and miniature deer and kissing Dutch children. But Skellville was something else entirely.

He's been plowing a loooooong time.

A life-size skeleton in mechanic's overalls greeted me at the gate, reminding me to pay my $1 admission. Back through the weeds I found a half dozen wrecked and rusted cars and tractors, each driven by a plastic skeleton in similar ratty attire. A family of dead, fleshless hillbillies stood on the porch of a small shack, another skeleton sat in an outhouse playing a banjo, and a dog skeleton backed up to a fire hydrant. Another four residents, much smaller than the others, sat around a circular picnic table pounding whiskey shots. Skulls and bones were everywhere.

It all made for a fun stop, but I still don't think I'd visit at night.

Piedt & Son Do-It-Yourself Lawn and Garden Supply, 2400 Michigan 139, Benton Harbor, MI 49022

Phone: (269) 925-0220

Hours: Monday–Friday 9 AM–5 PM, Saturday 9 AM–3 PM

Cost: $1/person

Website: www.skellville.net

Directions: North of I-94 on Scottdale Rd. (M-139), at Nickerson Ave.

Buchanan

Bear Cave

There aren't too many places where tourists can explore Michigan's deep caves without spelunking equipment. In fact, there's just one: Bear Cave. Formed 25,000 years ago through a tufa rock formation, it's not exactly mammoth. You enter it through a gift shop, a flight of narrow stairs dropping you 40 feet into the ground until you run out of cave about 150 feet in. The temperature is a constant 58°F year-round, a nice stop during a muggy summer day, which is the only time of year that it's open.

What it lacks in size, Bear Cave more than makes up in history. Before the Civil War, it was a station on the Underground Railroad. And in 1875, Ohio bank robbers stashed their ill-gotten booty in the cavern, an event that inspired the 1903 silent film *The Great Train Robbery*.

4085 Bear Cave Rd., Buchanan, MI 49107

Phone: (800) 388-7788 or (269) 695-3050

Hours: May–October, daily 10 AM–4 PM

Cost: Adults $3, Kids (6–12) $2

Website: www.zonecampingpass.com/locations/bearcave.aspx?zone=NE

Directions: Three roads north of Miller Rd., on the west side of the river.

Edwardsburg
Lunker's

What Cabela's (see page 159) is to hunting, Lunker's is to fishing, and then some. And because there is only one Lunker's, it still retains its small business charm even though the place is enormous.

A giant, rotating fish sign lures you to this anglers' Mecca. Inside, stuffed Canadian geese, suspended in flight from a barreled roof with a painted sky and sunset, make you feel like you're still outside. Forest sounds overlaid with 1970s music set the mood. A long wooden bridge winds through the aisles of spinners, bobbers, reels, and rods, back and forth over a plexiglass-topped "river" filled with mounted muskies and bass. Wildlife taxidermy rings the perimeter, most of it native species, but also an African lion and an ostrich cozying up to a grizzly bear.

At the far end of the building, beneath an 8,000-pound bass breaking through a brick wall, you'll find the Angler's Inn. The menu may be surf-and-turf, but the decorations are definitely surf. Each booth has its own fish tank, many with their own themes—the SpongeBob Tank, the Patriotic Tank, the Butterfly Tank, and so on. At the center of the room is a large cylindrical aquarium, the "Lunkquarium," where a spotted moray eel twists around and around a fake coral reef, magnified to anaconda proportions. It's the only way to dine!

26324 US Hwy. 12 East, PO Box 246, Edwardsburg, MI 49112
Phone: (269) 663-3745
Hours: Monday–Thursday 10 AM–8 PM, Friday–Saturday 8 AM–8 PM, Sunday 8 AM–5 PM
Cost: Free
Website: www.lunkers.com
Directions: East of M-62 on Main St. (Rte. 12).

Fennville
Betty, the Dead Dog

There's a customer tradition at Crane's Pie Pantry Restaurant: always wave to Betty as you enter. Not that she'll wave back, in part because she's a dog, but more so because she's dead. Eighty years dead. Betty lived in Chicago from 1930 to 1937, and when she passed away, her owner had her stuffed and mounted in a curled up pose. In time, the owner died (and was *not* stuffed) and willed the glassy-eyed pooch to a woman who baked pies at Crane's. She felt that Betty matched the restaurant's decor, and so the dog was given a permanent seat on the sleigh in the front entryway.

Betty isn't the only taxidermied critter on the premises; there are also Plymouth Rock and Buff Orphington chickens peeking out from a wall coop. Old-timey junk is everywhere: baby buggies, coffee percolators, and Kewpie dolls. Aviation enthusiasts will appreciate the airplane models and World War I doodads in display cases near the restrooms, newspapers announcing the landings of Lucky Lindy and the not-so-lucky *Hindenburg*. And don't miss the old Fennville traffic light. It was declared illegal in 1939 because it only had red and green signals, but no yellow caution. Meddling nanny-state bureaucrats!

Crane's Pie Pantry Restaurant & Bakery, 6054 124th Ave., Fennville, MI 49408

Phone: (269) 561-2297

Hours: May–October, Monday–Saturday 9 AM–8 PM, Sunday 11 AM–8 PM; November–December, Tuesday–Saturday 10 AM–6 PM, Sunday 11 AM–6 PM; January–March, Tuesday–Sunday 11 AM–4 PM; April, daily 11 AM–5 PM

Cost: Meals, $7–10; Pies, $10–15

Website: www.cranespiepantry.com

Directions: On M-89 (124th Ave.) between McVickers Ave. and Meade Ave.

Grand Haven

Grand Haven Musical Fountain

Each summer evening around sunset in Grand Haven you'll see thousands of tourists stumbling toward the waterfront like an army of sunburned zombies. My advice? *Follow them.* For if you do, you'll be treated to a fabulous display of a dying art form: the musical fountain. These hokey water shows were once audience favorites at Marine Worlds and Cyprus Gardenses, but today they're as endangered as the Florida manatee.

The Grand Haven Musical Fountain opened in 1962, the brainchild of William Booth II. More than 8,000 feet of pipe and nozzles shoot 40,000 gallons of waltzing water 125 feet into the evening sky, all to the rhythms of classical standards and pop favorites and illuminated by zillions of multicolored lights. Someone once calculated the number of visual variations and came up with roughly 1,875,352,500,000,000 possibilities. That's more than can fit into one 20-minute performance, which is why each season brings a new show theme and musical playlist.

Waterfront Stadium, Washington Ave. at Harbor Dr., Grand Haven, MI 49417

Phone: (616) 842-2550

Hours: June–September, Friday and Saturday, 8:30-ish PM

Cost: Free

Website: http://grandhaven.org/recreation/musical-fountain-schedule/

Directions: Fountain on Dewey Hill, across the Grand River; view from Waterfront Stadium or anywhere along Harbor Dr. from Howard Ave. to Columbus Ave.

Grand Rapids

The American Horse

Leonardo da Vinci was a true Renaissance man—he could do anything. But that doesn't mean he could do everything on schedule. Back in 1482, he was commissioned by Ludovico Sforza, the Duke of Milan, to create the world's largest horse sculpture out of bronze. Da Vinci got as far as making a clay model, but it was destroyed by invading French troops 17 years later, before he finished the work.

Fast forward five centuries, when Pennsylvania sculptor Charles Dent was asked to complete the project. He toiled away for 15 years, but died before it was ever cast. Another artist, Garth Herrick, kept the project going, but eventually the horse was turned over to Nina Akamu. After assessing the condition of Dent's model, Akamu decided to start from scratch. Three years later, on September 10, 1999, the 24-foot-tall bronze horse was unveiled at the Hippodrome de San Siro in Milan. An ungrateful Italian art critic called it "a typical American eyesore."

Oh, screw him. A month later *The American Horse*, cast from the same mold, was trotted out at the Frederik Meijer Gardens and Sculpture Park. Visitors loved it. They loved it even more when a second work, *Paletta Grande* ("Large Shovel"), was placed behind the horse, filled with a half-dozen gunnysack road apples. These two pieces are just a small part of more than 70 works found in this 125-acre park on the northeast side of Grand Rapids. Make an afternoon of it.

Frederik Meijer Gardens and Sculpture Park, 1000 E. Beltline Ave. NE, Grand Rapids, MI 49525

Phone: (888) 957-1580 or (616) 957-1580

Hours: Monday & Wednesday–Saturday 9 AM–5 PM, Tuesday 9 AM–9 PM, Sunday 11 AM–5 PM

Cost: Adults $12, Seniors (65+) $9, Kids (5–13) $6, Toddlers (3–4) $4

Website: www.meijergardens.org

Directions: North of I-96 on M-44 (Beltline Ave. NE).

Fluoridation!

On January 25, 1945, residents of Grand Rapids turned on their taps and got something they'd never had before: fluoride in their water. The city was the first in the United States to add the element to its public water supply as a dental health measure.

As more communities followed the practice, a backlash started, primarily from the far right who saw it as a vast Communist conspiracy. Dr. Charles Bett, one of fluoridation's most outspoken opponents, claimed that as a weapon it was "better THAN USING THE ATOM BOMB because the atom bomb has to be made, has to be transported to the place it is to be set off while POISONOUS FLUORINE has been placed right beside the water supplies by the Americans themselves ready to be dumped into the water mains whenever a Communist desires!" Who knew the Soviets were so anti-cavity?

Though most of Europe and voters in Portland, Oregon, have discontinued the practice, fluoride is still widely used in the United States. To honor its place in public health history, Grand Rapids erected a monument made of bright, white marble. Ironically, it corroded to the point where it had to be replaced by a new artwork, *Steel Water,* a 33-foot-tall column of blue waves along the riverfront.

JW Marriot Grand Rapids, 235 Louis St. NW, Grand Rapids, MI 49503

Phone: (888) 844-5947 or (616) 242-1500

Hours: Always visible

Cost: Free

Website: www.historygrandrapids.org/photo/752/fluoridation-sculpture-steel-w

Directions: Downtown, on the east bank of the river, one block south of Pearl St.

Gerald R. Ford Museum (and Library)

If you have any lingering resentment about the pardoning of Richard Nixon, it's time to put that aside, for it's no reason to miss this fascinating presidential museum. Not only is the Gerald R. Ford Museum a warts-and-all exploration of the former commander-in-chief (a rarity among presidential museums), it's chock-full of groovy 1970s artifacts.

After a brief viewing of *A Time to Heal* in the theater, the self-guided tour begins in a disco with swirling colored lights and a mod couple boogieing on the dance floor while Marvin Gaye's "What's Going On?" plays in the background. Adjoining display cases are filled with 8-tracks, bell-bottoms, mood rings, and WIN buttons. In the next room, you're whisked back to Grand Rapids in the early 1900s, 50-gallon drums from the Ford Paint & Varnish Company (his stepfather's business) stacked to the rafters. See Ford's little baby booties, christening gown, and Boy Scout sash covered in merit badges. And follow his football, legal, and navy careers before he ever ran for office.

Before long, Ford is elected to represent Michigan's 5th district, then serves on the Warren Commission and as House Minority Leader. And then the display cases get really interesting. You'll see one of Nixon's tape recorders, tools and recording devices used in the Watergate break-in, Spiro Agnew's resignation letter, and the former White House switchboard. Check out the hand-printed cheat sheet Ford used to take the oath of office and the powder blue dress Betty Ford wore that day. Then turn the corner and you're in a full-scale replica of the Oval Office, unelected but there nonetheless.

Though Ford held office for just over two years, they were quite eventful. The museum has the iconic rooftop staircase from the US embassy in Saigon, the gun Squeaky Fromme used in her assassination attempt, and an apology note from Sara Jane Moore, who also tried to off the president. "Although part of me regrets not being successful in this task," she wrote, "I am very thankful that I did not kill another human being." Some apology.

On it goes . . . mementoes from the nation's Bicentennial . . . a holographic tour of the White House . . . a re-creation of the Cabinet Room

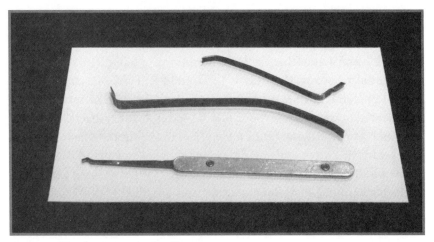

Tools used by the Watergate burglars. Photo by author, courtesy National Archives, Washington, DC, and the Gerald R. Ford Museum

where you can sit at the big, long table . . . the backup head for the San Diego Chicken.

303 Pearl St. NW, Grand Rapids, MI 49504
Phone: (616) 254-0400
Hours: Daily 9 AM–5 PM
Cost: Adults $7, Seniors $6, Kids (6–18) $3
Website: www.fordlibrarymuseum.gov
Directions: Just east of Rte. 131, south of I-196 (Gerald R. Ford Fwy.).

Oddly enough, Gerald Ford's presidential papers are not found at his presidential museum, but 130 miles away at his alma mater, the University of Michigan. The Gerald R. Ford Presidential Library opened in 1981, and is used primarily by scholars. They do put some documents on display in the lobby, but you have to make a formal request to search the archives in person. It's far easier to browse online.

1000 Beal Ave., Ann Arbor, MI 48109
Phone: (734) 205-0555
Hours: Monday–Friday 8:45 AM–4:45 PM
Cost: Free
Website: www.fordlibrarymuseum.gov
Directions: Just north of the intersection of Fuller Rd. and Glazier Way.

OTHER FORD SITES

Gerald Ford wasn't born in Grand Rapids, he was born in Omaha, Nebraska, as Leslie Lynch King Jr. on July 14, 1913. As it turned out, Leslie Lynch King *Sr.* wasn't much of a dad or husband, so Martha King fled to Illinois two weeks after giving birth. Within the year, she'd moved in with her parents in Grand Rapids at **1960 Terrace Avenue SE**. In 1916 Martha remarried, to Gerald R. Ford Sr., future heir to the Ford Paint & Varnish Company. At the time he was only a salesman. Leslie's parents called their child Gerald R. Ford Jr. even though he hadn't been adopted nor had his name changed. (He would do that in 1935.)

The Ford family lived at **630 Rosewood Avenue SE** from 1919 to 1921, but Ford spent his formative years, from 1921 to 1930, at **649 Union Avenue SE**. He had three half-brothers and was heavily involved in the Boy Scouts. (Ford made Eagle Scout, the only president to have done so.) Today's local chapter, the **Gerald R. Ford Council**, has a bronze statue of the future president outside its headquarters (3213 Walker Ave. NW, (616) 785-2662, www.michiganscouting.org/PresidentFord). He graduated from **South High School** (110 Hall St. SE, closed) in 1931 and went off to play football at the University of Michigan.

Rather than play professional football after graduation—he had offers from the Lions and the Packers—Ford went to Yale Law School. After that, he returned to Grand Rapids and set up his law practice, living at **1011 Santa Cruz Drive SE**. During World War II he served in the US Navy aboard the USS *Monterey* aircraft carrier in the South Pacific.

When he returned to Michigan, Ford met Elizabeth "Betty" Bloomer. She had been born in Chicago on April 8, 1918, but grew up in Grand Rapids, graduating from **Central High School** (421 Fountain St. NE) in 1936. Bloomer was recently divorced and was working at a downtown department store. She was also an accomplished dancer, sometimes referred to as the "Martha Graham of Grand Rapids." The wedding ceremony took place at **Grace Episcopal Church** (1815 Hall Street SE), on October 15, 1948. The couple owned their home at **1624 Sherman Street SE** from 1950 until 1979, from the first years Ford served in Congress until three years after he lost the 1976 election. They had four children together.

The Fords divided their twilight years between southern California and Grand Rapids. The president died on December 26, 2006; Betty Ford passed away on July 8, 2011. Both are buried in the courtyard of the museum.

Pond Ness Monster

The John Ball Zoo in Grand Rapids is nice enough, but you won't find too many animals that aren't in most zoos, *except* for the Loch Ness Monster in the pond near the entrance. *Nessie on the Grand* was originally created by Richard App in 2009 for ArtPrize (www.artprize.org), the city's big autumn art festival. The 100-foot creature was moved to its new home after the event, and can be seen here from spring to fall (it hibernates in winter). The zoo later installed a viewing platform, and *Nessie* was given glowing, electric eyes. Frightening, but not as scary as the jaguar that escaped from its cage in 1985 and killed one of the park's zoologists.

John Ball Zoological Gardens, 1300 W. Fulton St., Grand Rapids, MI 49504

Phone: (616) 336-4301

Hours: March–October, check website

Cost: Summer/Fall & Spring, Adults $8.50/$5, Seniors (62+) $7.50/$5, Kids (3–13) $6.50/$4

Website: http://nessieproject.wordpress.com and www.johnballzoosociety.org

Directions: Just east of I-196 (Gerald R. Ford Fwy.) on M-45 (Fulton St.).

Sanctuary Folk Art Gallery

The world needs more people like Reb Robert and Carmella Loftis. This creative couple had been making art for years, but in 1999 they opened a storefront gallery devoted to outsider and visionary works by (mostly) Michigan self-taught artists, the sort of artists found throughout this book. Paintings, collages, sculptures, and drawings cover every wall and surface, floor to ceiling, and are stacked up like cordwood in bins. Sanctuary Folk Art doesn't have the pretentiousness found in so many galleries, nor the shocking sticker prices—this stuff is quite affordable. They're constantly rotating in new pieces, so it's worth a stop whenever you're in town.

Sanctuary Art Gallery, 140 S. Division Ave., Grand Rapids, MI 49503

Phone: (616) 454-0401

Hours: Monday–Saturday noon–5 PM

Cost: Free

Website: http://sanctuaryfolkart.com

Directions: Three blocks south of Fulton St. on Rte. 131 Bus. (Division St.).

13 Weatherball

In olden times, back before cell phones and Wi-Fi and handy downloadable apps, you couldn't just find the day's forecast with a few keystrokes. You had to look out the window, preferably in the direction of the 13 Weatherball, instead of down at a small screen.

Of course, you also had to remember the following handy rhyme:

13 Weatherball red, warmer ahead.
13 Weatherball blue, cooler in view.
13 Weatherball green, no change foreseen.
Colors blinking bright, rain or snow in sight.

OK, not exactly Robert Frost, and the poem could do without the shameless channel plugs for local television station WZZM-13. But give the broadcasters credit—they rescued this poor ball from the scrap heap.

For 20 years, the Weatherball loomed over downtown Grand Rapids, high atop the Michigan National Bank Building. It was unceremoniously

---

HARBERT

➡ Writer Carl Sandburg lived at the **"Chickaming Goat Farm"** on Birchwood Court in Harbert from 1928, when he had it built, to 1945. He wrote his Lincoln biography while living there.

removed in 1987 and later spotted in a Kalamazoo junkyard. That's when WZZM came to the rescue. In 1999 the station restored its 288 neon lights and mounted it 100 feet above the busiest highway interchange in town.

I-96 & Rte. 131, Grand Rapids, MI 49544

No phone

Hours: Best after dark

Cost: Free

Website: www.wzzm13.com/weather/article/118804/14/The-Story-of-the-13-Weatherball

Directions: Southwest of the interchange.

Holland
Art at the Padnos Iron and Metal Company

Stuart Padnos used to walk through his scrap yard, seeing little more than the metal he'd collected and its worth as scrap. But then he began to notice

One tough junkyard dog. Photo by author, courtesy Padnos Iron and Metal Company

shapes and forms, and with the help of a welding torch began to transform cast-off materials into simple yet beautiful works of art. Huge, heavy, industrial works of art. You can see a number of his pieces along "Sculpture Row" (Pine Avenue) on the east side of the 35-acre Padnos recycling facility in Holland, scattered here and there and ever changing. Most of the sculptures are modern and conceptual, but others are figurative, like the huge junkyard dog guarding the facility's parking lot from atop a steel doghouse.

If you're willing to take a drive, you can see one of Padnos's largest works on the **Grand Valley State University** campus in Allendale (1 Campus Dr., (616) 331-5000, www.gvsu.edu). In honor of his wife Barbara, a graduate of GVSU, Padnos built a full-size, 21-piece marching band, decked out in powder blue uniforms and tooting away on rusty brass instruments. He also created a statue of a U of M football player for the **Gerald R. Ford Museum** in Grand Rapids (see page 111) and additional pieces for the **Frederik Meijer Gardens and Sculpture Park** (see page 110) in the same town. The Padnos Company generously contributed the copper used to sculpt the park's iconic horse statue (see page 109) as well.

185 W. Eighth St., PO Box 1979, Holland, MI 49423

Phone: (616) 396-6521

Hours: Daylight hours

Cost: Free

Website: www.padnos.com

Directions: Along Pine Ave. between Fourth and Seventh Sts., heading south.

Deep in Dutch

The town of Holland was founded in January 1847 by Dr. Albertus C. Van Raalte and 53 Dutch Calvinist separatists. These immigrants had fled their home country because of religious persecution, not because they were tired of wearing wooden shoes. In fact, they retained much of their Dutch heritage, including the shoes, as you will see at the town's history museum.

The Holland Museum has a tribute to the old country—the Dutch Galleries—where you'll find paintings and decorative arts . . . all very dark and serious. The local history section is much more lively, detailing the Great Fire of 1871, when the town was incinerated on the same night as the Great Chicago Fire; objects from the Netherlands Pavilion at the 1939 New York World's Fair; local maritime and agricultural displays;

HART AND SHELBY

➡ The towns of Hart and Shelby cohost the **National Asparagus Festival** each June (www.nationalasparagusfestival.org).

and stories of local businesses, such as the **world's largest pickle factory** (H. J. Heinz Company, 431 W. 16th St., (616) 396-6557, www.heinz.com), and churches, including the **Calvary Reformed Church** (995 E. Eighth St., (616) 392-8559, www.calvaryreformedholland.org), creators of the "WWJD?" bracelet in 1989.

Holland Museum, 31 W. 10th St., Holland, MI 49423

Phone: (616) 796-3329

Hours: Monday & Wednesday–Saturday 10 AM–5 PM

Cost: Adults $7, Seniors $6, Kids $4

Website: www.hollandmuseum.org

Directions: Just east of River Ave. on Tenth St.

If the Holland Museum strikes you as a bit dry, klomp on over to Dutch Village, the closest thing you'll find to a Dutch amusement park in the States. Kids (or small adults) can ride down a wooden shoe slide. Adults

can be cleared of any supernatural wrong-doing on an authentic "witch's scale"—they'll even give you a certificate showing you are not in cahoots with the Dark One. Take a ride on the Draaimolen carousel, swing on the Zweefmolen chair ride, or listen to Old World dance tunes on the Amsterdam "Golden Angel" Street Organ. Every hour the workers gather for a traditional folk dance in their noisy wooden shoes. And if you're hungry, check out the menu at

A big baby.

the windmill-shaped Queen's Inn Banquet Facility or the Hungry Dutchman Café.

Nelis' Dutch Village, 12350 James St., PO Box 1798, Holland, MI 49422
Phone: (616) 396-1475
Hours: April–October, daily 9 AM–6 PM
Cost: Adults $10, Seniors (59+) $9, Kids (3–15) $8
Website: www.dutchvillage.com
Directions: North of Lakewood Blvd. on Rte. 31.

The next stop on your tour of Holland is the DeZwaan windmill, the centerpiece of the town's 36-acre Windmill Island Gardens. This 12-story authentic Dutch windmill was built in 1761 in Krommenie, Holland, later moved to Vinkel, but had fallen into disrepair by the 1960s. The Dutch government allowed "The Swan" to be disassembled and shipped to the states in 1964, the first and only time a windmill has been allowed out of the Netherlands. Now restored, it mills flour you can buy at the gift shop.

Windmill Island Gardens also has an 1895 Dutch carousel, a mechanized Little Netherlands Village, tulip gardens, and Klompen dancers in the summertime. (If it's wooden shoes you're after, don't miss the local high school's Marching Dutchman Band; it's very easy to follow their tempo as they perform in local parades.)

1 Lincoln Ave., Holland, MI 49423
Phone: (888) 535-5792 or (616) 355-1030
Hours: April–September, daily 9:30 AM–6 PM
Cost: Adults $8, Kids (5–15) $5
Website: www.windmillisland.org
Directions: North from Seventh St. (Rte. 31 Business), northeast of the central business district.

Once you're pumped up on all things Dutch, it's time to head over to Veldheer's and naar winkel, naar winkel, naar winkel ("shop, shop, shop")! The company's DeKlomp Wooden Shoe and Delftware Factory is the only one of its kind in the United States. Artisans carve floatable footwear and paint blue-and-white porcelain knickknacks while you watch, so you know these aren't cheap Chinese knockoffs.

But Veldheer's is best known for its Tulip Gardens. Five million bulbs burst open each May during the city's Tulip Time Festival (www.tuliptime

.com). If you're tempted to pick a tulip in Holland, *don't*—it'll cost you a $50 fine. Instead, load up on bulbs (you can order them any time of year, but they won't be delivered until fall) to turn your own garden into a little patch of Holland, minus the red light district.

12755 Quincy St., Holland, MI 49424

Phone: (616) 399-1900 or (616) 399-1803

Hours: April–October, daily 9 AM–5 PM; open longer when blooming—call ahead

Cost: Free

Website: www.veldheer.com

Directions: Three miles north of town on Rte. 31.

Peninsular Pool

Who says vacations can't be educational? At a Holiday Inn Express in Holland, the kids can learn a little geography while playing Marco Polo. The indoor pool at this motel is shaped like the state of Michigan, or at least the lower mitten. Sorry, yoopers! And where the Great Lakes are supposed to be is a pebble-encrusted pool deck. Think of it as a topographical negative of the state—land is water and water is land. Plus, "Michigan" has a roof to keep off the lake-effect snow in winter.

Holiday Inn Express, 12381 Felch St., Holland, MI 49424

Phone: (616) 738-2800

Hours: Always visible from lobby

Cost: Free; Rooms, check website

Website: www.hiexpress.com

Directions: Two blocks east of Rte. 31 on Felch St.

Kalamazoo
Burger King King

Contrary to what you might have read in the *National Enquirer*, Elvis never worked at a Kalamazoo Burger King after his "death" . . . he only ordered at the drive-thru window. That is where local resident Louise Welling spotted him in the summer of 1988. He was driving a red Ferrari, hardly an inconspicuous vehicle for an undercover celebrity in buy-American Michigan. Nevertheless . . .

Welling also spotted the King twice more around town—first, dressed in a one-piece white jumpsuit while buying a fuse at **Felpausch's Food Center** (120 W. Prairie Street, (269) 649-1698) in nearby Vicksburg; and second, at the **J. C. Penney** in the Crossroads Mall (6580 W. Westnedge Ave., (269) 327-3500) in Portage. She also documented other sightings. A woman told her she'd seen Elvis being interviewed by a TV reporter as he walked up **Milham Avenue** toward Oakland Drive, also in Portage. Several other people spotted Presley in a police cruiser, and many heard, "I'm checking into the presence of Elvis" on their police scanners one evening.

Are you curious if he's still in the area? Well, be careful. A woman identified only as Kelly B. went in search around Kalamazoo. She tracked down a man named John Burrows—an alias often used by Presley—at a local apartment complex. When she confronted him, he denied it . . . but Kelly B. was positive it was the singer. And then she died under "mysterious circumstances" a month later. You've been warned.

Burger King, 3015 S. Westnedge Ave., Kalamazoo, MI 49008

Phone: (269) 343-2066

Hours: Monday–Friday 6 AM–11 PM, Saturday–Sunday 6 AM–1 AM

Cost: Free; Meals, $4–7

Website: www.bk.com

Directions: Just north of the Whites Rd./Cork St. intersection.

ELVIS EVERY YEAR

If you don't have the time to hang around a Kalamazoo Burger King waiting for the Peanut Butter and Banana Sandwich King to reappear, you can always head to Ypsilanti in July. Every year since 2000, fans have flocked to the city's Riverside Park (5 E. Cross St.) to watch tribute performers—or at least they *say* they're tribute performers—gyrate their hips and toss sweaty handkerchiefs into the crowd. For information, check out the **Michigan Elvisfest** website: www.mielvisfest.org.

Tim Allen—BUSTED!

Long before anyone knew him as Tim Taylor on *Home Improvement*, comedian Tim Allen was known to federal authorities as inmate 04276-040. Back in 1978 he was trying to supplement his income as a drug trafficker in southern Michigan, but on October 2 of that year was busted in the parking lot of the Kalamazoo Airport by the Michigan State Police. Allen, whose real name is Timothy Alan Dick, had tried to sell two undercover cops 1.4 *pounds* of cocaine.

In exchange for turning in several of his "business partners" and pleading guilty to drug trafficking, Allen was given a reduced sentence—three to seven years in the federal prison in Stillwater, Minnesota. He served two years and four months.

If you don't count eight seasons of crimes against good taste, Allen stayed on the right side of the law of the law until May 1997, when he was arrested for drunk driving after being pulled over for speeding 70 in a 40 mph zone near the intersection of Maple and Cranbrook roads in Beverly Hills, Michigan. He later paid a fine, was given one year's probation, and was ordered to attend substance abuse counseling.

Kalamazoo/Battle Creek International Airport, 5235 Portage Rd., Kalamazoo, MI 49002

Phone: (269) 388-3668

Hours: Always visible

Cost: Free

Website: http://azoairport.com

Directions: South of I-94 at Winters Dr.

Montague
World's Largest Weather Vane

Bob Dylan once sang that you don't need a weatherman to know which way the wind blows, which is particularly true in Montague. Since 1984, a 48-foot-tall weathervane has graced the north shore of White Lake, its 26-foot arrow faithfully pointing windward. It was built by Whitehall Metal Studios (www.whitehallproducts.com), a local business that specializes in more size-appropriate versions of the enormous weathervane.

Topping the 3,500-pound aluminum weathervane is a replica of the *Ella Ellenwood*, a Great Lakes schooner that ran aground, broke up, and

It's blowing that-a-way.

sank near Milwaukee in October 1901. A year after it went down, the ship's nameplate was found floating in the channel to Montague's White Lake, its home base. No one could say how it found its way across Lake Michigan without the aid of a beacon like the world's largest weathervane. You can see the old nameplate today at Montague City Hall.

Ellenwood Park, 8718 Water St., Montague, MI 49437

Phone: (231) 893-3903

Hours: Always visible

Cost: Free

Website: www.weathervaneweather.com/weathervane.htm

Directions: On Rte. 31 (Water/Dowling Sts.) just west of the lake.

Montague City Hall, 8778 Ferry St., Montague, MI 49437

Phone: (231) 893-1155

Hours: Monday–Friday 8 AM–5 PM

Cost: Free

Website: http://cityofmontague.org

Directions: One block west of Water St., one block north of Dowling St.

Muskegon
Buster Keaton Statue

Buster Keaton was born into show business. Literally. Both his parents were vaudeville performers and Buster—Joseph, actually—was born during an October 4, 1895, stopover in Piqua, Kansas. The Keatons ran the Mohawk Indian Medicine Company theater troupe in partnership with Harry Houdini. It was at the age of 18 months that the young boy earned his nickname; he fell down a long flight of stairs and didn't hurt himself, to which Houdini proclaimed, "That was a real buster!" (Vaudevillians called a dangerous, hilarious pratfall a buster.)

Keaton's parents put their son's unique talent to use, starting at the age of three. In a popular sketch, Buster would misbehave on stage, then

---

MUSKEGON

⇒ In 1986, a mysterious man dressed in a pinstriped suit appeared in Muskegon and started handing out $5 and $10 bills to strangers. He did this for a week before disappearing.

⇒ Muskegon is known as both the Sawdust Queen and the Red Light Queen.

---

get "punished" by his father who would heave him into the scenery, the audience, or the orchestra pit. Playing dead on landing, Buster learned how to maintain his signature deadpan expression during the chaos. Some handwringers in the audience complained that the act was child abuse, so they began billing him as "The Little Boy Who Couldn't Be Damaged." *Riiiiight.*

To the extent that The Three Keatons ever settled down, it was in Muskegon. In 1908 they established the Actors' Colony in the Bluffton neighborhood, where many performers liked to summer. The colony lasted about a decade before silent film changed the entertainment industry, drawing actors to the West Coast, including Buster.

Today Keaton is immortalized as a director, standing behind a movie camera, on the sidewalk outside a Muskegon theater. The bronze by Emmanuil Janet Snitkovsky was purchased in 2010 from the Hollywood Entertainment Museum when that establishment went belly-up.

Frauenthal Center for the Performing Arts, 425 W. Western Ave., Muskegon, MI 49440

Phone: (231) 722-2890

Hours: Always visible

Cost: Free

Website: http://frauenthal.org/

Directions: One block east of Shoreline Dr. (Rte. 31), at Third St.

Jonathan Walker, Slave Stealer—
the Man with the Branded Hand

In 1844, two decades before the Civil War broke out, abolitionist Jonathan Walker decided that he'd help free seven slaves who lived near his home in Pensacola, Florida. Unfortunately, his small ship was captured off the coast while en route to the Bahamas, and everyone aboard was returned to the United States. Later convicted in federal court, Walker was given a $150 fine and sentenced to one hour in the pillory and 15 days in jail. (He ended up serving 11 months until his fine was paid.) And, he was branded with "SS" on his right hand, marking him forever as a "Slave Stealer." He remains the only person to be ordered branded by a federal court.

After being freed, Walk returned to his native New England and started speaking on the abolitionist lecture circuit, flashing his scar for dramatic effect. A daguerreotype of his scar made the rounds when Walker wasn't available. Poet John Greenleaf Whittier immortalized Walker in his poem "The Man with the Branded Hand."

In 1850, Walker moved to Norton Shores, Michigan, where he ran a small fruit orchard. He died there on April 30, 1878, and was buried in Muskegon. Later that year, a cenotaph was placed over his grave bearing an engraving of the scar that made him famous.

Evergreen Cemetery, 391 Irwin Ave., Muskegon, MI 49442

Phone: (231) 724-6783

Hours: Daylight hours

Cost: Free

Directions: Seven blocks south of Apple Ave. (M-46) at Wood St., two blocks east of Terrace St.

Tornado over Kansas

If you're looking for a little culture on your next trip to Muskegon, head over to the city's art museum where you'll find *Tornado over Kansas,* one of the best-known works by the Regionalist John Steuart Curry. It was painted in 1929, and depicts a scene right out of the first reel of *The Wizard of Oz,* though it was created 10 years before the movie: as a twister churns up a wheat field in the distance, a poor farm family scurries for a storm cellar, mom carrying a baby, dad pulling a young girl, and two brothers holding three puppies and one very freaked-out cat. A chicken watches it all, unconcerned. Stupid chicken.

The artwork is just one of a small but impressive collection that includes works by Winslow Homer, Edward Hopper, Elizabeth Catlett, John Singer Sargent, Joos van Cleve, and Alfred Sisley.

Muskegon Museum of Art, 296 W. Webster Ave., Muskegon, MI 49440

Phone: (231) 720-2570

Hours: June–August, Tuesday & Thursday 10 AM–6 PM, Wednesday, Friday, and Saturday 10 AM–4:30 PM, Sunday noon–4:30 PM; September–May, Wednesday & Friday–Saturday 10 AM–4:30 PM, Thursday 10 AM–8 PM, Sunday noon–4:30 PM

Cost: Adults (18+) $7, Kids Free

Website: www.muskegonartmuseum.org

Directions: Three blocks east of Rte. 31, between Second St. and Third St.

USS *Silversides*

It might look like an old rust bucket today, but you wouldn't have wanted to be a Japanese ship facing down the USS *Silversides* in 1942. This 312-foot submarine was commissioned just eight days after Pearl Harbor, and by the end of the war had sunk 30 Japanese ships and incapacitated 14 more—the third highest of any American submarine in the war and the most of any sub still on the water.

Unless you're claustrophobic, take the tour below decks. See the torpedo room with sailors' bunks wedged around the bombs. Listen to the deafening "aaa-OOOO-gahhh" of the dive horn. Visit the officers' mess and hear the story of seaman George Platter, who had his gangrenous appendix removed on the table in December 1943 by shipmate Thomas Moore (a pharmacist by trade) and then returned to duty six days later. And watch for the ghost of Torpedo Man Third Class Mike Harbin, who was hit by enemy fire on May 10, 1942, and became the only person to die on the sub.

The USS *Silversides*.

The ship's dockside museum has a bit more elbow room, and many more exhibits, including periscopes, ship models, and machine guns for the kids. But if you're *really* interested in experiencing the life of a seaman, book a sleepover on the *Silversides*. The bunks are tight, which is why you can have 72 people in your party. It works best with Boy Scout troops.

1346 Bluff St., Muskegon, MI 49441

Phone: (231) 755-1230

Hours: September–May, Sunday–Thursday 10 AM–4 PM; Friday–Saturday 10 AM–5:30 PM; June–
   August, daily 10 AM–5:30 PM

Cost: Adults $15, Seniors (62+) $12.50, Kids (5–18) $10.50; Museum only, $6 (all ages)

Website: www.silversidesmuseum.org

Directions: Follow Lakeshore Dr. north to Beach St., then north to the museum at the channel.

SHIPS AHOY!

If you're afraid of water but still like BIG ships, there's a great observation platform at the **Soo Locks Visitors Center** (312 W. Portage Ave., (906) 632-3366, www.saultstemarie.com/soo-locks-46/) in Sault Ste. Marie. See a model of the famous locks and watch these enormous freighters move up and down the river. An even better view of the Soo Locks in action can be had from the nearby **Tower of History** (326 E. Portage Ave., (888) 744-7867, www.saulthistoricsites.com/tower-of-history-4/). Originally built to be a shrine to missionaries, it now operates as both a museum of local culture and a 20-story observation tower.

But if you're *not* hydrophobic, and your taste in ships is of the above-the-waterline variety, Michigan has several other floating museums just feet from shore:

SS *City of Milwaukee* and USCGC *Acacia*

99 Arthur St., Manistee, (231) 723-3587, http://carferry.com/

The SS *City of Milwaukee* was built in 1931 for the Grand Trunk Western Railroad, and for 50 years it transported cars across

Lake Michigan, 32 at a time. (It replaced the SS *Milwaukee*, which sank in a 1929 gale, killing all 52 crew aboard.) After being decommissioned in 1981, the 360-foot-long steamer found a permanent home on Manistee Lake, where it is open for tours. In October, all four decks are transformed into a haunted Ghost Ship, open on weekends. And moored alongside the SS *City of Milwaukee* is the USCGC *Acacia*, built in the early 1940s, which for 62 years operated as an icebreaker and maintained 210 buoys on the Great Lakes. Your ticket ($7 for adults, $5 for seniors and students) covers both vessels.

Museum Ship *Valley Camp*

401 E. Water St., Sault Ste. Marie, (906) 632-3658 or (888) 744-7867, www.thevalleycamp.com

This attraction claims to be the world's largest Great Lakes maritime museum, made all the more amazing because the entire museum is located *inside* the cargo holds of the ship. The 550-foot freighter transported iron ore and grain around the lakes from 1917 to 1967, but today it's permanently docked in the St. Mary's River, its cargo only ship models, old buoys, and other flotsam and jetsam. It also has four 1,200-gallon aquariums filled with local freshwater species and two battered (but never used) lifeboats from the *Edmund Fitzgerald*.

Icebreaker *Mackinaw*

131 S. Huron Ave., Mackinaw City, (231) 436-9825, www.themackinaw.org

The Icebreaker *Mackinaw* was ordered built 10 days after the bombing of Pearl Harbor, and would be used to keep war materials moving on the Great Lakes year-round. Trouble was, it didn't go into service until December 30, 1944, nearly at the war's end. But it still worked the lakes for 62 years, earning the nickname "Queen of the Lakes." In addition to seeing the captain's and crew's quarters, the engine room, and the bridge, you can check out 18 replicas of Great Lakes ships at the accompanying maritime museum.

Lightship *Huron*

Pine Grove Park, Thomas Edison Pkwy. & Prospect St., Port Huron, (810) 984-9768, www.phmuseum.org/Port_Huron_Museum/Huron_Lightship.html

It wasn't always practical to build a lighthouse everywhere ships might be in danger of running aground, which is why the Coast Guard used anchored lightships to guide freighters through hazardous waters. The *Huron* served this purpose from 1920 to 1970, most of its time stationed three miles from shore, six miles north of the Blue Water Bridge above the dangerous Corsica Shoals in Lake Huron. At night it would flash its beacon, and in misty weather blow its foghorn every 30 seconds. Today it sits dim and mostly quiet along the St. Clair River, open for tours.

Karl's Cuisine Café & Winery

447 W. Portage Ave., Sault Ste. Marie, (906) 253-1900, www.karlscuisine.com

OK, so this isn't exactly a museum. Or a ship. But it's *shaped* like a ship. Sitting just across Portage Avenue from the Soo Locks, this freighter-shaped building offers fine dining and a great view of passing ships from the open-air upper deck.

Newaygo
Roadside Fetus

Some people wear their politics on their sleeve, others share their beliefs on the back bumpers of their cars, but rare is the person who converts his or her entire front yard to make a *big* point. But northwest of Newaygo you'll find just that: "Suffer the Little Children" depicts a very large fetus in the palm of a giant hand rising from a pedestal. In front, 668 white

Not exactly subtle.

crosses are arranged to spell out ABORTION. According to an explanatory sign, they also represent the number of babies killed through abortion each hour of a 40-hour week. Another sign repeats Psalms 139:1, 13–16, a passage of scripture often quoted by foes of the practice. Pretty heavy stuff. But the scene is lightened up, just a little, with a bright yellow smiley face painted on an adjoining water tank.

1076 W. 48th St., Newaygo, MI 49337
Private phone
Hours: Always visible; view from street
Cost: Free
Directions: West of the Gordon Ave. intersection.

Niles
Sitting Bull and a Two-Headed Lamb

Most small-town museums are filled with stuff that you can find any-where—butter churns and photos of old buildings and school desks with slates and inkwells. *Yawn.* But occasionally they're chock-a-block with historical ephemera, like the Fort St. Joseph Museum.

The most fascinating exhibits here have nothing to do with the region. Best known are the 12 Lakota pictographs drawn in 1881 by Sitting Bull. They were given to Martha "Jennie" Quimby, wife of Capt. Horace Baxter Quimby, when the couple was stationed at Fort Randall in the Dakota Territory. The Quimbys later moved to Niles, and their descendants donated these rare documents of 1880s Indian life to the museum, which preserves them today.

Upstairs at the former Chapin mansion, you'll find a small display case that contains a spindle from George Washington's pew at Christ Church in Alexandria, Virginia; a small piece of copper sheathing from the USS *Constitution*, Old Ironsides (not Coppersides); and a one-inch length of the Nantucket transatlantic cable that carried the news of Lindbergh's successful landing in France. It's all watched over by the four glass eyes of Ditto, a stuffed two-headed lamb born on the nearby Bybee farm.

Fort St. Joseph Museum, 508 E. Main St., Niles, MI 49120

Phone: (269) 683-4700 x4012

Hours: Wednesday–Friday 10 AM–4 PM, Saturday 10 AM–3 PM

Cost: Free

Website: www.fortstjosephmuseum.org

Directions: On M-51 (Main St.) just east of Fifth St.

Nunica
Semi-Stonehenge

While there is still some debate about the origin and spiritual significance of Stonehenge, there's little debate about the one found today in Nunica: it was built by Fred and Pam Levin in 2007 to spruce up their front yard. At 13 feet tall, the Levins' Stonehenge is midway in scale between the English original and the *Spinal Tap* version. It was fashioned out of Styrofoam and sprayed with stucco, then anchored to the earth. Moss has begun to cover the base of the standing stones, making it look older than it really is.

As far as anyone knows, the Levins aren't druids, they just have a passion for ancient stonework. They plan to add a Native American medicine wheel for a garden, as well as a Cretan labyrinth for long, meandering walks on their property.

This beats lawn gnomes any day.

11591 Leonard Rd., Nunica, MI 49448

Private phone

Hours: Daylight hours; view from road

Cost: Free

Directions: South from I-96 on 112th Ave., then west on Leonard Rd., on the north side of the road.

Portage

Air Zoo

As you enter the Air Zoo through a curvy, cloudscape tunnel, you quickly realize that this isn't a typical airplane attraction. Inside, the museum's main exhibit hall is ringed by the *Century of Flight* mural—800 by 32 feet, the world's largest indoor mural (which took 14 months to paint)—and its dark floor is so reflective it gives you the feeling you're hovering in space. You're flying!

The cavernous hall is crammed with shiny, meticulously restored aircraft, including re-creations of the Wright Brothers' flyer and the Red Baron's Fokker tri-plane, fighter jets, barnstorming biplanes, khaki-green bombers, experimental aircars, and the world's only SR-71B Blackbird, capable of going Mach 3. That plane once made a flight from New York to London in less than two hours. The museum's east wing is split between two galleries, one featuring aircraft from both world wars and the other spacecraft and NASA ephemera, including spacesuits, a *Saturn V* rocket engine, dummy capsule trainers, and spacecraft mockups from Mercury to the Space Shuttle.

Want to take the controls? The Air Zoo has full-motion flight simulators (for an additional price), as well as hands-on exhibits where you can catch satellites, land space shuttles, and fly to Mars. They've also got carnival rides with aeronautical themes—mini hot air balloons, World War I biplanes, and more. After you're through, have a bite in the Kitty Hawk Café or max out your credit card in the well-stocked gift shop.

6151 Portage Rd., Portage, MI 49002

Phone: (866) 524-7966 or (269) 382-6555

Hours: Monday–Saturday 9 AM–5 PM, Sunday noon–5 PM

Cost: Adults $10, Kids (5 and up) $10; Entrance + Simulators, $16.50

Website: www.airzoo.org

Directions: South of Milham Ave. on the west side of the airport.

Celery Flats Interpretive Center

Have the kiddies not been eating their vegetables? Perhaps they haven't developed a deep enough appreciation for non-processed food. Well then, bring them to Portage where, in 1866, the modern "ivory pascal" variety of celery was first created. Soon, so much celery was being grown in the area that neighboring Kalamazoo was calling itself "Celery City." That's a fact bound to get children excited!

Not only will you learn about local agriculture at this quaint history center, but you can visit Stuart Manor, believed to be a station on the Underground Railroad, see works by local artists, or take in a musical performance at the open-air theater. But don't expect to see any actual celery flats—that's just a name for the area. Most of that production moved to Florida and California a lonnnng time ago.

7335 Garden Ln., Portage, MI 49002

Phone: (269) 329-4522

Hours: Park, daily 8 AM–Sunset; Center, June–August, Saturday 10 AM–3 PM, Sunday noon–5 PM

Cost: Park, Free; Center, Adults $3, Kids $2

Website: www.portagemi.gov/departments/parksrecreation/parksamenitieslisting
/celeryflats.aspx
Directions: East of Westnedge Ave. and Portage Creek on Garden Ln.

Rockford
Hot Dog Hall of Fame

Don't be confused by the name of this place—it's not where you'll find
shrines to the foot-long, the Chicago-style, the red snapper, or the Mexican Estilo Sonora. Instead, the Hot Dog Hall of Fame honors any *customer*
who can down 12 chili dogs (onions and mustard optional) in four hours
or less. Do that and your name, hometown, and number of wieners consumed will be etched on a tiny wall plaque along with 5,000 or so others.
If you can down 20, the Corner Bar will not only pick up the tab, but give
you a free T-shirt—XXL, one assumes.

This eating challenge dates back to 1967 when several Detroit Lions
tried to out-gorge each other, but soon customer free agents got into the
act. Balinda Gould holds the current amateur title, having downed 43
weenies in December 2005.

The Corner Bar, 31 N. Main St., Rockford, MI 49341
Phone: (616) 866-9866
Hours: Monday–Thursday 11 AM–10 PM, Friday–Saturday 11 AM–11 PM, Sunday 11 AM–9 PM
Cost: Free; Meals, $7–10
Website: www.rockfordcornerbar.com/historyHallofFame.html
Directions: Three blocks north of Division St., one block east of the river.

A *REAL* HOT DOG HALL OF FAME

If you'd rather look at large wieners than the folks who eat
them, there are a few jumbo dogs to visit in the state.

Big Wiener

Hefty's Coney Island, 26080 Grand River Ave., Redford, (313) 387-5977

It's certainly big, maybe six feet from tip to tip, thrusting out
above the entrance of this suburban Detroit fast-food joint, but

I've seen larger. And though Hefty's brags about its coneys, it doesn't have any chili spooned on top of its biggest dog. What gives?

Drive-In Dog

Cherry Bowl Drive-In Theatre, 9812 Honor Hwy., Honor, (231) 325-3413, www.cherrybowldrivein.com

The mustard-topped hot dog hanging on the fence outside this classic drive-in movie theater is obviously intended to imprint a message on your subconscious: Aren't you hungry? Maybe it's time to go to the concession stand . . .

Big Flat Kielbasa

Kowalski Sausage Company,
2270 Holbrook St., Hamtramck,
(313) 873-8200, www.kowality.com

That's gotta hurt!

Hamtramck is the epicenter of Polish American life in Detroit, so they prefer kielbasas to hot dogs. But this 20-foot-tall kielbasa has been run over by a steamroller, branded with the word KOWALSKI, and impaled on a two-pronged skewer. Is that any way to treat a wiener? Relax, it's just a sign, and has been here since the 1950s. Come to Hamtramck on Labor Day weekend and you'll get a smaller, plumper, tastier kielbasa at the city's annual Sausage Fest.

Wienermobile

The Henry Ford, 20900 Oakwood Blvd., Dearborn, (800) 835-5237, www.hfmgv.org

This wiener's got wheels! The first Oscar Mayer Wienermobile was built in Chicago in 1936, but the model on display at the Henry Ford (see page 263) was made during the 1950s from a

Dodge chassis and a very large and hollow "Yellow Band Wiener." If it makes you hungry, step next door to the Wienermobile Café, or plunk down $2 and you can create a scalding hot plastic replica from an adjacent Mold-a-Rama machine.

Saugatuck
Hand-Cranked Chain Ferry

If the coal ash–spewing SS *Badger* car ferry isn't your cup of organic tea, perhaps this environmentally friendly watercraft is more your speed. Instead of fossil fuel, it uses human muscle power as its means of conveyance, which is why it only goes 380 feet across the Kalamazoo River, not across the vastness of Lake Michigan. Once common in America, today it's the last watercraft of its type in the United States.

Saugatuck's first hand-cranked chain ferry opened in 1838, before the practical internal combustion engine, though the craft you'll be riding was built in the 1930s. The ferry has a filigreed canopy to shade you from the midday sun while crossing between Saugatuck and Douglas (and the imposing Mt. Baldhead dune). The ferry, usually cranked by a burly high school student, has the right of way on the river because the taut chain rises to the water's surface, endangering other boats' engines, keels, and paint jobs, to say nothing of people on the ferry. Once on the opposite shore, the chain goes slack and the captain blasts an all-clear horn.

360 Water St., Saugatuck, MI 49453

Phone: (269) 857-1701

Hours: June–August, daily 9 AM–9 PM

Cost: Each way, Adults $1, Kids (under 12) $0.50

Website: www.south-haven-to-saugatuck.com/Saugatuck-chain-ferry.html

Directions: At Main St. just east of Water St.

Shelby
Shelby Gem Stone Factory

Calling all cheapskates, or anyone who doesn't want to buy a diamond pulled from a mine by a South African teenager making a few bucks a day:

the Shelby Gem Stone Factory will make you a synthetic rock manufactured and cut right here in the U. S. of A. at a fraction—about 1/20th—of the price of a real one. Why not use the savings to upsize?

This business was started by Larry Kelly in 1970, and today is the largest manufacturer of synthetic gems in the world—rubies, emeralds, sapphires, aquamarines, diamonds, and more. Start your visit to the showroom/museum in the 50-seat theater—a movie details every step in the process. Then it's off to see piles of fake gems, from simulated 5,000°F diamond blobs, hot out of the oven, to imitation rubies being cut and polished. Ever see an amethyst the size of a baseball? You can at Shelby's!

1330 Industrial Park Dr., PO Box 155, Shelby, MI 49455

Phone: (231) 861-2165

Hours: Monday–Friday 9 AM–5:30 PM, Saturday noon–4 PM

Cost: Free; Gems, $175/carat

Website: www.shelbygemfactory.com

Directions: North of Fifth St./Woodrow Rd., east of 72nd Ave.

South Haven
The Blueberry Store

Blueberry jam. Blueberry syrup. Blueberry muffins. Blueberry caramel corn. Blueberry taffy. Blueberry lollipops. Blueberry maple granola. Blueberry gumballs. Blueberry coffee. Blueberry tea. Blueberry scones. Blueberry pie filling. Blueberry salsa. Blueberry cornbread. Blueberry mustard. Blueberry BBQ sauce. Blueberry sausage and brats. Dried blueberries. Frozen blueberries. Chocolate-covered blueberries. Blueberry soap. Blueberry bubble bath gel. Blueberry body butter. Blueberry dog treats. Blueberry clove pet cologne. Blueberry candles. Blueberry aprons. Blueberry earrings. Blueberry shot glasses. Blueberry temporary tattoos. Blueberry license plate frames. . . .

OK, that's about enough. Basically, if it's made from blueberries, resembles blueberries, honors blueberries, or even mentions blueberries, it's for sale at the Blueberry Store. The shop is located in downtown South Haven, the "Blueberry Capital of the World." Every August since 1969, the town has hosted the National Blueberry Festival (www.blueberryfestival .com), which includes a Blueberry Parade, a Blueberry Pie Eating Contest, a Blueberry Cook-off, a Blueberry Pancake Breakfast, and the crowning of a Little Miss Blueberry. If she's in town, Violet Beauregarde always wins.

525 Phoenix Rd., South Haven, MI 49090

Phone: (269) 637-6322

Hours: Monday–Saturday 10 AM–7 PM, Sunday 10 AM–6 PM

Cost: Free

Website: www.theblueberrystore.com

Directions: One block west of Broadway St., southeast of the river.

The Caboose Inn

Do it in a caboose.

Vacation is a time for adventure, for exploring new worlds, for new experiences. So if you've ever thought about doing it in a caboose, come to South Haven—there are two units to choose from. A few years ago, Bob and Pat Burr bought a pair of decommissioned railroad cabooses, parked them beside the town's old depot, and turned them into one-bedroom B&Bs. The rooms aren't much wider than the queen-sized beds inside, but they're long rooms and include small kitchenettes and outdoor decks. You can also climb up their ladders into their windowed cupolas for a look outside.

The cabooses are managed by the Old Harbor Inn across the street. It has a more nautical vibe, if that's your thing.

Old Harbor Inn, 515 Williams St., South Haven, MI 49090

Phone: (800) 433-9210 or (269) 637-8480

Hours: Always visible; April–October

Cost: April–May, Sunday–Thursday $89/night, Friday–Saturday $99/night; June–August,
    Sunday–Thursday $159/night, Friday–Saturday $189/night; September–October,
    Sunday–Thursday $99/night, Friday–Saturday $129/night;

Website: www.oldharborinn.com/accommodations/cabooseinn.php

Directions: On the northeast corner of the Dyckman Ave. bridge.

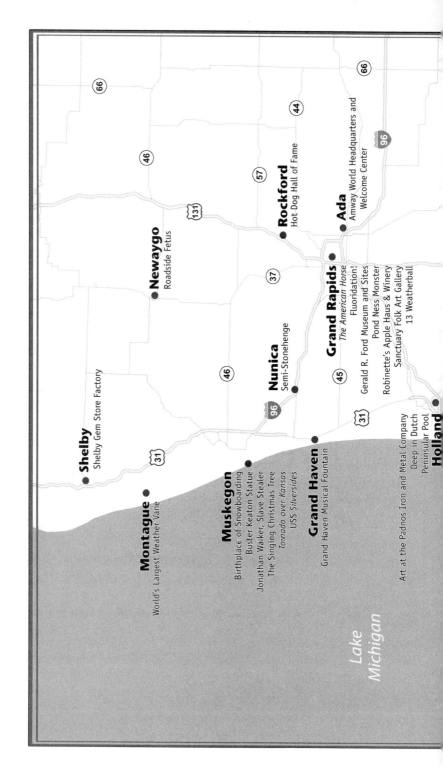

Montague
World's Largest Weather Vane

Muskegon
Birthplace of Snowboarding
Buster Keaton Statue
Jonathan Walker, Slave Stealer
The Singing Christmas Tree
Tornado over Kansas
USS Silversides

Grand Haven
Grand Haven Musical Fountain

Shelby
Shelby Gem Store Factory

Newaygo
Roadside Fetus

Nunica
Semi-Stonehenge

Grand Rapids
The American Horse
Fluoridation!
Gerald R. Ford Museum and Sites
Pond Ness Monster
Robinette's Apple Haus & Winery
Sanctuary Folk Art Gallery
13 Weatherball

Rockford
Hot Dog Hall of Fame

Ada
Amway World Headquarters and
Welcome Center

Art at the Padnos Iron and Metal Company
Deep in Dutch
Peninsular Pool

Holland

Lake Michigan

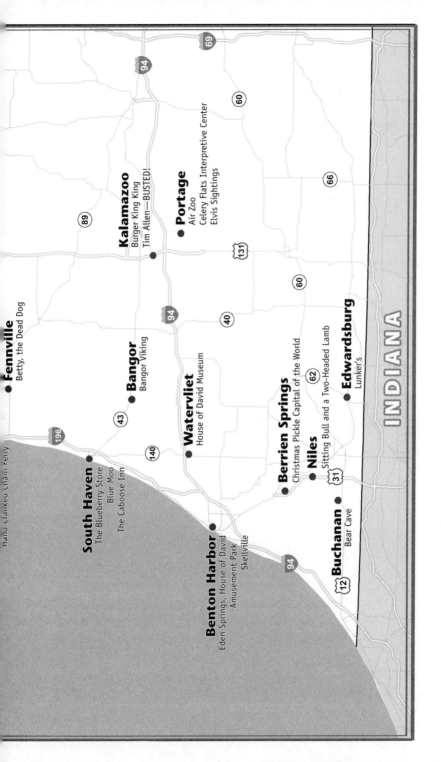

Fennville
Betty, the Dead Dog

Hand-cranked Chain Ferry

South Haven
The Blueberry Store
Blue Moo
The Caboose Inn

Benton Harbor
Eden Springs, House of David
Amusement Park
Skellville

Bangor
Bangor Viking

Watervliet
House of David Museum

Kalamazoo
Burger King King
Tim Allen—BUSTED!

Portage
Air Zoo
Celery Flats Interpretive Center
Elvis Sightings

Berrien Springs
Christmas Pickle Capital of the World

Niles
Sitting Bull and a Two-Headed Lamb

Edwardsburg
Lunker's

Buchanan
Bear Cave

INDIANA

MAP OF WESTERN MICHIGAN **141**

4

Central Michigan

*C*entral Michigan. Palm of the mitten. Heart of the state. It's where you'll find the center of government—the capitol in Lansing—as well as its moral heart. Where was the hotbed of the Underground Railroad? The birthplace of the US Peace Corps? An animal hospital that makes prosthetic feet for injured roosters? Central Michigan, that's where.

That said, the region also has a dark, sinister side. It is home to museums of bugs and dentistry, stores dedicated to the dark arts, and a little place called Hell.

Are you inspired, or frightened? Better read on . . .

Adrian

Laura Smith Haviland Statue and Grave

Few people were as devoted to the antislavery cause in Michigan as Adrian's Laura Smith Haviland. A Quaker from Canada, she (along with Elizabeth Margaret Chandler) established the state's first abolitionist group, the Logan Female Anti-Slavery Society, in 1832. And in 1839 she founded the Raisin Institute, Michigan's first integrated school, with her husband, Charles, and brother Harvey.

In 1845, an erysipelas epidemic left Haviland widowed with seven children, yet the personal loss seemed to energize her. "Aunt Laura" became the busiest conductor in the area's Underground Railroad, often employing disguises—as a farmer, a nurse, a schoolteacher, and even as a man—to help passengers reach their destinations. She eventually had a $3,000 bounty put on her head by southern slave catchers, though it didn't stop her from lecturing across the Midwest, always carrying a "knee-stiffener" leg iron given to her by former slaves to show the brutality of the so-called peculiar institution; you can see it today at the Michigan Historical Museum in Lansing (see page 175).

Haviland died in 1898 and was buried north of Adrian at the **Raisin Valley Friends Cemetery** (3552 N. Adrian Hwy.). A statue of her was placed in front of City Hall in 1909, which was relocated to a courtyard adjoining the local history museum in 2011.

Lenawee County Historical Museum, 110 E. Church St., Adrian, MI 49221

Phone: (517) 265-6071

Hours: Always visible; Museum, Tuesday–Friday 10 AM–2 PM, Saturday 10 AM–4 PM

Cost: Free

Website: www.ci.adrian.mi.us/Community/Adrian-Art-Discovery/Laura-Smith-Haviland.aspx

   and http://freepages.history.rootsweb.ancestry.com/~keller/museum/work/

Directions: At the intersection of Rte. 223 (Main St.) and M-52 (Church St.).

Ann Arbor
Birthplace of the Peace Corps

The initial concept of what became the Peace Corps was batted around by Minnesota Senator Hubert Humphrey in the late 1950s, but it was not until presidential candidate John F. Kennedy posed a series of rhetorical questions to students at the University of Michigan did the program begin to take shape. On a campaign trip through the state on October 14, 1960, he stopped in Ann Arbor to spend the night. Though it was 2 AM, about 10,000 students turned out to greet him, and he was coaxed into an impromptu speech. "How many of you are willing to spend 10 years in Africa or Latin America or Asia working for the US and working for freedom?" he asked. "How many of you who are going to be doctors are willing to spend your days in Ghana?"

Two attendees, the newly married Judy and Al Guskin, took Kennedy's words to heart and formed a committee of graduate students, Americans Committed to World Responsibility. On October 21, they published an article in the *Michigan Daily* asking how many readers would volunteer to serve the poor around the world. Petitions flooded in, and the Guskins delivered them to the Kennedy campaign. On November 2, less than a week before the election, Kennedy announced in a speech at San Francisco's Cow Palace that he would support this effort. The agency was created by executive order on March 1, 1961, and signed into law on September 22 the same year.

In the 50 years since its founding, 210,000 Peace Corps volunteers have served two-year commitments in 140 countries around the world. Today you can stand on a brass medallion embedded into the steps of the Michigan Union where Kennedy made that first speech.

Michigan Union, 530 S. State St., Ann Arbor, MI 48109

Phone: (734) 764-4636

Hours: Always visible

Cost: Free

Website: http://uunions.umich.edu/munion/ and www.peacecorps.gov

Directions: At the intersection of State St. and University Ave.

Giant Garlic

If you're the type of person who is self-conscious about your breath, the decoration outside this Cajun/Creole eatery might make you anxious. It's an enormous head of garlic, about 10 feet in diameter, that dangles just above the main entrance to the restaurant. Not every item on the menu includes garlic—iced tea, for example, does not—but most do. At least you'll be in good, smelly company.

There is no similarly scaled breath mint over the exit.

Just follow your nose.

Quarter Bistro & Tavern, Westgate Shopping Center, 300 S. Maple Rd., Ann Arbor, MI 48103

Phone: (734) 929-9200

Hours: Always visible; Restaurant, Monday–Saturday, 11 AM–12 AM; Sunday 10 AM–2 PM

Cost: Free; Meals, $10–30

Website: www.thequarterbistro.com

Directions: Two blocks south of Jackson Ave., just east of I-94.

Mini-Museums of the Catholepistemiad, University of Michigania

When the University of Michigan was established in Detroit in 1817, it was given the auspicious title Catholepistemiad, or University of Michigania, but then somebody with an underdeveloped flair for the dramatic came up with its far less interesting current name. Boooooooo! But luckily, not everybody has abandoned this institution's original sense of style. Take, for example, the curators of these four specialty museums and collections on campus.

The **Kelsey Museum of Archaeology** houses more than 100,000 artifacts from the ancient Middle East and Mediterranean—falcon and cat mummies, Roman sculptures, Grecian urns, small sphinxes, magical amulets, the coffin of Djehutymose, and a full-scale re-creation of the painted "Room of the Mysteries" from Pompeii.

Kelsey Museum of Archaeology, 434 S. State St., Ann Arbor, MI 48109

Phone: (734) 764-9304

Hours: Tuesday–Friday 9 AM–4 PM, Saturday–Sunday 1–4 PM

Cost: Free (but donations are welcome)

Website: www.lsa.umich.edu/kelsey

Directions: On State St. north of University Ave.

The Catholepistemiad's College of Dentistry has its own minimuseum, tucked away in a lobby on the building's ground floor. The **Sindecuse Museum of Dentistry** has more than 15,000 artifacts related to the profession's history, from 1700s to today, but not a lot of room to display

---

ANN ARBOR

⇒ One in every 750 Americans has a degree from Ann Arbor's U of M.

⇒ Ann Arbor's **Michigan Stadium** (1201 S. Main St.), also known as the Big House, seats 109,901 fans and is the largest college stadium in the country.

⇒ Some Ann Arborites believe a lake monster is responsible for the mysterious thawed hole that often appears in the ice of **Pleasant Lake,** southwest of town, during the dead of winter.

---

them. That's why half of the museum space is dedicated to rotating exhibits. On one side of the room is an "operatory" where you'll see chairs, X-ray machines, hygienists' tools, and spit basins to show you just how much the profession has improved with years of practice. On the other side, you'll find the Sindecuse's latest exhibition. On a recent visit, it was Women in Dentistry—their pliers, prosthetics, and tooth-related souvenirs, such as the elaborately carved walrus tusk Leonie von Zesch received from thankful, too-often-toothless Inuit villagers.

Sindecuse Museum of Dentistry, University of Michigan School of Dentistry, Kellogg Building, 1011 N. University Ave., G-565, Ann Arbor, MI 48109

Phone: (734) 763-0767

Hours: Monday–Friday 8 AM–6 PM

Cost: Free

Website: www.dent.umich.edu/sindecuse

Directions: Just east of the intersection of N. University Ave. and Fletcher Ave.

As with the Sindecuse Museum of Dentistry, most of the pieces in the **Stearns Collection of Musical Instruments** are tucked away under lock and key, but they do show off some of their 2,500+ artifacts in display cases at the south end of the music building and the lobby of the Hill Auditorium. If you're lucky, you'll see Tibetan drums made out of human skulls, peacock vina, idiophones, Hawaiian rattles, composite sitars, and a rare quadruple-reed serunai from Malaysia—there's something for every music lover!

Stearns Collection of Musical Instruments, Earl V. Moore Building of the School of Music, UM North Campus, 1100 Baits Dr., Ann Arbor, MI 48109

Phone: (734) 936-2891

Hours: Monday–Friday 9 AM–5 PM

Cost: Free

Website: www.music.umich.edu/research/stearns_collection/index.htm

Directions: Two blocks southeast of Broadway on Baits Dr., at the south end of the music building.

You have to be a researcher or a very convincing imposter to view the items in the **Joseph A. Ladabie Collection**, but anyone can see its artifacts online. Ladabie was a turn-of-the-century anarchist, and this collection is dedicated to the nation's radical and protest history—pamphlets, buttons, photos, letters, and scrapbooks. They even have UM alum Ted Kaczynski's Unabomber Manifesto and his other kooky writings.

Joseph A. Ladabie Collection, Harlan Hatcher Graduate Library, 913 S. University Ave., Ann
   Arbor, MI 48109
Phone: (734) 936-2314
Hours: By appointment only
Cost: Free
Website: www.lib.umich.edu/labadie-collection
Directions: Within the library at State St. and University Ave.

The Wave Field

Architect Maya Lin is certainly best known for designing the Vietnam Veterans Memorial in Washington, DC. But visitors to the University of Michigan can see another one of Lin's works, this one built in 1995, tucked in the courtyard behind an engineering building on the school's north campus.

The Wave Field is a 90-by-90-foot landscape covered with dozens of three-dimensional sine waves, looking like a very large prairie dog town or the open ocean, only covered in green grass. It's a great place to lie out and get a tan, because one side of every hill is always facing the sun. Or, if you like to picnic, you can spread out in relative privacy while others are just a few yards away, blocked from view by a four-foot mound. Because of its location away from the main campus, it's often empty anyway.

François-Xavier Bagnoud Building, UM North Campus, 1320 Beal Ave., Ann Arbor, MI 48109
Phone: (734) 764-3310
Hours: Always visible
Cost: Free
Website: http://public-art.umich.edu/the_collection/campus/north/38 and www.mayalin.com
Directions: South on Draper Dr. from Hayward St., then follow around the building to the right.

Batavia and Coldwater

Grave of Lizzie Whitlock, the Original Circus Fat Lady

Her stage name was Lottie Grant, but her real name was Lizzie Whitlock. She was born Elizabeth Stice in Iowa in 1853, and by the time she was a teen she was working the sideshow circuit as the Fat Lady. Not only that, but she was a rattlesnake charmer whose talents eventually led to tours with the Ringling Brothers Circus.

Whitlock could also charm the fellas, though her husbands never seemed to last very long. Her first spouse, George Parker, died while trying to harpoon a seal. Hubby number two, Charles Love, was a trapeze artist, and not a very skilled one—he fell to his death. Her third husband, Frank Whitlock, was a carnival barker and ticket-taker who somehow survived their short marriage; they divorced before he was gored by an elephant or blown to bits by a cannon.

Having saved a considerable sum from her nationwide appearances, she retired to Batavia and opened a retail shop, the Beehive Shoe Store, in nearby Coldwater. When she passed away in 1899 at the age of 45, she tipped the scales at over 650 pounds. A pallbearer was sent through the front porch while carrying her casket out of the house on the way to the township cemetery. You can see a pair of her size 24 shoes today at the Wing House Museum in Coldwater.

Batavia Township Cemetery, N. Batavia & Lindley Rds., Batavia, MI 49036

Phone: (517) 278-7445

Hours: Daylight hours

Cost: Free

Directions: North of Rte. 12 (Chicago Rd.) on Batavia Rd.

Wing House Museum, 27 S. Jefferson St., Coldwater, MI 49036

Phone: (517) 278-2871

Hours: Third Saturday of every month, noon–4 PM or by appointment

Cost: Free

Website: www.branchcountyhistoricalsociety.org

Directions: One block south of the train tracks, at Hooker St.

Bath

The Bath School Bombing

Even in today's world, it's hard to find or imagine a person as evil as Andrew P. Kehoe. Enraged over what he felt was a too-high property tax that cost him his farm (a fiction—his own financial mismanagement was to blame), he methodically plotted vengeance against the entire community.

All that's left.

Kehoe and his wife lived on a farm on Clark Road near Bath. They inherited the property (in part) from his wife's uncle, and purchased the balance from other family members. Driven by anger over the town's new Bath Consolidated School, approved in 1921, Kehoe ran for school board trustee in 1924 and won. He was voted treasurer because, despite his clear personality faults, everyone knew he was a tightwad. And later, when the new school needed maintenance, Kehoe offered to do the wiring work and was hired as a contractor. This gave him 24-hour access to the building he hated more than anything in the world.

On May 18, 1927, Kehoe's plot unfolded. First he killed his wife, Nellie, and set their home and barn on fire, with the animals still inside. At 9:45 AM, when all the town's children were in class, a timer detonated dynamite Kehoe had tucked throughout the north wing, causing half the building to collapse. The whole town rushed to the scene to rescue the wounded.

Kehoe then arrived in his pickup truck, and motioned to school superintendent Emory Huyck to come over. Huyck immediately suspected Kehoe was involved in the explosion, and went over to confront him. While Huyck stood on the running board, Kehoe fired a gun into another cache of explosives in the cab, killing them both, along with the town's postmaster, a local farmer, and an eight-year-old boy who had just survived the first blast.

In all, Kehoe killed 43—37 children, 2 teachers, 3 bystanders, and his wife. Another 58 were injured, though it could have been much worse. In combing through the wreckage, investigators found another 504 pounds of dynamite wired through the rest of the building; somehow it had failed to detonate. There were about 275 people in the school when the north wing exploded.

The town removed the cupola from the Bath Consolidated School and later made it the centerpiece of a memorial park built on the site. Artifacts from that fateful day can be found in a display-case museum at the nearby middle school.

James Couzens Memorial Park, Main & High Sts., Bath, MI 48808
No phone
Hours: Daylight hours
Cost: Free
Website: http://freepages.history.rootsweb.ancestry.com/~bauerle/disaster.htm
Directions: Three blocks north of Clark Rd., one block west of Oak St., south of High St.

Bath School Museum, Bath Middle School, 13675 Oak St., Bath, MI 48808
Phone: (517) 641-6781
Hours: By appointment
Cost: Free
Directions: One block east of the memorial park.

Battle Creek
Historic Bridge Park

There was a time, about 100 years ago, when truss bridges were state of the art in road construction. American steel was booming, and so was the industrialization of the country. But nothing lasts forever, particularly

No bridge too far.

when it's made of rustable steel. After tearing down and replacing many old structures, the Calhoun County Road Commission decided it should preserve some of its most beautiful bridges, and Historic Bridge Park was born.

Under the direction of Vern Mesler, five local truss bridges were disassembled, restored, and rebuilt over Dickinson Creek, just north of where it dumps into the Kalamazoo River. Battle Creekers can now see the 20 Mile Road Bridge, the 133rd Avenue Bridge, the Bauer Road Bridge, the Gale Road Bridge, and the Charlotte Highway Bridge, just as they looked a century ago, all along the same scenic footpath. And, as a bonus, the park includes the stone arch Dixon's Bridge, which is still used by railroads today.

14930 Wattles Rd., Battle Creek, MI 49014

Phone: (800) 781-9841 or (269) 781-9841

Hours: Daily 8 AM–8 PM

Cost: Free

Website: www.historicbridges.org/info/bridgepark/

Directions: Just east of the river on Wattles Rd., which connects 9 Mile Rd. to 9½ Mile Rd.

Sojourner Truth's Grave

Isabella Baumfree was born a slave in New York in 1797, and was sold several times before fleeing to freedom with her infant daughter in 1826. A year later she no longer had to worry about being captured and returned; all New York slaves were emancipated by the New York State Emancipation Act of 1827. Baumfree returned to her former owner to retrieve her five-year-old son, Peter, only to learn that he had illegally sold him to an Alabama plantation . . . *after* the boy was technically free. Baumfree registered a complaint with local authorities, and was able to get her former owner thrown into jail. Charges were dropped when, remarkably, her son was returned to her in 1828.

Baumfree ended up in New York City where, at an 1843 service at the Mother A.M.E. Zion Church, she stood up and announced she would be changing her name to Sojourner Truth. "Sojourner, because I am a wanderer; Truth, because God is truth," she explained. When she wasn't touring the country lecturing against slavery and for women's rights, Truth made a home in Battle Creek, starting in 1857. Her final home, where she lived from 1867 until her death in 1883, stood at 38 College Street; it burned down in 1898.

Truth died in Battle Creek on November 26, 1883, and was buried in Oak Hill Cemetery; a granite cairn was erected over her plot in 1929. (Dr. John Harvey Kellogg, Will Kellogg, C. W. Post, and Ellen White, co-founder of the Seventh-Day Adventist Church, are also buried in Oak Hill.) Kimball House Museum is the final repository of many of Truth's personal belongings, including a painting of her meeting with Abraham Lincoln, a silk dress given to her by Queen Victoria, and her only known signature.

Oak Hill Cemetery, 255 South Ave., Battle Creek, MI 49014

Phone: (269) 964-7321

Hours: Daily 8 AM–sunset

Cost: Free

Directions: East on Burnham St. to South Ave., then south one block.

Kimball House Museum, 196 Capital Ave. NE, Battle Creek, MI 49017

Phone: (269) 966-4157

Hours: By appointment

Cost: Adults $5, Kids (12 and under) $3

Website: www.heritagebattlecreek.org

Directions: One block east of Division St. on Capital St., four blocks north of the river.

Wellville

The next time you sit down for a bowl of cereal, think of the breakfast food pioneers who made your meal possible and who made Battle Creek the "Cereal Capital of the World." The story begins in the 1850s, when Ellen and James White, J. N. Andrews, and Joseph Bates began developing a new Christian religion based in part on visions Ellen White was having. In addition to theological concerns, she saw images of herself eating fruits and nuts, which led her to a life of vegetarianism. The foursome officially founded the Seventh-day Adventist Church in Battle Creek on May 21, 1863.

At first, the church had about 3,500 followers, one of whom was Dr. John Harvey Kellogg. In 1876, he became medical superintendent of the Western Health Reform Institute, later known as the Battle Creek Sanitarium (and lampooned as Wellville by the writer T. C. Boyle). The sanitarium was owned by the church, and advocated its unique philosophies on proper, healthy living: vegetarianism, brisk walks and breathing exercises, artificial sunbaths, sexual abstinence (particularly from onanism), and—put down your spoon for a moment—daily yogurt enemas. Among the sanitarium's famous visitors: George Bernard Shaw, Amelia Earhart, Thomas Edison, Henry Ford (who would follow Edison anywhere), Sarah Bernhardt, and soon-to-be-president Warren G. Harding, who recovered here from five different nervous breakdowns between the ages of 22 and 35.

Kellogg and his brother Will also developed new ways to prepare nuts and grains. Granulacerelomia, often shortened to just Granula, had been invented by Seventh-day follower James Caleb Jackson in 1863; the Kellogg brothers introduced Granola, an obvious knockoff, in 1881. In 1894, they stumbled on the recipe for corn flakes, which they originally called Granose, after accidentally allowing a batch of corn paste to go stale, which caused it to flake when it was rolled out for dough. As demand for their cereals increased, they formed the Sanitas Food Company in 1897. Later, in an argument over whether their recipes could be sweetened, sugar-loving Will broke away and formed the Battle Creek Toasted Corn Flake Company, today known as Kellogg's.

Meanwhile, Charles William "C. W." Post passed through Battle Creek after an 1891 nervous breakdown. He enjoyed the sanitarium's food so much he launched the Postum Cereal Company in 1895. Post introduced Grape Nuts, essentially small granola, in 1897; and Elijah's Manna in 1904, renamed Post Toasties—essentially corn flakes—three years later. The Postum Cereal Company became General Foods in 1929.

As medical fads and practices changed, the Battle Creek Sanitarium faded away. Its massive main building went into receivership in 1933, and during World War II it was converted into the Percy Jones Army Hospital. Today, it houses the **Hart-Dole-Inouye Federal Center** (74 N. Washington Ave.). Those interested in the Kelloggs should visit Historic Adventist Village, which has many of the sanitarium's old medical devices, including the Electric Light Bath Cabinet, the Oscillo-Manipulator, the Kneading Machine, the Foot Vibrator, and the Colonic Machine. Look, but definitely don't touch.

Battle Creek still holds the title of "Cereal Capital of the World" (or sometimes the "Cereal Bowl of America"). Every second Saturday in June since 1956, the city has thrown the World's Longest Breakfast Table celebration. Three hundred picnic tables—2,700 feet in length—are lined up along the town's main drag for the most important meal of the year.

Dr. John Henry Kellogg Discovery Center, Historic Adventist Village, 482 Van Buren St., Battle Creek, MI 49037

Phone: (269) 965-3000

Hours: April–May, Sunday–Friday 10 AM–5 PM, Saturday 2–5 PM; November–March, Sunday–Friday 10 AM–4 PM, Saturday 2–4 PM

Cost: Free, donations accepted

Website: www.adventistheritage.org

Directions: Four blocks north of the river, at Kendall St.

Brooklyn
St. Joseph's Stations of the Cross Shrine

St. Joseph's Church southeast of Brooklyn is a very old parish, established in 1854 by Irish immigrants. And it was already over 80 years old when parishioners, led by their pastor Monsignor Joseph Pfeffer, decided to fix up the place, choosing (oddly) a Spanish motif. They also expanded the grounds to five acres, and included outdoor stations of the cross. But rather than just install the traditional 14 tableaus, they decided to re-create the entire *Via Dolorosa*—the Sorrowful Way—starting with the temple of Pontius Pilate, leading down past the balconied homes of Jerusalem, and finally to the crucifixion at Calvary.

For the job, the church hired Mexican artisans Dionicio Rodriquez and Ralph Corona, both skilled in *el trabajo rustico*, a technique of molding and embellishing concrete to resemble trees, wood, and other natural materials. Work started in 1932, but wasn't completed until 1936. Though some parts of this remarkable folk art site have been damaged in recent years, most of the concrete stations, bridges, railings, and archways remain standing, including the last station embedded with stones from around the world. (If you like the handiwork here, be sure to check out the nearby McCourtie Park, page 185.)

8743 US Hwy. 12, Brooklyn, MI 49230

Phone: (517) 467-2183

Hours: Daylight

Cost: Free

Website: www.stjosephshrinebrooklyn.catholicweb.com

Directions: Where Rte. 12 meets Egan Hwy.

Camden
Tristate Corner

In the United States, there are 37 places on dry land (not in a river or lake) where three states intersect at the same point. Most aren't marked by anything special, just benchmark medallions from the US Geologic Survey, but at the intersection of Michigan, Indiana, and Ohio you'll find a stone monument. It was placed there by the Hillsdale County Historical Society in 1977, and while they get an A for effort, they get a C for execution. The actual intersection is about 130 feet south of the stone. The only thing that prevents them from getting an F is that the inscription on the marker states how far off it is.

Cope Rd., Camden, MI 49232

No phone

Hours: Always visible

Cost: Free

Website: www.hillsdalehistoricalsociety.org

Directions: South from Camden on M-49, west on Territorial Rd. (Indiana Rte. 120), turn south on Cope Rd., then two miles ahead on the left.

Chelsea
Birthplace of "JIFFY" Baking Mixes

The Chelsea Milling Company was founded in 1887, but it wasn't until 1930 that it first made the familiar product that you probably have in your cupboard right now: "JIFFY" mix! It was invented by Mabel White Holmes, who became the company's president after her husband fell from a too-tall silo. She wanted to create "a mix that is so easy, even a man could do it," and she succeeded. The general baking mix was her first, but the company later added mixes for muffins, cakes, crusts, biscuits, brownies, and frostings.

"JIFFY" mixes are still manufactured in the town where they were invented—1.6 million boxes *each day*. You can find the plant by looking for the 50-foot-tall "little blue box" painted on the side of its grain tower west of downtown. Plant tours are available with an appointment, and on your visit you'll learn some fascinating facts. For instance, did you know that neither the blueberry nor the raspberry muffin mixes contain actual blueberries or raspberries? They're dyed apple chunks!

201 N. Main St., PO Box 460, Chelsea, MI 48118

Phone: (800) 727-2460 or (734) 475-1361

Hours: By reservation, Monday–Friday 9 AM–3 PM

Cost: Free

Website: www.jiffymix.com

Directions: On M-52 (Main St.), just north of the railroad tracks.

Colon
Abbott Magic Company

It's said that a good magician never reveals a trick, but the truth is, most in the business will reveal a trick . . . for a price. The Abbott Magic Company, founded in 1934 by Australian Percy Abbott and American Recil Bordner, proves the point. If you're willing to shell out enough quarters pulled from some kid's ear, any trick on the shelves is yours.

Though it looks small, Abbott's is the world's largest distributor to the magic trade. Eight years before Abbott's opened, Harry Blackstone Sr. made Colon his summer home. With an endless parade of magicians coming through town to meet the conjurer (including Abbott), it seemed like the perfect location to set up shop. Today Colon calls itself "Magic City."

The current store is hard to miss—it's the spooky black structure covered in skeleton stencils. Helpful staff will demonstrate the merchandise—floating balls, dove pans, vanishing wands, and straitjackets—but don't expect them to reveal the secret until your credit card clears. During the summer, they put on a 45-minute show every Saturday at 1 PM, and each August they host a four-day Magic Get-Together, which includes Vent-o-Rama, a gathering of ventriloquists and their dummies.

124 St. Joseph St., Colon, MI 49040

Phone: (269) 432-3235

Hours: Monday–Friday 9 AM–5 PM, Saturday 9 AM–4 PM

Cost: Free

Website: www.abbottmagic.com

Directions: South of State St. (M-86) on St. Joseph St., one block west of Blackstone Ave.

If you're interested in magic history, stop by the local museum for a modest display of material related to Blackstone, Abbott, and the black arts. Hours are limited, so plan your visit accordingly.

Colon Community Museum, 219 N. Blackstone Ave., Colon, MI 49040

Phone: (269) 432-2462

Hours: June–August, Tuesday, Thursday, and Sunday 2–4:30 PM, or by appointment

Cost: Free

Website: http://colonmi.com/magiccapital.html

Directions: One block north of State St. (M-86).

And before you leave town, stop by the Lakeside Cemetery, on the western shore of Sturgeon Lake, where 20-some famous magicians are buried. (There's no truth to the rumor that their assistants are also buried here in sawed-in-half coffins.) Both Harry Blackstones have plots, each under a pedestal with a granite flame. Other permanent residents include Bill "The Magnificent Fraud" Baird and Ricki "America's Greatest Pickpocket" Dunn, whose headstone proudly announces, "Ricki Dunn was a Thief." John "Little Johnny" Jones's marker nervously admits, "Now I Have to Go and Fool St. Peter." Good luck with that.

Lakeside Cemetery, Colon and N. Farrand Rds., Colon, MI 49040

No phone

Hours: Daylight hours

Cost: Free

Directions: At the intersection of M-124 (Colon Rd./State St.) and M-145 (N. Farrand Rd.).

Dundee
Predator Peak

The two enormous bears fighting over a moose carcass on a pedestal in front of Cabela's, the outdoorsman superstore off US Route 23, are hard to miss. The pair comprises what is reportedly the world's largest bronze wildlife sculpture. Impressive, to be sure, but wait until you get inside Cabela's itself.

From the store's entrance, you'll spot an enormous indoor mountain covered in stuffed wildlife, and as you draw closer you'll notice that about half of the critters are just moments from being maimed and devoured by the other animals. Don't cry, kids—it's just survival of the fittest! A grey fox stalks a pair of prairie chickens. A badger and coyote fight over a dead pheasant. A bobcat chases a snowshoe hare. A diamondback rattlesnake confronts a herd of antelope. A cougar pounces from a rock ledge onto a buffalo, and another jumps a whitetail deer. A pack of white wolves battle a polar bear for a dead muskox, while two other wolves circle a still-living (but-not-for-long) calf. High above, a mountain goat appears primed to jump to its death. Even the herbivores battle it out: two bull moose lock horns for dominance over the herd.

And what about man—nature's most dangerous predator? Step over to the south wall and find a display of adorable and mostly tiny deer from around the world, all gunned down by the store's owners, Mary and Dick Cabela. The details of when they were "taken" are clearly spelled out on adjacent signage. The store also has an enormous freshwater aquarium stocked with local species, but sadly, no piranhas.

Cabela's, 110 Cabela Blvd. East, Dundee, MI 48131
Phone: (734) 529-4700
Hours: Bear sculpture, always visible; Store, Monday–Saturday 8 AM–9 PM, Sunday 10 AM–6 PM
Cost: Free
Website: www.cabelas.com
Directions: West of US Rte. 23, north of Tecumseh Rd. (M-50).

East Lansing
Magic Johnson in Bronze

Earvin "Magic" Johnson Jr. was the greatest basketball star to come out of Michigan State University, and nobody will ever forget that, certainly not as long as there's a 12-foot bronze of him shooting out of a volcano in front of the school's basketball arena. Titled *Always a Champion*, the sculpture is mounted atop a black granite pyramid listing his eight lifetime championships, from high school to the pros to the Olympics.

Could it be Magic?

And though he left MSU for the NBA after his sophomore year, the face on the statue makes him look decades older than he looks today.

The fact that Johnson was raised just miles away from campus certainly endeared him with State fans. Born in Lansing on August 14, 1959, he grew up at **814 Middle Street**. His father worked at General Motors and his mother was a school custodian; they had seven children. Johnson attended **Dwight Rich Junior High** (2600 S. Hampden Dr.) and **Everett High School** (3900 Stabler St.), where he earned the nickname "Magic" after a 36-point, 18-rebound, 16-assist game. At MSU, he led his team to the 1978–79 NCAA championship, defeating Larry Bird and the Indiana State squad in the tournament's final game.

Breslin Student Events Center, 534 Birch Rd., East Lansing, MI 48824

Phone: (517) 432-1989

Hours: Always visible

Cost: Free

Website: www.breslincenter.com

Directions: North on Birch Rd. from Shaw Ln., on the south side of the building.

Sparty, the World's Largest Terra Cotta Statue

When it was first sculpted by professor Leonard D. Jungwirth in 1945, *The Spartan* was made from terra cotta. Jungwirth had no choice—all the nation's bronze was being used for the war effort. But far from being a lesser monument, people soon realized that the 10½-foot hunky Greek warrior broke the record for tallest terra cotta statue in the world. It was installed along the Red Cedar River for State fans to venerate on their way to games. And venerate they did.

Unfortunately, terra cotta doesn't hold up well to Michigan winters and rival Big Ten vandals. Sparty, as he became known, was restored in 2005 and moved indoors to the Spartan Stadium annex. A sturdy bronze replica has been placed at the original statue site.

Terra Cotta Sparty, 1 Spartan Way., East Lansing, MI 48824

Bronze Sparty, E. Kalamazoo St. & Red Cedar Rd., East Lansing, MI 48824

Phone: (800) GO-STATE

Hours: Terra cotta, game days; Bronze, always visible

Cost: Free

Website: www.msuspartans.com/trads/msu-trads-sparty.html

Directions: Terra cotta, inside the stadium annex; Bronze, northwest of Spartan Stadium.

MSU Creepy Crawlies

Calling all insect lovers—crawl on over to Michigan State for two bug-themed attractions. First and foremost is Bug House, run by the university's Department of Entomology. Though open primarily for elementary school groups by appointment, the Bug House does have several open houses each year, so check the website.

And what will you see? Thousands of dead creatures pinned to corkboard and scientifically labeled, a live butterfly room, and terrariums filled with walking sticks, hissing cockroaches from Madagascar, and—ohmigod—whatever that thing is that looks like a giant leaf. The exhibit is maintained and hosted by student volunteers who will enthusiastically fish out the grossest squirming specimens for you to hold. Yikes!

Bug House, 146–147 Natural Science Building, 288 Farm Ln., East Lansing, MI 48824

Phone: (517) 355-4662

Hours: Check website for open house dates

Cost: Free, but donations encouraged

Website: www.ent.msu.edu/bughouse

Directions: South of E. Circle Dr. on Farm Ln.

If your love of insects only extends to the colorful, nonthreatening, nonbiting kind, come to Butterflies in the Garden. Open seasonally, visitors walk through a room filled with caterpillars, cocoons, and butterflies sucking nectar, munching on host plants, and flitting around in the warm greenhouse. The indoor exhibit is just one of the 25 themed gardens that are part of the school's 4H Children's Gardens, so even if you find butterflies icky, let the kids have fun while you visit the cactus exhibit. Wimp.

Butterflies in the Garden, 4H Children's Gardens, A240-B Plant & Soil Science Building, 1066
 Bogue St., East Lansing, MI 48824

Phone: (517) 355-0348

Hours: Summers, Monday–Friday 2–4 PM, Saturday–Sunday 10 AM–4 PM

Cost: Free

Website: http://4hgarden.cowplex.com/Butterflies/

Directions: Southwest of the intersection of Wilson Rd. and Bogue St.

Elsie

Elsie the Bull

Elsie might be a milk cow in other parts of the country, but in Elsie, Michigan—originally named after Elsie Amelia Tillotson, the first child born to settlers in the area—Elsie is a bull. When boosters bought a big boy bovine and named it Elsie, the gender question was settled for good. The creature's breed, however, was not. The 10-foot-tall fiberglass animal is clearly a Black Angus, yet it's been painted to look like a Holstein, the cow-of-choice at the nearby Green Meadows Farm dairy. Confused? Perhaps you have mad cow disease.

A lotta bull.

Village Hall, 125 W. Main St., Elsie, MI 48831

Phone: (989) 862-4273

Hours: Always visible

Cost: Free

Website: www.elsie.org

Directions: On Main St. just west of County Rd. 505.

COW-A-BUNGA!

Elsie isn't the only colossal cow in these parts. In fact, they come in all breeds, sizes, colors, and states of dismemberment.

Scared Steer

Country Smoke House, 3294 Van Dyke Rd., Almont, (810) 798-3064, www.countrysmokehouseinc.com

It's kinda disturbing that a giant Hereford steer would lure visitors to this butcher shop, given the cutting and gutting and grinding and sausage stuffing going on inside. Yes, most of what is processed at the Country Smoke House is wild game, but there's plenty of beef in the coolers. Is this steer worried he might be next?

Cheesy Cow

Williams Cheese Co., 998 N. Huron Rd., Linwood, (800) 968-4492,
www.williamscheese.com

Unlike the steer in Almont, this huge Holstein in Linwood draws shoppers to a nonlethal dairy emporium. In fact, she stands beside a large, three-legged stool and invites you and anyone else to pull on her teats. Talk about friendly!

Cows High and Low

Jilbert Dairy, 200 Meeske Ave., Marquette, (906) 225-1363,
www.jilbertdairy.com

Another friendly cow standing beside a milk stool can be found at the ice cream picnic area at Jilbert Dairy in Marquette. A second fiberglass mooer balances atop a narrow scaffold above the milk-holding tank adjacent to the barn, which would probably be both a health and a safety code violation if it were real.

Rolling Cow

Carney Roundup Rodeo, US Route 41, Carney, (906) 639-2618,
www.carneyrounduprodeo.com

Because it's mounted on a flatbed trailer, the black-and-white Holstein spotted outside the Carney Roundup Rodeo could be anywhere in the western UP, so don't be surprised if you pass it on the highway going 60 MPH.

Texas Longhorn

Tom's Western Store, 8982 W. M-21, Ovid, (989) 834-5446,
www.tomswesternstore.com

An out-of-state Texas longhorn balances atop a sign outside this saddle, boot, hat, and tack shop. A tan quarter horse stands in front of the sign, at ground level. How it chased the bull up that pole is anyone's guess.

Carry Dairy Cow

Carry Dairy, 979 Ecorse Rd., Ypsilanti, (734) 483-5648

Another mega-mooer, this one a brown-and-white Guernsey, has been standing on the roof of this Ypsilanti convenience store since 1962.

Blue Moo

Sherman Dairy Bar, 1601 Phoenix Rd., South Haven, (269) 637-8251, www.shermanicecream.com

Here in South Haven, the Blueberry Capital of the World, much of what you see is blue ... but the *cows*? Actually, just one cow is blue, and she stands on the roof of an ice cream outlet a few blocks east of the main highway.

Kow Kong

13099 Mack Ave., Detroit, No phone

It's just a head, but it's an *enormous* head that protrudes from an abandoned ice cream stand once run by Wilson & Sons Dairy. It looks like a Guernsey, tan and white, but it was once covered in spots—Eminem shot it with a paintball gun in *8 Mile*. (Don't get angry; the movie crew restored the cow before they shot it, so the cow came out ahead.)

Steer Face

Bonser's of Custer, 2391 E. State St., Custer, (231) 757-2264

The steer head poking through the wall of this small-town supermarket is more of a face than a head: the big scary face of a long-ago butchered fiberglass Hereford.

Concrete Steer

Freel's Market, 1139 W. Lake St., Tawas City, (989) 362-6900

The Hereford steer on a cinder block pedestal outside Freel's Market in Tawas City is much smaller than a real Hereford steer. It is interesting, however, because it was not pulled from a fiberglass mold, but crafted out of concrete by local sculptor Gordon Clute (see page 92).

Coney Island Steer

Tom Z Flint Original Coney Island, 401 W. Court St., Flint, (810) 768-0000

Another concrete steer, also smaller than the real thing, stakes out the corner of a Coney Island's parking lot in Flint.

Hastings
Crash at Airport Sand & Gravel

Seeing an airplane crashed nose-down into a hill near an airport can be rather unnerving, but don't worry if you're in Hastings—it's just a sign! Bruce Firlik, owner of Airport Sand & Gravel, purchased a Luskin Taildragger that was damaged in an East Coast hurricane, patched it up, and used it to mark the entrance to his quarry. Contrary to the 1940s plane's name, Firlik pointed its tail high into the air, allowing him to write AIRPORT SAND & GRAVEL across the wide, red wings.

1950 W. State Rd., Hastings, MI 49058

Phone: (269) 945-5767

Hours: Always visible

Cost: Free

Directions: Northwest of town on M-37 (W. State Rd.), on the road to the airport.

Hell
Come to Hell

You know what? You can go to hell. Or, more correctly, Hell . . . Michigan! Founded in 1841, nobody's quite sure how it got its name, though two stories persist. In the first, German stagecoach travelers passing through would get out to stretch their legs and proclaim, "*So schön hell!*"—"So bright and beautiful!" But in the other, founder George Reeves was asked what they should call it when it was incorporated. "Name it Hell for all I care!" he bellowed, and they did.

This dinky burg has seized on the latter story. Stop on by the Halloween-themed Hell Country Store, where you'll find the community's post office. Bring your letters and bills to get the "I've Been to Hell" postmark, or come in April and they'll cancel your IRS filing with "Taxes from Hell." Next door, Screams Ice Creamatory sells sundaes served in coffin-shaped dishes. Toppings—buttersnot, bat droppings, ghost poop, and more—can be found in a genuine wooden casket from Transylvania. Step out back and snap a gag photo of your face poking through a Devil, Bigfoot, or three-headed Hydra painted cutout. And for the over-21 crowd, mosey over to the flame-façade Dam Site Inn, a restaurant and honky-tonk (heavy on the honkies) where you can buy a degree or T-shirt from Dam U.

All they need is your evil face.

This is the only Hell on earth (if you don't count Scranton, Pennsylvania). To get to Hell, follow the main road southwest out of Pickney. It's paved. With *asphalt*.

Hell Country Store & Spirits, 4025 Patterson Lake Rd., Hell, MI 48169

Phone: (734) 878-3129

Screams Ice Creamatory, 4045 Patterson Lake Rd., Hell, MI 48169

Phone: (734) 878-2233

Dam Site Inn, 4095 Patterson Lake Rd., Hell, MI 48169

Phone: (734) 878-9300

Hours: Call ahead

Cost: Free

Website: www.gotohellmi.com

Directions: Just west of the intersection of Patterson Lake Rd. and Silver Hill Rd.

HELL BY ANOTHER NAME

There are many other Michigan communities with equally hellish names. Have you ever been to Agnew, Bumbletown, Cement City, Colon, Crapo, Crisp, Devils Corner, Devils Elbow, or Devils Lake? How about Dick, Disco, Germfask, Hard Luck, Hemlock, Killmaster, Locust Corners, Pigeon, Pompeii, Rainy Beach, or Ransom? Or perhaps Rock, Slapneck, Sleepy Hollow, Teapot Dome, Temperance, or Willard?

Hickory Corners
Gilmore Car Museum

Michigan is filled with auto museums, but none is more impressive than the far-from-Detroit Gilmore Car Museum. Why? Because it's not really *a* car museum, it's *five* unique museums: the Model-A Ford Museum, the Pierce-Arrow Museum, the Lincoln Motorcar Museum, the Classic Car Club of America Museum, and the Cadillac-LaSalle Club Museum. It is also home to the Tucker Historical Collection, the Franklin Collection, and the Checker Motors Archive. In all, there are more than 400 mint condition vehicles displayed in 24 buildings and barns located on the 90-acre campus.

Want more? The Gilmore has the "Gnome-Mobile" from the Disney movie of the same name, a children's antique pedal car exhibit, and more than 1,500 hood ornaments. It also has a refurbished 1930s Shell Gas Station, a replica of the Wright brothers *Flyer*, and a 1941 Blue Moon Diner, where you can still order lunch and rest your feet. Because you'll need to.

Gilmore Car Museum, 6865 Hickory Rd., Hickory Corners, MI 49060

Phone: (269) 671-5089

Hours: Monday–Friday 9 AM–5 PM; Saturday–Sunday 9 AM–6 PM

Cost: Adults $12, Seniors (62+) $11, Kids (7–15) $9

Website: www.gilmorecarmuseum.org

Directions: Just east of M-43, north of Sheffield Rd.

Jackson

Birthplace of the Republican Party

On July 6, 1854, a group of Michigan abolitionists—Whigs and Free Soilers and disaffected Democrats—gathered in Jackson to form a new party. So many showed up (about 1,500) they decided to move the meeting to a grove on Morgan's Forty at the edge of town. There, under the oaks, the first "convention" chose a slate of candidates and produced a document stating, in part, "We will cooperate and be known as Republicans." It was the first time the new party's name was put to paper. The Republican Party was born.

The slate went on to sweep Michigan's 1854 election, and the Republicans would dominate state politics for years to come. In 1910, President Taft dedicated a historic marker and a boulder to mark the site, which today is a park the size of a house lot in a run-down neighborhood that many would just as soon forget.

Second & Franklin Sts., Jackson, MI 49201

No phone

Hours: Daily 7 AM–10 PM

Cost: Free

Website: www.jacksonrepublicans.com

Directions: Two blocks south of Rte. 127 on Second St.

Cascade Falls

Though the Grand River flows through the center of Jackson, it has nothing to do with the city's famous Cascade Falls, a man-made waterfall with a redundant name. Planning for the popular Jackson attraction started in 1929, led by "Captain" William Sparks, but construction wasn't completed until the spring of 1932. Sparks based the design on the cascades at Ciutadella Park in Barcelona, Spain. Each minute 2,000 gallons of water tumbles over 16 successive falls, past six enormous fountains and through three reflecting pools, most of it illuminated. The entire structure is 500 feet long, 60 feet wide, and drops 64 feet over its length.

Cascade Falls is only open at night during the summer, all the better to appreciate the 1,350-bulb, ever-changing colored light show and the music blasted over the new and improved speaker system. Watch it all from the adjoining amphitheater or hike the 126 steps on either side of the pools and be sprayed by the mist. Wednesday nights are Family Nights with live music, and several times a year you can enjoy fireworks; check the website for dates.

Sparks County Park, 1992 Warren Ave., Jackson, MI 49203

Phone: (517) 788-4320

Hours: June–August, Thursday–Tuesday 8–11 PM, Wednesday 7–11 PM; open 6 PM on fireworks nights

Cost: Adults $4 ($6 with fireworks), Kids (10 and under, with paid adult) free; Family Night (Wednesday), $7/family

Website: www.co.jackson.mi.us/departments/Parks/parks_description/cascade_falls_park.asp

Directions: At the west end of Denton Rd., south of Spring Arbor Rd.

Grave of Mr. Chicken

Had Mr. Chicken had his accident anywhere else but Jackson, Michigan, he might have ended up breaded, deep fried, and sold off by the bucket. But Jackson was the hometown of Dr. Timothy England, veterinarian extraordinaire, who would do anything to save a poor critter.

In December 1996, back when Mr. Chicken was named Colonel Sanders, the bird was trapped outside in a blizzard. His feet were frozen solid, and England had to amputate; he even used a transfusion of parrot blood to help the plucky clucker pull through. England then outfitted the rooster with two prosthetic feet made from green plastic. Before long, Mr. Chicken was back and strutting. England adopted the rooster and gave him a new, if not particularly original, name.

The story made it onto CNN, the pages of *Newsweek*, and newspapers across the world. Sadly, Mr. Chicken didn't have much time in the spotlight; he was mauled by a raccoon while defending his coop in June 1997. England buried him with his feet on, as he would have wanted.

Crossroads Animal Hospital, 3232 N. Dettman Rd., Jackson, MI 49201

Phone: (517) 784-1111

Hours: Always visible

Cost: Free

Website: www.mycrossroadsvet.com

Directions: Just northwest of the intersection of Rte. 127 and I-94.

BIG CLUCKERS

The grave of Mr. Chicken is nice enough, but it is a little difficult to find—just a small headstone at a remote animal hospital. Wouldn't it be nice if somebody donated a large statue to
honor this brave bird?

Luckily, there seem to be two shelf-ready fiberglass models
available. A short and stocky version can be found outside the
Original Tony's Restaurant (518 W. Washington Ave., (989) 681-
5621) in St. Louis, a place that brags it is the "Home of the Giant
Steak Sandwich." Really? *Steak*? The same white chicken stands
outside the **Davison Bacon & Sausage Works** (9090 Lapeer Rd.,
(810) 654-0920, www.baconandsausage.biz) in Davison and
the **Cherry Bowl Drive-In Theatre** (see page 71) in Honor.

The second chicken model stands much taller than its feath-
ered cousin, mostly because it struts proudly on two bright
yellow feet. This model can be found on the sidewalk outside
Bob's Lounge (114 W. Fourth St., (989) 386-7884) in Clare and
the **Borg Poultry Farm** (10600 S. Meridian Rd., (517) 448-2473)
in Hudson. Come to think of it, this clawed version might be
inappropriate given Mr. Chicken's drumstickless later life.

The only unique big chicken statue in Michigan happens to
share the same name as his Jackson cousin. Mr. Chicken wears
a black top hat and stands atop the sign of a restaurant that
bears his unoriginal name. **Mr. Chicken** (6000 N. Telegraph Rd.,
Dearborn Heights, (313) 277-0100, www.mrchicken.com) has
been serving up pressure-cooked chicken in suburban Detroit
since 1961.

Lansing
Climbing Giraffe

There was a time when some Meijer stores would use oversized fiberglass
animal statues in their parking lots to help customers find their cars. No,

the statues didn't roam the lots with a beacon, they just stood there, but they provided easy-to-remember visual clues when you returned from shopping, frazzled and confused.

As you can imagine, these animals were also targets for vandals, pranksters, and bad drivers. Meijer eventually phased them out, with the exception of one defiant giraffe that has climbed onto the portico roof of an adjoining gas station on the west side of Lansing and is refusing to come down.

Meijer Gas, 5125 W. Saginaw Hwy., Lansing, MI 48917

Phone: (517) 321-1302

Hours: Always visible

Cost: Free

Website: www.meijer.com

Directions: On M-43 (Saginaw Hwy.), one block west of Elmwood Rd.

This smokestack ain't goin' nowhere.

Large Lansing Lugnut

Professional baseball has been a part of the Lansing sports scene since 1889. Owing to its home base being in the state capital, the team was called the Senators until disbanding in 1941. By the time pro baseball returned to the city in 1996, politicians had fallen in the public eye, so the new team was called the Lansing Lugnuts.

Its fans obviously approved of the new name, setting minor league attendance records its first year. Big Lug, a purple dinosaur with lug nuts for nostrils, is the team's mascot. And adjoining the stadium, atop an old smokestack, the franchise has screwed on the world's largest lug nut. How they did it is unclear; the world's largest tire iron is nowhere to be found.

Larch St. & Michigan Ave., Lansing, MI 48912

Phone: (517) 485-4500

Hours: Always visible

Cost: Free

Website: www.lansinglugnuts.com

Directions: One block from Cooley Law School Stadium, just east of the river.

Malcolm X's Boyhood Homes

Though he was born in Omaha, Nebraska, in 1925, Malcolm X (Little) spent most of his childhood years in Lansing, and they weren't exactly happy. Earl and Louise Little moved their family to town in 1928, purchasing a home at Grand River Avenue and Waverly Road. Local developers later claimed this neighborhood, known as Westmont, was restricted to whites, and took the Littles to court. A judge ruled in 1929 that the Littles could legally *own* the land, just not *live* there, and ordered them to vacate. But before authorities could evict the family, the white supremacist Black Legion burned their home to the ground. To add insult to injury, police charged Earl Little with arson, a charge that was later dropped.

The Littles then rented a home at 401 Charles Street, near East Lansing, and lived there until late 1930, when they moved to a home Earl built at 4705 Logan Street. Here, Malcolm was enrolled at Pleasant Grove Elementary. Then on September 28, 1931, when Malcolm was six, his father was run over and killed by a Michigan Avenue trolley. The family believed the Black Legion responsible, but the coroner ruled it a suicide. As such,

---

LANSING

➡ Actor Steven Seagal was born in Lansing on April 10, 1952.

➡ An 18-inch crocodile was caught in the **Michigan State Capitol Building** in Lansing in June 1968.

➡ Three Lansing sisters were once arrested after running through the streets naked, smeared with mustard, after they "got filled with the Holy Spirit" while reading the Bible.

Louise Little was unable to collect Earl's life insurance money, and the family began a downward spiral into crushing poverty. Louise had a mental breakdown in 1939 and was committed to the Kalamazoo asylum. Malcolm lived for a time with a local family, but was eventually sent to a foster home in Mason; his seven siblings were scattered to other locations.

Today a marker stands at the former site of the Littles' home on Logan Street, today known as Martin Luther King Jr. Boulevard.

Historic Marker, 4705 S. Martin Luther King Jr. Blvd., Lansing, MI 48910

No phone

Hours: Always visible

Cost: Free

Website: www.malcolmx.com

Directions: Two blocks south of Cavanaugh Rd./Mary Ave. on M-99 (MLK Blvd.), at Vincent Ct.

Moon Tree

Anyone who has seen *Invasion of the Body Snatchers* knows that visiting the Moon Tree is probably a bad idea, but you should be OK if you keep a safe distance and express no emotions. Planted on the lawn of the Michigan State Capitol Building is a weeping beech grown from a seed that was carried to the moon aboard the *Apollo 14* module. The seed never made it down to the lunar surface, it just orbited, so in theory it couldn't have been impregnated with some alien DNA looking for a ride back to Earth . . . but you never know. In 1976 a sapling grown from the seed was planted on the statehouse lawn by Governor George Romney for the nation's bicentennial.

But that's not all. The park surrounding the capitol building is a forest of historic horticulture. You can find a Mothers Against Drunk Driving silver maple, a Martin Luther King Jr. sugar maple, an Earth Day white pine, and a Pioneers for Women's Suffrage ginkgo planted by Eleanor Roosevelt in 1934.

115 W. Allegan St., Lansing, MI 48933

Phone: (517) 373-0170

Hours: Always visible

Cost: Free

Directions: On the southeast lawn of the Capitol Building along the diagonal sidewalk; look for the plaque.

Stevie Wonder's Piano and Harmonica

For once in my life, I can say there's an exhibit at the Michigan Historical Museum that'll make everyone shout, *Shoo-be-doo-be-doo-da-day!*— a Chickering baby grand piano from the Michigan School for the Blind, upon which Stevie Wonder's fingertips learned to play classical music. Isn't it lovely? Its ebonies and ivories are probably responsible for bringing a little sunshine to your life, so if you really love him, won't you stop by? And heaven help us all, there's also a Hohner Chromatic Harmonica sitting on the piano bench! Wonder signed, sealed, and delivered it to the museum in 1988, the year before he was inducted into the Rock and Roll Hall of Fame.

Of course, the piano is just part of what you'll find at the Michigan Historical Museum. As the state's repository of all the good, old stuff, you can also see relics from oddball entries throughout this book, including a length of wire from the Mackinac Bridge main cable (see page 78); a gas mask from the Flint Sit-Down Strike; a club used to beat labor leaders at the Battle of the Overpass, as well as Richard Frankensteen's bloody shirt from the battle; a slave's "knee stiffener" used by Laura Smith Haviland to shock audiences during her antislavery crusades (page 143); and the 1957 Corvette showcase from the Detroit Auto Show (page 253).

Isn't it lovely? Photo by author, courtesy the Michigan Historical Museum

Michigan Historical Museum, 702 W. Kalamazoo St., Lansing, MI 48915

Phone: (517) 373-3559

Hours: Monday–Friday 9 AM–4:30 PM, Saturday 10 AM–4 PM, Sunday 1–5 PM

Cost: Adults $6, Seniors (65+) $4, Kids (6–17) $2

Website: www.michigan.gov/museum

Directions: One block west of Pine St., three blocks north of I-496.

Marshall
American Museum of Magic

It's no surprise that the American Museum of Magic is located less than 40 miles from Michigan's magic vortex, Colon (see page 157). After all, it was Harry Blackstone who got journalist and Marshall native Robert Lund interested in the entertainment form. Lund and his wife went on to collect more than 250,000 pieces of paranormal paraphernalia covering 400 years of magic history, including milk cans from which Houdini escaped, Harry Blackstone's "Levitating Skull," 350 different magicians' kits, and 3,000 vintage posters from magic shows. Every square inch of the walls in this former three-story storefront is papered with colorful playbills for performers who took their last bows years ago.

While here, you'll learn about the great conjurers, as well as some not-so-great, at least at the moment when it mattered. Take, for example, the story of Chung Ling Soo, a turn-of-the-century magician who introduced the bullet-catching trick to European audiences. At a London show in 1918, he caught a bullet in his chest instead of his hands when the prop malfunctioned. During the coroner's inquest it was discovered that Soo wasn't Chinese after all, but a white guy from the States named William Robinson. That explained why his last words weren't in Mandarin, but English: "Oh my God. Something's happened. Lower the curtain."

If you're a serious magician or researcher, the museum also owns the **Lund Memorial Library**, which contains thousands of books on the history of magic. It is housed offsite, but is available to serious visitors with an appointment.

107 E. Michigan Ave., PO Box 5, Marshall, MI 49068

Phone: (269) 781-7570

Hours: Museum, April–May, Thursday–Saturday 10 AM–4 PM; June–August, Tuesday–Saturday 10 AM–4 PM; September–October, Thursday–Saturday 10 AM–4 PM; Library, by appointment

Cost: Adults $5, Kids (5–12) $3.50

Website: www.americanmuseumofmagic.org

Directions: Downtown on Business I-94 (Michigan Ave.) at Jefferson St.

Crosswhite Boulder

On January 26, 1847, four slave catchers showed up in Michigan at the door of fugitive slaves Adam and Sarah Crosswhite. Four years earlier, the couple had escaped the Kentucky plantation of Francis Giltner when they learned he planned to sell off their four children, and Giltner wanted them back. Word quickly spread among Marshall's abolitionist community, and soon the Crosswhites' home was surrounded by 200 citizens.

Outnumbered, the leader of the slave-catching posse demanded to know who each of the troublemakers were, so the townsfolk lined up and told him, even providing correct spellings as he recorded each name in a book. During this brave, boring, and time-consuming distraction, the Crosswhites slipped out of town and on to Canada.

The affair, however, was far from over. Giltner sued everyone written in the book at a federal court in Detroit, though each case was ultimately dismissed, except against Charles T. Gorham, a Marshall banker. He was found guilty of stealing the slaves and ordered to pay $1,926—about $45,000 today. The fine was paid by Zachariah Chandler, a Detroit businessman who later represented Michigan in the US Senate.

As a direct result of the Crosswhite incident, the Fugitive Slave Act was passed in 1850, making it a federal crime to assist runaways. The spot where the Crosswhites were freed is now marked by a boulder just east of downtown Marshall. It stands about 900 feet south of where their cabin stood.

Triangle Park, 801 E. Michigan Ave., Marshall, MI 49068

No phone

Hours: Always visible

Cost: Free

Website: www.marshallmi.org/attractions/17

Directions: On I-94 Bus. (Michigan Ave.) at Lincoln St.

Honolulu House Museum

It didn't take long for Judge Abner Pratt, the first US Consul to the Sandwich Islands (today known as Hawaii), to go native. He was only on post for two years, from 1857 to 1859, but by the time Pratt returned to his

Aloha!

Michigan hometown, he had resolved to makes some changes. First, he insisted on wearing Polynesian clothing wherever he went, no matter the weather. And second, in 1860 he had a Hawaiian home built just west of downtown Marshall.

As you might expect, the floor-to-ceiling windows on the Honolulu House turned out to be better looking than they were practical; it's one thing to let cool breezes blow through on Oahu, but quite another in Michigan. The same held true for his attire. Three years after his dream home was finished, Pratt was caught in a snowstorm on the way back from Lansing. Wearing little more than a white linen suit, he contracted pneumonia and perished soon after. The Honolulu House was eventually sold off, and some idiot with no taste painted over all its interior tropical murals.

Today, the exterior of Honolulu House has been returned to the same color palette as Pratt originally intended. The Marshall Historical Society, which is headquartered here, is slowly restoring the interior too, which you can see during a tour of the building.

107 N. Kalamazoo Ave., Marshall, MI 49068
Phone: (269) 781-8544

Hours: May–October, daily 11 AM–4:30 PM; April, November–December, Saturday–Sunday
  11 AM–4:30 PM
Cost: Adults $5, Kids $5
Website: www.marshallhistoricalsociety.org
Directions: On the northwest corner of the intersection of Michigan and Kalamazoo Aves.

US Postal Service Museum

The US Postal Service has been the butt of jokes for years, though it's never clear why. Why don't *you* try to get a letter from a metal box in some small town to the front door of any home or business in the United States . . . in two or three days . . . for just 49¢ . . . hmmm?

As you will learn if you come to Marshall, the post office has a long and mostly distinguished history, starting with its founder, Benjamin Franklin. Mike Schragg, the town's former postmaster who retired in 2002, details it all in seven basement rooms of the town's old (but still working) office. The museum opened in 1987 and contains canceling machines, mail-sorting cubbies, uniforms, mail sacks, antique PO boxes, three-wheeled "Mailster" carts, and old postcards and letters. Out back, in a nearby garage, he also has a 1931 Model A postal delivery truck and a horse-drawn mail buggy.

The museum is only open by appointment, but give Schragg a call and he or one of his volunteer docents will meet you, through snow or rain or heat, but *not* gloom of night.

202 E. Michigan Ave., Marshall, MI 49068
Phone: (269) 979-2719
Hours: By appointment
Cost: Free
Website: www.marshallmi.org/attractions/8
Directions: Downtown on I-94 Bus. (Michigan Ave.) at Madison St.

Monroe
Custer Town

George Armstrong "Autie" Custer was born in New Rumley, Ohio, on December 5, 1839, though he would spend many years in Monroe, the hometown of his wife-to-be. Custer first came to Michigan at the age of seven and was raised by his half sister, Ann Reed, and her husband, David, who lived at Monroe and Fifth Street. Young "Autie" attended the New Dublin School and the Stebbins Academy for Boys, and excelled at neither. After going back to Ohio for a few years, he returned with his family in 1852 and lived in Monroe for the rest of his life—when he wasn't off fighting, of course. Custer married Elizabeth "Libby" Bacon at the **First Presbyterian Church** (108 Washington St., (734) 242-1545, www.monroefirst .org), on February 9, 1864. The Custers lived in a home at Monroe and Second Streets, which was later moved to 703 Cass Street.

The original home site is now home to the town's historical museum, which today has the world's largest collection of Custer family artifacts. You'll see the Custer family Bible and George's baby dress, a lock of his golden hair, and specimens from George's amateur taxidermy collection. From his military career, the museum has his West Point uniform (where he ranked last in a class of 34), binoculars, bowie knife, Remington rifle, and buffalo hide coat from an 1868 winter campaign out west. Civil War buffs will enjoy the faithful reproduction of the "surrender table" upon which Lee and Grant scribbled out terms for the end of the conflict; the actual table was purchased for $20 from Wilmer McLean by Thomas Custer, George's brother, who was present at the negotiations in Appomattox Court House, Virginia. (The original table is now in the Smithsonian.) And finally, from Little Big Horn, you'll see bullets from Water Carriers' Ravine marble marker stones that were once placed where George and his siblings Thomas and Boston fell, riddled with arrows and bullets, as well as Libby's black mourning dress. She got a lot of mileage out of that one.

Monroe County Historical Museum, 126 S. Monroe St., Monroe, MI 48161

Phone: (734) 240-7780

Hours: June–September, daily 11 AM–5 PM; October–May, Tuesday–Sunday noon–5 PM

Cost: Adults $4, Kids (5–17) $2

Website: http://historicmonroe.org/museum/index.htm

Directions: One block south of Front St. (along the river) on M-125 (Monroe St.).

Custer's, shall we say, *uneven* military carrier is memorialized in Monroe by a bronze statue of the general, astride a horse, along the north bank of the river. It is titled *Sighting the Enemy*, and it was created by sculptor Edward C. Potter. Custer looks resolute, not terrified, so one can assume this depicts him at Gettysburg rather than Little Big Horn. President Taft, Governor Warner, and Custer's widow were all on hand for its 1910 unveiling.

The statue has been the victim of single-minded vandals over the years. Every so often city officials discover that the horse's prominent testicles have been painted bright orange. Nobody knows why.

Elm Ave. & Monroe St., Monroe, MI 48161

No phone

Hours: Always visible

Cost: Free

Directions: Just north of the river on M-125 (Monroe St.), at Elm St.

Onsted

Mystery Hill

For decades, Michigan's Irish Hills was the state's big tourist getaway, close to Detroit and chock-full of tacky attractions—dinosaur parks and miniature golf courses and hokey Wild West towns—fun for the whole family. But most of those businesses have long since closed, with the exception of one of the biggies: Mystery Hill.

It was discovered in 1953, and by "discovered," the owners really mean "built." Small groups are led around and through a cattywampus shack where nothing meets at right angles. The forced perspective created by its windows, doors, walls, and floors make you think some things are level when they're really not. Your tour guide pours water into a trough and it runs uphill; walks up a ladder that's flush against the wall, but doesn't need to grab the rails; swings a one-way pendulum; and balances a broom at an angle in the middle of the room. It's disorienting, but ultimately explainable.

OWOSSO

➡ Republican presidential loser Thomas Dewey was born in an apartment over his grandfather's grocery at 323 W. Main Street in Owosso on March 24, 1902. He grew up at 421 W. Oliver Street.

Mystery Hill also has a funky gift shop, a miniature golf course, a remote control car racing track, and a hunk of stone from Castle Blarney, which you can kiss for good luck before you enter.

7611 US Hwy. 12, Onsted, MI 49265

Phone: (517) 467-2517

Hours: June–August, Tuesday–Sunday 11 AM–7 PM

Cost: Adults $8, Kids $7

Website: www.mysteryhillirishhills.com

Directions: At the intersection of Michigan Ave. (Rte. 12) and Wamplers Lake Rd. (M-124).

I Want *YOU* . . . to stock up on flaming explosives.

Ottawa Lake
Big Uncle Sam

What could be more American than a fireworks store just across the border from a state where fireworks are illegal? How about a four-story Uncle Sam statue with an observation platform? Well, in Ottawa Lake, you can have *both*.

The 42-foot-tall (if you count the hat) fiberglass Sam started his life in California—details are sketchy—then moved to a Toledo restaurant where he held a hamburger in his outstretched hand. Years later, when he was sold to a septic tank company, the sandwich was removed and his suit painted black. The business thought Abraham Lincoln would be a better spokes-statue.

Finally, Uncle Sam's red, white, and blue outfit was restored in 2001 when the big guy was purchased by this fireworks emporium. They also added a viewing platform where you can either watch cars on the Route 23/223 on-ramp or stare at Sam's enormous striped crotch.

All American Novelties, 6263 Sterns Rd., Ottawa Lake, MI 49267

Phone: (734) 854-3752

Hours: Always visible

Cost: Free

Directions: Exit 1 off Rte. 23/223 at Sterns Rd.

Potterville
Joe's Gizzard City

Anyone who has eaten a chicken gizzard knows they can be tough, *really* tough. This muscle is actually the "second stomach" of the chicken—the ventriculus—which grinds the bird's food using small pebbles (gizzard stones) it has already swallowed. You'd be tough, too, if you did this all day.

But the gizzards on the menu at Joe's Gizzard City are anything but hard to chew. The trick is to pressure cook the gizzards, and they come out as fluffy and tender as baby chicks, without the bones and beak, of course—served Traditional, Cajun, Garlic & Herb, Naked Fried, or Naked Nuked. For anyone who likes Joe's special batter, but not gizzards, the restaurant also offers deep-fried battered burgers. Oh, yeah . . .

Every year on the third weekend in June the entire town of Potterville joins together for a **Gizzard Fest** (www.gizzardfest.com). Events include a parade, the crowning of a Gizzard Princess, and a gizzard-eating competition where participants try to see who can eat two pounds of gizzards the fastest. Burp!

120 W. Main St., Potterville, MI 48876

Phone: (517) 645-2120

Hours: Café, Monday–Friday 6:30 AM–2 PM, Saturday 7 AM–noon, Sunday 8 AM–noon; Restaurant, Monday–Thursday 10:30 AM–11 PM, Friday–Saturday 10:30 AM–1 AM, Sunday noon–10 PM

Cost: Meals, $8–12

Website: www.gizzardcity.com

Directions: Three blocks west of Hartel Rd. (M-100) at N. Dunbar St.

Toll-free fun.

St. Louis
Little Mac

If the thought of driving over the Mackinac Bridge (see page 78) makes you a bit nauseous—and you're not alone in this—you might want to do a practice run on the Little Mac. You can't drive your car over it since it's just a footbridge, but that'll save you the $4 toll. The bridge spans two connected ponds on the east side of a self-storage facility on the west side of St. Louis, which is also smaller than its namesake. If you were to jump from the high point at the center of Little Mac's "roadbed," it's only about five feet down to the water, which is probably half as deep as the bridge is high.

Mini-Mac Storage, 8200 N. Begole Rd., St. Louis, MI 48880

Phone: (989) 681-4315

Hours: Always visible

Cost: Free

Website: http://minimacstoragecenter.com

Directions: North of Rte. 127/M-46 (Monroe Rd.) on Begole Rd.

Saranac
Birthplace of the Roadside Table

If you think about it, the concept of a road—a flat, cleared path to get from one point to another—seems fairly obvious. But a roadside *table*, a place to stop and enjoy a picnic or a little fresh air? That took some imagination. Back in 1929, Ionia County engineer Allan Williams took some leftover guardrail planks and hammered them together to make a small table for a pullout on a Route 16 right-of-way. And drivers loved it.

Before long, roadside tables were going up all over Michigan, and then across the United States. The modern interstate rest stop is its most visible incarnation. Ironically, there is no longer a roadside table where the first one was erected, just a historic marker to remind travelers how hospitable the open road once was.

Grand River Ave. & Morrison Lake Rd., Saranac, MI 48881

No phone

Hours: Daylight hours

Cost: Free

Directions: South of town, just east of Morrison Lake Rd., north of I-96.

Somerset Center
El Trabajo Rustico Bridges

Yes, it's concrete.

W. H. L. McCourtie loved concrete, and it was easy to see why: as founder of the Trinity Portland Cement Company in Cement City (of course), the building material made him a fortune. So when McCourtie decided to expand the grounds around his Aiden Lair estate in Somerset Center, what do you think he chose to create the rustic log bridges, benches, and trees? Not wood!

Instead, McCoutrie brought in two men from Texas who were skilled in the Mexican folk art known as *el trabajo rustico*, where cement is fashioned to look like logs, branches, rope, wooden planks, stone, or thatched grass—anything natural that doesn't look like cement. (More *trabajo rustico* work can be found at the nearby St. Joseph's of the Cross Shrine, page 155.) For three years, starting in 1930, George Cardoso and Ralph Corona built 17 bridges over a creek running through the estate, each one unique. They also constructed rustic benches, two large ponds (one for swimming, the other for trout), and two cement tree trunks that disguise the chimneys rising from an underground apartment, rathskeller, and five-car garage.

McCourtie would open up the grounds for the Somerset Homecoming each year, though he died soon after the project was completed. The estate fell into disrepair and the grounds filled with weeds. They were even used as a buffalo pen, yet the solid-as-a-rock bridges survived. Rescued in 1987, today they are the centerpiece of an underappreciated, underused, and beautiful park.

McCourtie Park, 12715 E. Chicago Rd., PO Box 69, Somerset Center, MI 49282

Phone: (517) 688-9223

Hours: Daylight

Cost: Free

Website: www.visitlenawee.com/page25.html

Directions: Off Rte. 12 (Chicago Rd.) at S. Jackson Rd.

Tecumseh
Rusty Dino Bones and Earthen Caterpillars

You can find dinosaur skeleton puzzles made from thin, die-cut plywood at most natural history museums. Artist Martin Kailimai used these toy models as inspiration for two much larger steel versions that now mark the entrance to the Tecumseh flea market. Here, a 10-foot-tall Apatosaurus battles with a much smaller, perhaps 5-foot-tall, Tyrannosaurus rex. You can look at them as either large versions of small models, or small models of large dinosaurs.

Less difficult to describe, in terms of relative size, are the two earthen caterpillars located just behind the dinos. The Tecumseh Trade Center has added eyes, noses, and smiles to two weed-covered berms, making them look like 40-foot-long insects. They're huge!

Tecumseh Trade Center, 9129 Tecumseh Clinton Hwy., Tecumseh, MI 49286

Phone: (734) 216-6010

Hours: Always visible; Flea market, Saturday–Sunday 9 AM–5 PM

Cost: Free

Website: www.thetecumsehtradecenter.com

Directions: North of town on Evans St. (Tecumseh Clinton Hwy.), on the southwest side of the airport.

Ypsilanti
Iggy Pop's Childhood Trailer Park

James Newell Osterberg Jr. had a fairly typical American childhood. Born in Muskegon on April 21, 1947, he grew up in a trailer park on the west side of Ypsilanti. Like many kids in the 1960s, he played in basement and garage bands starting in middle school—Megaton Two, the Prime Movers, and the Iguanas, from which he later derived the stage name you recognize today: Iggy Pop.

Osterberg attended Ann Arbor High School (renamed **Pioneer High School**, 601 W. Stadium Blvd.) where he was on the golf and debate teams, and worked afternoons as a stock boy at **Discount Records** (300 S. State St., closed). He attended the University of Michigan for a year, but dropped out and moved to Chicago to break into the blues scene. After attending a 1967 Doors concert in Ann Arbor, he decided to change the tone of his on-stage performance, adapting Morrison's surly demeanor to become a "street walking cheetah with a heart full of napalm," as he proclaimed in the classic song "Search and Destroy."

Pop and his bandmates came up with their name, the Psychedelic Stooges, while living in Ann Arbor at **1324 Forest Court** and watching a Three Stooges TV marathon; they shortened it to the Stooges when they signed on with Elektra Records in 1968. Iggy reportedly phoned Moe Howard to clear the name—the annoyed Howard said he didn't give a damn, but told Pop never to use "Three" with the name, then hung up on him. With a little more cash in hand, they moved into what they would call the **Fun House**, or Stooge Manor (2666 Packard Rd., torn down), which became the scene of much rock 'n' roll debauchery and an album of the same name.

Iggy Pop would go on to invent the stage dive, and less popular concert antics like smearing himself with peanut butter and rolling around in broken glass on stage. The Stooges broke up in 1974, but reformed in 2003.

Coachville Gardens Mobile Park, 3423 Carpenter Rd., Ypsilanti, MI 48197

Phone: (734) 971-1370

Hours: Always visible

Cost: Free

Website: www.iggypop.com

Directions: North of Ellsworth Rd., northeast of the I-94/Rte. 23 interchange.

St. Louis ●
Big Clucker
Little Mac

Saranac ●
Birthplace of the Roadside Table

Bath
The Bath
School Bombing

Lansing ●
Climbing Giraffe
Large Lansing Lugnut
Malcolm X's Boyhood Homes
Moon Tree
Stevie Wonder's Piano and Harmonica

Hastings ●
Crash at Airport Sand & Gravel

Maso
Big Vanilla Co
Santa's Giant Mail

Hickory Corners ●
Gilmore Car Museum

Potterville ●
Joe's Gizzard City
The Real Potterville

Battle Creek ●
Historic Bridge Park
Sojourner Truth's Grave
Wellville

Jacks
Birthplace of the Republican Pa
Cascade F
Grave of Mr. Chic

Marshall ●
American Museum of Magic
Crosswhite Boulder
Honolulu House Museum
Turkeyville U.S.A.
US Postal Service Museum

Somerset Center ●
El Trabajo Rustico Bridges

Colon
Abbott Magic Company
Colon Community Museum
Lakeside Cemetery

Jerome
Jerome County Market
Jumping Deer

Batavia ●
Grave of Lizzie Whitlock,
Circus Fat Lady

Coldwater
Capri Drive-In Theater
Wing House Museum

Camden ●
Tristate Corner

INDIANA

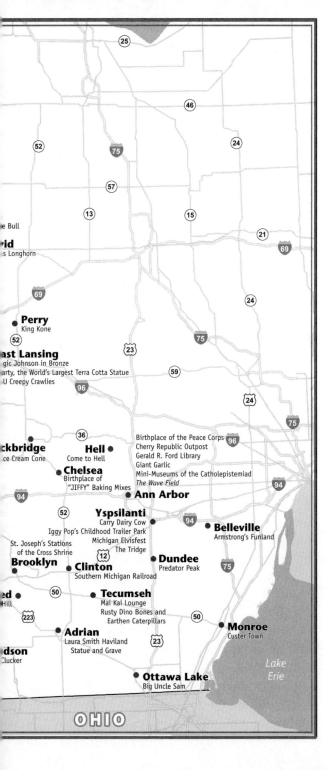

e Bull
id
s Longhorn

25

46

52

75

24

57

13

15

21

69

69

● **Perry**
King Kone

52

ast Lansing
gic Johnson in Bronze
arty, the World's Largest Terra Cotta Statue
U Creepy Crawlies

23

59

96

24

75

24

75

36

Birthplace of the Peace Corps
Cherry Republic Outpost
Gerald R. Ford Library
Giant Garlic
Mini-Museums of the Catholepistemiad
The Wave Field

96

ckbridge
ce Cream Cone

● **Hell** ●
Come to Hell

● **Chelsea**
Birthplace of
"JIFFY" Baking Mixes

● **Ann Arbor**

94

94

Yspsilanti
Carry Dairy Cow ●
Iggy Pop's Childhood Trailer Park
Michigan Elvisfest
The Tridge

52

94

● **Belleville**
Armstrong's Funland

St. Joseph's Stations
of the Cross Shrine
Brooklyn

12

● **Clinton**
Southern Michigan Railroad

● **Dundee**
Predator Peak

75

50

● **Tecumseh**
Mai Kai Lounge
Rusty Dino Bones and
Earthen Caterpillars

50

ed ●
Hill

223

● **Adrian**
Laura Smith Haviland
Statue and Grave

23

● **Monroe**
Custer Town

dson
lucker

● **Ottawa Lake**
Big Uncle Sam

*Lake
Erie*

OHIO

5

Eastern Michigan

$\mathcal{G}$eographically speaking, eastern Michigan is one of the most distinct regions of the state—it sticks out like a thumb . . . literally! Without it, the state would just be a bunch of differently sized fingers and an empty palm. What's special about that?

And, like the thumb, most of what you find in eastern Michigan is unlike anything you'll find anywhere else. It gave birth to one-of-a-kind entertainment icons like Stevie Wonder, Madonna, and Michael Moore. It's home to Michigan's only authentic Japanese Tea House, and a swinging bridge dedicated to mothers-in-law, and the world's largest figural neon sign, the massive Bean Bunny of Saginaw. And where can you find a gigantic can of Duff Beer, life-sized replicas of *Star Wars* characters, and the nude painting that sent Carry Nation into a hatchet-swinging rage? You got it: eastern Michigan!

Armada and Grand Rapids
Big Apples of Your Eye

Michigan is filled with u-pick-em orchards, so it can be hard to decide where to find the best apples. The *biggest* apples, however, can be found at two different establishments, one in the east and the other in the west. You certainly wouldn't want to eat them, though they do make for interesting photographs.

The eight-foot apple atop the roof of Blake Farms' main building looks a bit lumpy, as if it has a cellulite problem. You'd be a bit lumpy, too, if you'd been in business since 1946. Though its apples get all the attention, Blake's also offers strawberries, raspberries, peaches, cherries, pumpkins, and Christmas trees, in season.

Blake Farms Big Apple Orchard, 71485 North Ave., Armada, MI 48005

Phone: (586) 784-9710

Hours: Always visible

Cost: Free

Website: www.blakefarms.com

Directions: South of town, north of 33 Mile Rd.

The huge apple found at Robonette's Apple Haus & Winery north of Grand Rapids is much smoother than its eastern cousin, though this plump pomme has only been around since 1973. It stands nine feet tall and is made from urethane foam coated with fiberglass. And since it's at ground level in the picnic area, it's much more photo-friendly.

Even though its giant apple is new, Robinette's has been in business for more than a century. It does not have the fruit selection of Blake's, but they do have wine and hard cider. Lots of it. So let the kids get lost in the corn maze or wear themselves out on Robinette's big Jumping Pillow; mommy and daddy are getting likkered up in the barn.

Robinette's Apple Haus & Winery, 3142 4 Mile Rd. NE, Grand Rapids, MI 49525

Phone: (800) 400-8100 or (616) 361-5567

Hours: Always visible; Store, Monday–Friday 8 AM–6 PM, Saturday 8 AM–6:30 PM,
   Sunday noon–6:30 PM

Cost: Free

Website: www.robinettes.com

Directions: West of M-44 (Beltline Ave. NE) on 4 Mile Rd.

Bay City
A Star Was Born

And lo, in the City of Bay, there came a child, a material girl. Her father Silvio and mother Madonna had traversed afar, from Pontiac. And when the non-virgin mother went into labor, she was taken to Mercy Hospital where, on August 16, 1958, she gave birth to her third child, a girl, and they wrapped her in a swaddling bustier, calling her Madonna Louise Ciccone, or just Little Nonni. And later, just Madonna.

Though born in Bay City, Madonna's only childhood memories of the town came from visiting her grandparents, who lived at **1204 Smith Street**. Her parents had been married here in 1955, at **Visitation Church** (1106 State St.), and when her mother died of breast cancer in 1963, she was buried in the family plot at **Calvary Cemetery** (2977 Old Kawkawlin Rd.).

Then, when Madonna first became famous in 1985, city hall was prepared to give her the key to the city, but the mayor rescinded the offer after she posed nude for *Playboy*. He also nixed a plan to erect a 13-foot statue of the singer. She got back at them by telling *Today Show*'s Jane Pauley that she was born in "a little smelly town in northern Michigan. Like New Jersey. There's a lot of chemical dumps there or something."

Birthplace of the material girl.

And little has changed. There's nothing to mark Madonna's birth in Bay City today. Even Mercy Hospital has a new name, the Bradley House Retirement Center, though Mercy Hospital is still engraved on the outer wall.

Bradley House Retirement Center, 100 15th St., Bay City, MI 48708

Phone: (866) 379-8263

Hours: Always visible

Cost: Free

Directions: One block west of Washington Ave. (M-84), south of downtown, east of the river.

Bridgeport
Junction Valley Railroad

When it comes to little trains, somebody's gotta be the biggest, and in Michigan that's the Junction Valley Railroad. This ¼-scale miniature railroad attraction has almost four miles of track, crossing 16 bridges with 865 feet of trestles, past 30 downsized buildings, and through a 100-foot tunnel. They've got nine working engines that fit into a 10-stall roundhouse, as well as 75 cars in which you can ride, knees under your chin. It was all built by William "Pa" Stenger Jr. and his family, who also run the diesel truck repair shop next door. (Beware: you can almost miss the entrance to the JVR with so many semis parked around the entrance.)

Bring a lunch and make a day of it—the park has a large picnic area near the center of all the action. Come on weekends during October and they've got a Halloween Spook Train that passes 80 different eerie scenes over the course of two miles. And if you've caught the model railroading bug, they also have a large hobby shop for basement layout enthusiasts.

7065 Dixie Hwy., Bridgeport, MI 48722

Phone: (989) 777-3480

Hours: June–August, Monday–Friday 10 AM–4 PM, Saturday 10 AM–5 PM, Sunday 1–5 PM;
 September, Saturday–Sunday 1–5 PM; October, check website

Cost: Adults $6.50, Seniors $6.25, Kids $5.50

Website: www.jvrailroad.com

Directions: At the intersection of Junction Rd. and Dixie Hwy.

CHUGGING AROUND MICHIGAN

The Junction Valley Railroad isn't the only miniature or tourist train around. In addition to the ⅛-scale trains at Turkeyville U.S.A. (see page 279), here are a few more attractions to choo-choo-choose from:

Michigan AuSable Valley Railroad

230 S. Abbe Rd., Fairview, (989) 848-2225, www.michiganausablevalleyrailroad.com

Built in 1994–96 by the owners of a railroad hobby catalog, the ¼-scale Michigan AuSable Railroad travels over more than a mile's worth of track that includes a 115-foot tunnel and two wooden trestles, one 220 feet long. The attraction is best appreciated in fall, for the tracks wind through a jack pine forest overlooking the Comins Creek Valley.

Huckleberry Railroad

Crossroads Village, 6140 Bray Rd., Flint, (800) 648-PARK,
www.geneseecountyparks.org/pages/crossroads

Though it's a full-sized train, the Huckleberry Railroad has a miniaturized route, a 40-minute excursion from Crossroads Village, out around Mott Lake, and back. The 1857 train got its name because the old-timey steam locomotive moved so slowly that you could easily jump off, pick huckleberries, and hop back on. That activity is strongly discouraged today.

Toonerville Trolley

7195 County Rd. 381, Soo Junction, (888) 77-TRAIN,
www.trainandboattours.com

The Toonerville Trolley is a 24-inch narrow gauge train that runs 5½ miles through the forest from Soo Junction to the banks of the Tahquamenon River. From there, riders can board the *Hiawatha* riverboat for a 21-mile sightseeing cruise to Upper Tahquamenon Falls (see page 15), but that's not required. The train ride alone takes about two hours, but with the river cruise, almost seven.

Southern Michigan Railroad

320 S. Division St., PO Box K, Clinton, (517) 456-7677,
www.southernmichiganrailroad.com

Calling itself "The Little Railroad That Could," the Southern Michigan Railroad is a former branch line that runs between Clinton and Tecumseh, saved from destruction in 1985 by three high school students with big plans. Today it offers regular rides in summer as well as Fall Colors Tours, Ride and Dines, Crazy Hat Days, and a Santa Special.

Chesaning
Chesaning Showboat Star Walk

Hosting a Showboat Festival on the banks of the Shiawassee River must have sounded crazy in the midst of the Great Depression. The town didn't even have a boat! Still, the city ordered a $600 sternwheeler from the Swartzmiller Lumber Company, which had never before made a watercraft. Joe Swartzmiller delivered the boat, and the music festival raked in an $87.10 profit.

The annual Showboat Music Festival has expanded considerably since then, and today is held every July at a 6,000-seat outdoor amphitheater, with a snazzier *Shiawassee Queen* showboat and stars, stars, stars! More than 60 celebrities have left their handprints in the cement sidewalk surrounding the local Chamber of Commerce building, including Rich Little (twice), Lesley Gore, Bobby Vinton, Charlie Callas, Neil Sedaka, Debbie Reynolds, Wayne Newton, the Smothers Brothers, Weird Al Yankovic, and Willie Tyler & Lester. Sounds more like the Love Boat Festival.

Chesaning Chamber of Commerce, 218 N. Front St., PO Box 83, Chesaning, MI 48616

Phone: (989) 845-3055

Hours: Always visible

Cost: Free

Website: www.facebook.com/showboatmusicfest

Directions: One block north of Rte. 57 (Broad St.) just west of the river.

Croswell
Be Good to Your Mother-in-Law Bridge

If Croswell's swinging footbridge was accurately named, it would be called the Get to Work on Time Bridge. Built in 1905 by David Wise and the local Oddfellows lodge, the 139-foot structure connected local workers with the Michigan Sugar Company plant (which donated the cables) across the river. But then wise-guy Wise placed a sign over the eastern entrance admonishing all to be good to their mothers-in-law—nobody knows why—and the name stuck.

The bridge has been refurbished three times, most recently in 2006. The span bows considerably over the Black River, and sways with every

You should probably be good to *everyone* until you reach the other side.

step you take on its 455 slats. Warning signs on both ends limit pedestrians to 50, which seems about 45 people too many. Each year in June the town celebrates the longest suspension footbridge in the state with a Swinging Bridge Festival. Bring your mother-in-law!

River Bend Park, 45 N. Maple St., Croswell, MI 48422

Phone: (810) 679-2299

Hours: Always visible

Cost: Free

Website: www.cityofcroswell.com

Directions: One block south of Harrington Rd., one block west of Howard St., at Anderson Ave.

Emmett

Giant Duff Beer Can and South Paw Left-Handed Cigarettes

When you cruise through downtown Emmett, which is only about two or three blocks long, it's hard to miss the 10-foot-tall can of Duff Beer in

Can't get enough of that wonderful Duff.

a vacant lot, or the smaller (but still huge) pack of South Paw Left-Handed Cigarettes. The can is open, suds spilling out the top, and four cigarettes rise out of the pack, as if some giant is getting ready to enjoy a show with a smoke and a cool one.

And maybe one is! As it turns out, this isn't a vacant lot at all, but the once-a-month venue for outdoor music performances organized by Richard C. Hess, owner of the adjoining business, Waldenburg Heirloom Furniture. By day, Hess restores antiques and creates new furniture pieces. But he's also a big supporter of local artists, and this impromptu concert space is just a part. Stop by on the third Saturday of each month for a show, or any of the other 29 days to see the supersculptures.

Waldenburg Heirloom Furniture, 3137 Main St., PO Box 312, Emmett, MI 48022

Phone: (810) 384-1163

Hours: Always visible; Store, Friday–Saturday noon–5 PM, by chance, or appointment; Music, 3rd Saturday of each month (call ahead)

Cost: Free

Directions: North of the I-69 Exit on M-19 (Main St.).

Flint
The Big Girl

Businesses may come and go, especially in Flint, but the Big Girl is here to stay. She stands 15 feet tall, high atop a sign in a parking lot on Corunna Road, so high there's no good way to get a photo of her without getting a shot up her very short skirt.

Back when this was the Colonial Coney Island and Family Restaurant, it sort of made sense that she was carrying a tray with a milk shake. Later it became Ali Baba Mediterranean Cuisine, though she was not retrofitted with a hijab. On a recent visit, there was a sign saying the building would soon house a "Health Food Store," so one assumes she'll no longer be shaving her legs.

2913 Corunna Rd., Flint, MI 48503
No phone
Hours: Always visible
Cost: Free
Directions: On M-21 (Corunna Rd.) at Knight Ave.

Citizens Bank Weather Ball

Like the city of Grand Rapids (see page 115), Flint also has a weather ball to let its population know how to prepare for the day ahead. It sits on the roof of Citizens Bank, a glass orb atop triangular neon signs with the letters C and B, right in the center of downtown. To make sense of its prognostications, Flint's forecaster also has a rhyme that people must memorize:

> When the Weather Ball is red, higher temperatures ahead.
> When the Weather Ball is blue, lower temperature is due.
> Yellow light in Weather Ball means there'll be no change at all.
> When colors blink in agitation, there's going to be precipitation.
> (*Or alternately*: When colors come and go, it's going to rain or snow.)

Ouch—that's pretty awful, even by weather ball standards. This is what happens when poetry is turned over to a bank.

328 S. Saginaw St., Flint, MI 48502
Phone: (810) 766-7795
Hours: Best after dark
Cost: Free
Website: www.citizensbanking.com
Directions: Two blocks south of the river, at Kearsley St.

Happy Halfwit at the Dort Mall

From the outside, the Dort Mall doesn't look like much, just a half dozen vintage "satellite" neon signs in an empty parking lot and a tired 1970s

Dort Mall or *Dork* Mall?

façade guarded by a Muffler Man statue in a Hawaiian shirt and a straw hat, with a face like Alfred E. Newman. People call him the Happy Halfwit. But wait until you step inside.

The owners of this mall have covered the walls and ceilings of the main corridors in classic auto and oil company signage, commercial advertisements, nautical antiques, old Zambonis, welded sculptures, small aircraft, personal helicopters, and more. *Star Wars* fans will appreciate the life-size replicas of Darth Vader, C-3PO, R2-D2, and a storm trooper, all museum quality and safely stowed behind geek-proof plexiglass. A large, classic empty carousel spins near the center of the building, which is only half occupied by tenants, including a Coney Island restaurant, a hockey equipment outlet, and a huge head shop.

Dort Mall, 3600 S. Dort Hwy., Flint, MI 48507

Phone: (810) 744-3338

Hours: Always visible

Cost: Free

Directions: On M-54 (Dort Hwy.), north of Atherton Rd., at the mall's southeast entrance.

Keith Moon's Holiday Inn Bash

Rock 'n' roll road stories are like fine wine—they get better over time. But the tale of Keith Moon's 21st birthday bash in Flint on August 23, 1967, is almost too good to be embellished. First off, it was actually his 20th birthday—he just told everyone it was his 21st so he could legally drink . . . not that it really mattered. After the Who finished opening for Herman's Hermits at **Atwood Stadium** (701 W. Third Ave., (810) 766-7463, www.cityofflint.com/atwood/atwood.htm), the band returned to the Holiday Inn near the airport, where things got out of hand.

Back in their suite, a food fight erupted when a drum kit–shaped cake was delivered from Premier Percussion; Moon had kicked in many of their drums over the years, and they appreciated the business and publicity. Soon roadies were chasing groupies through the hall with fire extinguishers, cherry bombs were being thrown down toilets, and general public nakedness ensued. And sometime later that evening Moon found himself inside a Lincoln Continental in the parking lot, where he knocked the transmission into neutral. The car rolled through the lot and a retaining fence and into the swimming pool. Moon calmly waited for the pressure to equalize as the interior filled with water, then opened the car door and swam back to the party.

By this time, the motel had called the sheriff. The cops arrived to find Moon being de-pantsed by the Hermits, and when he tried to flee he slipped on some cake, fell, and knocked out his front teeth. At the hospital later that night, he had to have a broken tooth stump removed without anesthetics; he was too drunk to be given a painkiller. The next morning, the sheriff personally escorted Moon to the tour plane with a final warning: "Sonny, don't ever dock in Flint, again," to which Moon replied, "Dear boy, I wouldn't dream of it."

All totaled, the band had done $40,000 worth of damage, equal to about $280,000 today. The Holiday Inn later became a Days Inn, and was eventually torn down. An Econo Lodge stands on the site today.

Econo Lodge, 2215 W. Bristol Rd., Flint, MI 48507

Phone: (810) 341-1330

Hours: Always visible

Cost: Free

Website: www.econolodge.com/hotel-flint-michigan-MI316

Directions: Just west of I-75 at the Bristol Rd. exit.

Michael Moore's Flint

Nobody is more closely associated with Flint than the very funny and always provocative Michael Moore. Born in Flint on April 23, 1954, he grew up in suburban Davison where he attended **St. John's Elementary**

School (404 N. Dayton St., closed) and **Davison High School** (1250 N. Oak Rd.), following a brief and unsuccessful stint at Saginaw's **St. Paul's Seminary** (2555 Wieneke Rd., today Nouvel Catholic Central High School).

At the age of 18, Moore was elected to the Davison School Board, and was at the time the youngest person elected to public office in the United States. He had run a single-plank campaign: fire the high school principal who had given generations of Davison students so much grief. (After Moore's victory, the principal resigned before Moore got the chance to can him.) In 1976 he established the Davison Hotline, a no-judgment teen crisis center in Burton whose newsletter grew to become a muckraking newspaper, the *Flint Voice*, after Moore sweet-talked $200,000 in fundraising concerts out of singer Harry Chapin. It later became the *Michigan Voice* when it expanded to cover statewide news, and led to Moore's short editorship at *Mother Jones*.

Moore's first film is his best known. *Roger & Me* tells of the destruction of America's middle class at the hands of profit-hungry corporations, in this case General Motors, run at the time by Roger Smith. Moore tries unsuccessfully to meet with Smith, showing up three times at **GM Headquarters** in Detroit (3044 W. Grand Blvd., today named Cadillac Place), where he was always barred from reaching the executive's 14th Floor. He's also politely escorted out of the **Grosse Pointe Yacht Club** (788 Lake Shore Rd.) in Grosse Pointe Shores, and the **Detroit Athletic Club** (241 Madison Ave.).

Back in his hometown, Moore finds the well-to-do fiddling while Flint burns—at a Great Gatsby Party at **Applewood Estate** (1400 E. Kearsley St.), a Jailhouse Rock bash to open the brand-new and soon-to-be-filled **Genesee County Jail** (1002 S. Saginaw St.), and various golf courses and country clubs. The newly unemployed and struggling former GM employees try to survive by evicting their former coworkers from their homes, selling their blood at the **Flint Plasma Company** (500 S. Saginaw St., since moved), or raising rabbits for "pets or meat."

Meanwhile, city and state officials direct millions of taxpayer dollars into several ill-conceived development schemes, including the **Water Street Pavilion** (303 S. Saginaw St., today University Pavilion), the quickly bankrupt **Hyatt Regency** (1 Riverfront Center West, today Riverfront Res-

"We Shall Stay Free."

idence Hall), and **AutoWorld** (Harrison St. at the Flint River, torn down). The dancing GM robot from that attraction can be found today at Flint's **Sloan Museum** (1221 E. Kearsley St., (810) 237-3450, www.sloanlongway .org/sloan-museum), which is about all that's left to see in Flint from this classic movie.

At the time it was released, some criticized Moore for his essay-style documentary, claiming that he took sides in the story and placed some events out of order. But do yourself a favor: watch it again and try to deny that everything he predicted about the fate of this country hasn't already come true. Let's just hope what he wrote in cement in the sidewalk in front of the *Michigan Voice* headquarters is also true: WE SHALL STAY FREE.

Former *Michigan Voice* Headquarters, 5005 Lapeer Rd., Burton, MI 48509

No phone

Hours: Always visible

Cost: Free

Website: www.michaelmoore.com

Directions: On the northeast corner of the intersection of Lapeer and Genesee Rds.

Paul's Pipe Museum

Listen up, kids: just because Paul Spaniola opened his pipe shop in 1928 at age 15, and is still puffing away a century later, don't think you'll be as lucky. Pipe smoking is a smelly, dirty, unhealthy habit, and if nothing else, think of all you could purchase with the money you'd blow on 84 years' worth of tobacco.

OK, with that out of the way, it's time for all you grownups to stop on by Paul's Pipe Shop and Pipe Hospital in downtown Flint. Everything on the ground floor is for sale, but upstairs you'll find a dozen glass cases brimming with unique and antique tampers, lighters, tins, bags, ashtrays, advertisements, and of course, pipes of all shapes, sizes, and models. The building is also home to Paul's Institute of Pipe Smoking. Spaniola certainly knows enough to be dean—he's a six-time World Pipe Smoking Champion. To claim the title, smokers compete to see who can make 3.3 grams of tobacco burn the longest, which, I suppose, is one way to minimize the damage to your lungs. But then again, it takes a lot of practice.

Paul's Pipe Shop and Pipe Hospital, 647 S. Saginaw St., Flint, MI 48502

Phone: (810) 235-0581

Hours: Monday–Friday 9 AM–7 PM, Saturday 9 AM–5 PM

Cost: Free

Website: www.paulspipeshop.com and www.iapsc.net/museum.html

Directions: Between Second and Third Sts., west of I-475.

Frankenmuth and Pinconning

Cheesy Mega Mice

You might think using large rodents to market your products is a bad idea, but look what it did for Walt Disney. Then again, he wasn't selling food, like these two Michigan establishments.

The Frankenmuth Cheese Haus has a big-eared mouse mascot that's every bit as adorable as Mickey. He's burrowed his way into a wedge of concrete cheddar sitting in front of this dairy store, with only his head sticking out in front—perfect for photos.

Frankenmuth Cheese Haus, 561 S. Main St., Frankenmuth, MI 48734

Phone: (989) 652-6727

Hours: Always visible; Store, June–August, daily 9:30 AM–9:30 PM; September–May,
daily 9:30 AM–6 PM

Cost: Free

Website: www.frankenmuthcheesehaus.com

Directions: On M-83 (S. Main St.), three blocks north of the river.

However, the 2 nine-foot-tall mice outside Wilson's Cheese Shoppe in Pinconning look more rat-like. They're chocolate brown and have large, black eyes, and hold partially gnawed wedges between their tiny paws. One sits on a flatbed trailer with no wheels; the other peers down at you from a perch over the building's entrance.

Wilson's Cheese Shoppe, PO Box 657, 130 N. M-13, Pinconning, MI 48650

Phone: (800) CHEESE-5 or (989) 879-2002

Hours: Always visible; Store, Monday–Thursday & Saturday 8 AM–8 PM, Friday 8 AM–10 PM,
Sunday 8 AM–7 PM

Cost: Free

Website: www.wilsoncheese.com

Directions: Just south of North St. on Mable St. (M-13).

Grindstone City
Grindstone Memorial

Even though you probably know nothing about grindstones or this Michigan town, if the answer in Final Jeopardy was "This Michigan community produced more grindstones than any other town in the Midwest," you'd probably guess "What is Grindstone City?" And you'd be right!

Captain Aaron G. Peer shipped the first grindstone from this area in 1836. Because of its unique surrounding geology, the town got a reputation for supplying the best 4,750-pound, six-foot-diameter rocks around. But as mills moved to other methods of pulverizing wheat into flour in the 1900s,

---

LAKEPORT

➡ The Students for a Democratic Society wrote their manifesto, the Port Huron Statement, in June 1962 at old labor camp, today part of **Lakeport State Park** (7605 Lakeshore Rd., (810) 327-6224).

the quarrying business dried up. Today old stones can be found scattered around this near ghost town, used for driveway markers and mailbox pedestals. One 5,000-pound stone, however, has been inscribed as a memorial to the town's founders, a silent reminder that no industry lasts forever.

Copeland & Rouse Rds., Grindstone City, MI 48467

No phone

Hours: Always visible

Cost: Free

Directions: North of M-25 (Grindstone Rd.) on Rouse Rd.

Ignore the name—this is a Whippy Dip.

Hemlock and Perry
Whippy Dip and King Kone

As roadside architecture goes, the Twistee Treat Ice Cream stand, prefabricated in the shape of a fat vanilla soft-serve cone, is a relatively modern addition. The chain started in Florida in 1983, but went bankrupt in the early 1990s. By then, many of those who had purchased franchises had renamed their stores, despite the Twistee Treat brand being resurrected (and dying) several more times.

Michigan has two former Twistee Treats, and neither retains its original name. One is found on the west side of Hemlock. Owners Kathy and Alfred Smith call their store Hemlock Whippy Dip. It's still vanilla, but has pink, green, and chocolate brown swirls.

16675 Gratiot Rd., Hemlock, MI 48626

Phone: (989) 642-4222

Hours: Always visible; Store, April–September, Monday–Saturday 11 AM–9:30 PM, Sunday noon–9:30 PM

Cost: Free; Cones, $1.70–3.20

Directions: East of Brennan Rd. on M-46 (Gratiot Rd.), on the west side of town.

The second Twistee Treat can be found on the south side of Perry; it goes by the name King Kone. It, too, is vanilla, but has a giant red cherry on top.

12030 S. M-52, Perry, MI 48872

Phone: (517) 625-4004

Hours: Always visible; Store, June–September, daily 12:30–9:30 PM

Cost: Free; Ice cream, $1.65 and up

Website: http://twisterssoftserveicecream.com/index_kingkone.html

Directions: Just south of Bath Rd. on Main St. (M-52), at the south end of town.

I SCREAM FOR ICE CREAM CONES!

There's nothing better than an ice cream cone on a hot summer day, except perhaps winning the lottery, finding a Picasso for $5 at a yard sale, or striking oil while digging in your backyard. But how likely are any of those prospects? Instead, stop on by one of these dairy bars for a cold soft-serve in the shadow of a giant fiberglass cone, and enjoy a frosty treat while waiting for your unrealistic fantasies to pan out.

Boy with a Cone

Marion's Dairy Bar, 111 E. Bay St., East Tawas, (989) 362-2991, www.facebook.com/marionsdairybar

A towheaded boy in blue overalls holds a single-scoop cone high above his oversized head at this store on the eastern shore. A former A&W statue, he has been repainted to draw customers to Marion's, an East Tawas institution since 1945.

Burk's Igloo Ice Cream Cone

Burk's Igloo, 10300 Conant St., Hamtramck, (313) 872-6830

The crude, two-story, pink cone holding up the front of this roadside stand is as flat as the waffle it appears to made from, only it's made of plywood. Burk's Igloo also has three happy, hand-painted penguins to greet you. How they got to the North Pole, where igloos are found, is anyone's guess.

Turkey Cone?

Gobblers of Gaylord, 900 S. Otsego Ave., Gaylord, (989) 732-9005, www.gobblersofgaylord.com

Though Gobblers specializes in turkey meals, the store is fronted by an eight-foot-tall chocolate-and-vanilla twistee cone atop a brick pedestal in the parking lot. Or is it a white-and-dark pureed meat twist? Lick it and see.

Two-Scooper

Sundaes Afternoon, 406 Center St., Omer, (989) 653-2043, https://www.facebook.com/pages/Sundaes-Afternoon/220910181271832

A two-scoop cone—strawberry and chocolate—rises high on the sign outside this Omer establishment. Not surprisingly, given the store's name, you can also buy sundaes here.

Big Vanilla Cone

Super Twist, 575 N. Cedar St., Mason, (517) 676-6140

It towers above the surrounding landscape like a conical white flame, mounted on the peak of the Super Twist stand, but it's just an eight-foot vanilla soft-serve cone.

Giant Ice Cream Cone

Stage Stop Restaurant, 555 W. Main St., Stockbridge, (517) 851-7666

As colossal cones go, this giant vanilla soft-serve seems kinda puny at a mere six feet tall. It's mounted on a pole to discourage pranksters.

Holly

Carry Nation at the Holly Hotel

Carry Nation came to Holly on August 29, 1908, but unlike the town's visitors these days, she wasn't shopping for antiques, she was shopping for souls. Nation was joined by an army of umbrella-swinging followers bent on purging demon rum from this sinful railroad burg. At the time, most of the saloons in Holly could be found along Martha Street, which had earned the nickname "Battle Alley" in 1880 after the crew from a traveling circus engaged in a massive street brawl. (To be fair, there were also nightly drunken fistfights even when the circus wasn't in town.)

Nation did not have an umbrella that day, but she *was* toting her infamous hatchet, and she set her sights on the Holly Hotel. Not only did it have a large, popular saloon, but it also had a scandalous painting of a nude woman hanging behind the bar. Even though Nation wore a long, black dress, she was able to vault the bar while screaming, "Naked Jeze-

What all the fuss was about. Photo by author, courtesy Holly Hotel

bel!" She was stopped before she destroyed the artwork, but she successfully wiped out the liquor shelves.

The owner of the Holly Hotel swore out a warrant for Nation's arrest, and she was thrown in the local jail to cool down. She was eventually released and left Holly to continue her crusade against other Sodoms and Gomorrahi. As for the painting, it burned up in a 1913 fire, though it was re-created in 1979 based on sketches by historian Vera Cook Husted. It still hangs in the hotel today.

For many years, Holly celebrated a Carry Nation Festival on the first weekend after Labor Day, in which the infamous day's events were re-created. Because of budget cuts, it has been on hiatus, but locals promise they'll bring back the hatchet-swinging zealot in the future.

110 Battle Alley, Holly, MI 48442

Phone: (248) 634-5208

Hours: Monday–Saturday 2–10 PM, Sunday 10:30 AM–8 PM

Cost: Free; Meals, $30–50

Website: www.hollyhotel.com

Directions: One block south of Maple St., one block east of Saginaw St., at Broad St.

Dr. Death Gets His Start

Everyone has to start somewhere, and for Dr. Jack Kevorkian, his start was in a VW van at Groveland Oaks County Park on June 4, 1990. He brought Janet Adkins, a 54-year-old woman with early-onset Alzheimer's disease, here and hooked her up to a "suicide machine" he had demonstrated (without a patient) on the *Donahue* show. Adkins saw the episode and had contacted him for assistance in killing herself. So while Kevorkian and Adkins's friend Carroll Rehmke watched, Adkins pushed a button that allowed sodium thiopental to flow into her veins, knocking her out, followed by a dose of potassium chloride, which stopped her heart.

For the next ten years, Kevorkian would drive the nation's euthanasia debate, often recklessly so. He assisted in an estimated 130 more suicides, even though Michigan lawmakers banned the practice in 1993. His final provocative act took place on September 17, 1998, when he administered a lethal injection into Thomas Youk, who suffered from ALS. The very-assisted suicide was filmed and later broadcast on *60 Minutes.*

In 1999, a jury found Kevorkian guilty of Youk's second-degree murder, and he was sentenced to 10 to 25 years in prison. Kevorkian served eight years, and was released from the Lakeland Correctional Facility in Coldwater on June 1, 2007, on the condition he never perform assisted suicide again. He didn't, and died of kidney and respiratory failure on June 3, 2011, in Royal Oak. He was buried in Troy at the **White Chapel Memorial Park Cemetery** (621 W. Long Lake Rd., (248) 362-7670, www.whitechapelcemetery.com).

Groveland Oaks County Park, 14555 Dixie Hwy., Holly, MI 48442

Phone: (248) 634-9811

Hours: Daily 8 AM–9 PM

Cost: $10/day

Website: www.destinationoakland.com/parksandtrails/parks/grovelandoaks/Pages/default.aspx

Directions: East of I-75 at Grange Hall Rd., then north on Dixie Hwy.

Lennon
Krupp's on the Corner

With so many sites in this book dedicated to odd homeowners who have chosen to turn their front lawns into sculpture gardens, political statements, or weird wonderlands, you just might feel inspired to do the same at your place. But where to start?

Here's your answer: Krupp's on the Corner. This lawn ornament superstore was started by Jean and Carl Krupp in 1952. Originally they sold concrete birdbaths, but then Jean began making bird- and doghouses out of the leftover wood crates. From there, their inventory snowballed to include every outdoor concrete item imaginable—fountains, planters, benches, tables, Japanese pagodas, Greek statuary, jockeys, gnomes, gargoyles, deer, pigs, and Buddhas. Madonnas are lined up like an invading army, flanked by Mexican children leading burros, and more than a few nude Davids.

And that's just outside. Inside, crammed into several interlocking machine sheds, you'll find wind chimes and cartoon whirligigs, inspirational garden signs and goofy frog statues, colored glass gazing balls and metal butterflies . . . on and on, room after room.

In other words, there's no excuse to keep that boring lawn of yours. None.

2011 S. Sheridan Rd., Lennon, MI 48449

Phone: (810) 621-3752

Hours: Monday–Saturday 10 AM–6 PM, Sunday noon–6 PM

Cost: Free

Website: http://kruppsonthecorner.com/

Directions: At the intersection of M-13 (S. Sheridan Rd.) and M-21 (W. Corunna Rd.).

Lexington
Belly Bomber Hall of Fame

J. Wellington Wimpy, usually referred to as just Wimpy, is the patron saint of burger lovers everywhere. Seldom seen without a hamburger in his hand or mouth, this popular *Popeye* cartoon character has inspired many gluttons over the years. A Lexington café that bears his name even has a Belly Bomber Hall of Fame for anyone who can replicate his voracious appetite. All you have to do is down a dozen burgers in one sitting and you're inducted.

Wimpy's Place was established in 1987, and is not affiliated with the Wimpy's hamburger chain that originated in the 1930s (and still survives in England). The burgers here are fantastic *and* inexpensive, which is why so many have chosen to pursue this gastronomical honor.

Wimpy's Place, 7270 Huron Ave., Lexington, MI 48450

Phone: (810) 359-5450

Hours: Daily 7 AM–5:30 PM

Cost: $1.79/burger

Website: www.wimpys-place.com

Directions: Just west of M-25 (Main St.) on M-90 (Huron Ave.).

Midland
John Pratt Mosaic House

John Pratt had a difficult life. Born and raised in Midland, after graduating high school he ran off to New York, where he worked during the 1960s as a Macy's window dresser. He later opened an antique shop specializing in Tiffany lamps. But then Pratt started hearing voices telling him to be silent, and he stopped talking for two years. Eventually he returned to Michigan to live with his parents. After they died, his schizophrenia caused him to spiral even further downward.

Pratt's troubles with the law eventually led him to Midland-Gladwin Community Mental Health Services, which got him the medical help he needed. As part of his recovery, he turned to his love of dance and clowning to express himself. He also decided to convert his parents' cinder block home into a canvas for a stunning mosaic he created that resembled one of his old Tiffany lamps. He covered every square inch of the building with shards of broken pottery, mirrors, marbles, stones, and found items, creating dozens of religious and floral images and his motto: LIVE AND LET LIVE. Pratt saw the mosaic as an analogy for taking the pieces of his shattered life and making a thing of beauty.

When Pratt died in 1997, he willed his home to the agency that saved him; it is currently managed and maintained by Creative 360, a Midland arts nonprofit that today offers tours of the newly renamed John Pratt Mosaic House.

102 E. Isabella Rd., Midland, MI 48640
Contact: Creative 360, 1517 Bayliss St., Midland, MI 48640
Phone: (989) 837-1885
Hours: Daylight hours; Tours, by appointment
Cost: Free; Tours, $8–10 (depending on tour group size)
Website: www.becreative360.org/john_pratt2.htm
Directions: Just west of town on M-20 (Isabella Rd.).

The Tridge

If a bridge connects two banks of a river, then a structure that connects *three* sides of a river must be called a tridge, right? But where would you find such a tridge?

In Midland, that's where! Built in 1981, the Tridge is a set of three footbridges that meet over the confluence of the Tittabawassee and Chippewa Rivers. Each arm of this spiderlike structure is 180 feet long, and they all meet at a central concrete pillar.

Midlanders love their Tridge, since it connects the city's popular Midland Area Farmer's Market to the Pere Marquette Rail-Trail, St. Charles

On the Tridge, you have options.

Park, and Chippewassee Park, all southwest of downtown. Each Labor Day, Midlanders mock the Mackinac Bridge Walk (see page 78) by hosting their own crossing ceremony, led by the mayor. And at Christmastime, Santa arrives over the Tridge on foot, not pulled on a sleigh by reindeer (see page 291).

Chippewassee Park, Ashman & Ann Sts., Midland, MI 48640

Phone: (989) 837-3300

Hours: Always visible

Cost: Free

Website: www.midlandonline.com/moladmin/articles/articledisplay.cfm?art_id=75

Directions: Head southwest on Ashman St. from downtown to the river.

ANOTHER TRIDGE!

Believe it or not, Michigan actually has *another* Tridge, but it doesn't get as much attention as the one in Midland, perhaps because it's hidden beneath the Cross Street Bridge—or is it Bidge?—in Ypsilanti. The three-arm wooden footbridge connects Depot Town to Riverside Park and Frog Island Park.

Owosso
Curwood Castle

It's been said that a man's home is his castle, but for author James Oliver Curwood his writing studio actually *was* a castle. Built in 1922, Curwood Castle functioned as Curwood's creative retreat. The building was designed to resemble a French château, but it had no living or eating quarters, leaving him alone to work on his novels in the tower overlooking the Shiawassee River.

Curwood was born in Owosso on July 12, 1878, and though he often traveled to Alaska and the Canadian Yukon to gather material for his outdoorsy books, he always returned to Michigan to write. At the height of his popularity in the 1910s and '20s, Curwood was the highest paid author in the world, with 18 of his novels made into movies. A once avid hunter, he later became a conservationist, writing in *The Grizzly King*, "The greatest thrill is not to kill but to let live."

Ironically, it was nature that ultimately killed him. While on a fishing trip to Florida, Curwood was bitten by a spider, suffered an allergic reaction, and died from the infection at his home on Williams Street on August 13, 1927. He was buried on Owosso's Oak Hill Cemetery (see the following entry). Today his writing studio/castle has been restored and is open to the public as a museum.

226 Curwood Castle Dr., Owosso, MI 48867

Phone: (989) 725-0597

Hours: Tuesday–Sunday 1–5 PM

Cost: Free

Website: www.shiawasseehistory.com/curwood.html

Directions: One block north of M-21 (W. Main St.), one block east of M-52 (Shiawassee St.), just west of the river.

Grave of the Jefferson Nickel Designer

Take a look at the nickels in your pockets; if any were minted between 1966 and 2003, you should be able to find a small "FS" just below the portrait of Thomas Jefferson. Those are the initials of Felix Schlag, who in 1938 won a national design competition to replace the "buffalo nickel." Schlag was a German immigrant—he fought for the Kaiser in World War I—who was working at the time as a sculptor in Chicago. He received $1,000 for the design, and the first "Jefferson nickels" went into production in 1938.

Schlag's initials were not part of the original design, but the US Mint added them in 1966. Schlag died in Owosso on March 9, 1974, and was buried at Oak Hill Cemetery (Section Y, Block 1). The Michigan State Numismatic Society later replicated both sides of the Jefferson nickel for a memorial placed over his grave.

Oak Hill Cemetery, 1101 S. Washington St., Owosso, MI 48867

Phone: (989) 725-5495

Hours: Daylight hours

Cost: Free

Directions: Two blocks south of the east end of Gute St., where it intersects Washington Ave.

Oliver, the Dress-Up Bear

You think it's tough getting your kids into their school clothes in the morning? Try wrestling a Santa suit onto an eight-foot-tall brown bear! The fiberglass statue outside Owosso Carpet Center wears a different outfit every month, depending on the season or holiday. Store owners Diane and Jim Krajcovic named their ursine model Oliver after local author James Oliver Curwood (see page 215), who wrote *The Grizzly King*, which was later made into the movie *The Bear*.

Owosso Carpet Center, 2090 W. M-21, Owosso, MI 48867

Phone: (989) 725-6931

Hours: Always visible

Cost: Free

Directions: West of Delaney Rd. on W. Main St. (M-21).

BUNCHES OF BEARS

Oliver isn't the only roadside bear statue to be found in Michigan, nor the only one that wears clothes. On the south side of Tawas City, a dressed-up polar bear guards the entrance to the **North Star Motel** (1119 W. Lake St./US 23, (989) 362-2255, www.helensnorthstarmotel.com). Two bare grizzly bears, both made from the same fiberglass mold, stand on their hind legs over the rocky entrances to **The Bear Company** T-shirt stores, one in Traverse City (896 Munson Ave., (231) 929-9933) and the other in Mackinaw City (200 S. Nicolet St., (231) 436-9944). Another pair of bears battle to the death on a pedestal in front of **Cabela's** (110 Cabela Blvd. East, (734) 529-4700, www.cabelas.com) in Dundee; together, they're the world's largest bronze wildlife sculpture. And a slightly less vicious creature, a lumbering 22-foot-tall black bear made by John Radlovic in 2000, stands near the entrance to the **Big Bear Campground** (Main St. & US Rte. 2, (906) 420-4335) in Vulcan.

Port Austin
Kooky Golf

While it is certainly true that none of the 18 holes found at Kooky Golf are anywhere as dramatic as those at most modern miniature golf courses with their erupting volcanoes and other hi-tech nonsense, you have to appreciate the handmade obstacles and meticulously clean greens at this low-key attraction. It's the kind of place you'd build yourself if you had the time and carpentry skills—the windmill and doghouse, rocket and pinball machine weren't purchased in some ready-to-assemble putt-putt kit. And here and there are

One of a kind.

painted plywood cutouts of a giraffe, a clown, the Pink Panther, and more, all thrown together in a silly non-theme. Kooky Golf also has a half-dozen pirate paintings with their faces removed for gag photos, from a swash-buckling Captain Morgan to a buxom wench, her jacket open to the navel. You won't see that at Pirates' Cove.

283 W. Spring St., Port Austin, MI 48467
Phone: (989) 738-8612
Hours: June–August, daily 10 AM–10 PM
Cost: $5/game
Website: www.lakevistaresort.com/Kooky%20Golf.htm
Directions: On Rte. M-25 (W. Spring St.), at Omelia St.

MORE MINIATURE GOLF

Putt-putt courses aren't hard to find in Michigan—just follow any highway close to a lake and you're bound to find one. The trouble is, many look so similar because, well, they're drawn up by landscape designers from someplace like Hilton Head Adja-cent. But if you're looking for something different, something you haven't seen before, try these courses, each of which look cobbled together from discarded fast-food mascots, cement lawn statues, and the active imaginations of their creators.

Armstrong's Funland

8787 Belleville Rd., Belleville, (734) 699-3550

There are two things to enjoy at Armstrong's Funland: the ice cream and the homemade golf course. The obstacles found on the 18 holes were built when the course opened in 1980, and include a saloon, jailhouse, castle, windmill, clock tower, can-non, and space rocket. The final hole is a clown's grinning face; sink your ball into his nose and you win a free game. Golfers at Funland are asked to adhere to a set of course rules such as: no more than four players per team, place all cigarette butts in the proper receptacles, and no profanity. If any of these are deal breakers for you, take your putter somewhere else.

Jawor's Miniature Golf

32900 Gratiot Ave., Roseville, (586) 293-9836, www.jaworgolf.com/mini-golf/

Jawor's is a large golfing establishment with a driving range and a pro shop, but it's the two 18-hole, statue-covered mini courses that are the most interesting. None of the holes or obstacles look like they've been altered since the place opened in 1954. They've got Pinocchio, a purple stegosaurus, a boxing kangaroo, a chubby pig in a suit and bowtie, a menacing gorilla, a huge skull, a dancing dunce, two pink elephants, a violet crocodile, and more, each annually slathered with a fresh coat of bright paint.

Port Huron

Knowlton's Ice Museum of North America

Did you know that ice harvesting was once the 10th largest industry in the United States? That's just one of the fascinating facts you'll learn at this specialized museum of a bygone age. Your visit starts with a 14-minute film on how ice was harvested from lakes and rivers during the winter, stored in sawdust-filled warehouses, and sold to homeowners during the warm months. Then you're free to take the self-guided tour of the facility. Six antique ice wagons form the center of the collection, but there are more than 5,000 other ice-related artifacts on display, including saws, picks, tongs, sleds, iceboxes, milk jugs, advertisements, and more. It'll all make you appreciate the convenience of modern refrigeration.

317 Grand River Ave., Port Huron, MI 48060

Phone: (810) 987-5441

Hours: June–September, Thursday–Saturday 11 AM–5 PM; October–May, Saturday 11 AM–5 PM

Cost: Adults $5, Seniors $4, Kids (6–12) $2

Website: www.knowltonsicemuseum.org

Directions: One block north of the river, one block east of Huron Ave. (I-94/69 Bus.).

Thomas Edison Depot Museum

"That hole of Port Huron . . ."

When Thomas Edison was 30 years old he wrote to his father, recalling the childhood hometown where his dad still lived: "I don't want you to stay in that hole of a Port Huron, which contains the most despicable remnants of the human race that can be found on earth."

The Edisons had moved to Port Huron in 1854 when Thomas was seven, living near the southwest corner of Thomas and Erie Streets (today Thomas Edison Parkway)—about 800 feet north of the commemorative boulder in **Pine Grove Park** (Michigan and Prospect Sts.). It was here in Port Huron that Tom received his only formal schooling; a teacher labeled him "addled" because of his deafness, the result of a childhood bout with scarlet fever, so he quit after three months and was taught at home by his mother.

She did a good job. In 1859, at the age of 12, Thomas got a job selling candy and newspapers onboard the Grand Trunk Railroad during runs between Port Huron and Detroit. He used the money he earned to buy materials for chemistry experiments, which included his first electric battery in 1861. On February 3, 1862, Edison began selling his own paper, the *Weekly Herald*, which he printed in the baggage car—the world's first newspaper published from a moving train.

Edison left town for Stratford Junction, Ontario, when he was 16 years old, and his parents moved to a new house in Port Huron a year later. His childhood home burned down in 1867, and the foundation was covered over by a railroad line. (The site was excavated in 1979.) A small Edison museum stands today in the shadow of the Blue Water Bridge, housed in the old Fort Gratiot Depot. An attached Grand Trunk baggage car contains a replica of the press Edison used to print his newspaper.

510 Edison Pkwy., Port Huron, MI 48060

Phone: (810) 455-0035

Hours: May–September, Saturday–Sunday 10 AM–4 PM

Cost: Adults $7, Seniors (60+) $5, Kids $5

Website: www.phmuseum.org/Port_Huron_Museum/Thomas_Edison_Depot.html

Directions: Along the waterfront beneath the Blue Water Bridge (I-94/69).

Saginaw
Bean Bunny and the Neon Sign Park

There's no doubt about it—the giant neon rabbit atop the abandoned bean elevator north of downtown Saginaw is B-I-G. In fact, at 50 feet long it's the world's largest figural neon sign. Take that, Las Vegas! Built for the Michigan Bean Company in 1947–48, the sign advertised its famous Jack Rabbit Beans. The rabbit is pink and hops over the word BEANS, spelled out in 12-foot-tall green neon.

There's a charming story about how the MBC came up with its product's name. Back in the 1920s, Harry Houdini was touring Michigan and stopped in Saginaw, where he gave young Phyllis Reidel a rabbit from one of his tricks. She loved the little bunny, but her parents wouldn't let her keep it, so she gave it to her grandparents who lived on a farm. When she later returned, Phyllis discovered that they had eaten it. To cheer her up, her father, an executive at MBC, named the company's bean line after the stewed animal.

After MBC closed the elevator, the bunny sign fell into disrepair and went dark in 1985. It was later restored and relit on July 4, 1997. The grain elevator is still abandoned, but with donations the sign has been kept in service. It is part of a citywide effort to retain some of Saginaw's classic commercial signage, which includes a **Neon Sign Park** downtown, behind the Ippel Building (Court Street and Michigan Avenue). Check out the animated Brenske Plumbing Heating & Supply Company marquee, a faucet that leaks a bright red drop every few seconds, as well as other illuminated signs mounted high above the Ippel Building's parking lot.

Bunny Bean Sign, 1741 N. Niagara St., Saginaw, MI 48602

No phone

Hours: Best after dark

Cost: Free

Website: http://jameshowephotography.com/blog/2010/12/michigan-bean-bunny-saginaw.html/

Directions: Three blocks south of I-675, two blocks east of Michigan Ave., on the west side of the river.

Japanese Cultural Center, Tea House, and Gardens of Saginaw

If you were asked to make a list of three American cities in which you could participate in an authentic Japanese tea ceremony, you would probably say San Francisco, or Seattle, or Portland, Oregon. But Saginaw, Michigan?

As a matter of fact, yes! Since 1985, in collaboration with its sister city of Tokushima, Japan, Saginaw has offered a monthly tea ceremony "to promote intercultural understanding and peace through a bowl of tea." It takes place in an authentic sukiya (rustic) tea house designed by architect Tsutomu Takenaka, constructed entirely without nails by Japanese artisans.

A docent will lead you through each step of the ceremony, from the removal of your shoes to the proper way to kneel on the tatami mats. The monthly event is quite popular and inexpensive, so call ahead for reservations. And wash your socks.

Japanese Cultural Center, 527 Ezra Rust Dr., Saginaw, MI 48601

Phone: (989) 759-1648

Hours: Gardens, April–October, Tuesday–Saturday noon–4 PM; Tea Ceremony, Second Saturday of each month at 2 PM, except December

Cost: Gardens, Free; Tea Ceremony, $3/person

Website: www.japaneseculturalcenter.org

Directions: At Court St., east of the river.

Stevie Wonder's Childhood Home

Steveland Morris Judkins was born in Saginaw's **St. Mary's Hospital** (800 S. Washington Ave., (989) 907-8000, www.stmarysofmichigan.org) on May 13, 1950. Because he was six weeks premature, the blood vessels in his eyes had not yet fully developed, and the oxygen in his incubator caused his retinas to detach, a condition then known as retrolental fibroplasia, or RLF (but today called retinopathy of prematurity, or ROP). Forty-five days after being born, little Steveland came home to Farwell Street, later renamed and renumbered to be 1315 N. Fifth Avenue. His mother gave little Steveland a pair of bongo drums, which he cradled like a teddy bear while he slept in his crib.

Steveland's parents, Calvin and Lula Mae Judkins, had a dysfunctional relationship to say the least. Calvin began pimping his wife shortly after they married, and sometime in 1953 they got into a fight when he ordered her to go buy him a pack of cigarettes—Calvin was stabbed. They later got back together on Lula Mae's terms: they would move to Detroit and get away from Calvin's no-good friends.

Calvin left Lula Mae not long after the move, and she returned to her maiden name of Hardaway. Her children got new names as well, including Steveland, though his name changed spelling and order depending on who was using it—Steveland Hardaway . . . Stevland Hardaway Morris . . . nothing ever really stuck until 1961, when he was proclaimed Little Stevie Wonder by Motown producer Clarence Paul. But that's another story (see page 249).

Stevie Wonder's childhood home was torn down years ago, but a stone marker on a pedestal was later placed at the site. An adjoining Juneteenth Cultural Center & Museum, built at the same time as the monument was installed, has recently closed its doors, so there's not much more to see than a rock in a vacant lot.

1315 N. Fifth Ave., Saginaw, MI 48601

No phone

Hours: Always visible

Cost: Free

Website: www.steviewonder.net

Directions: One block south of Washington Ave. at Farwell St.

All that marks Saginaw's greatest export.

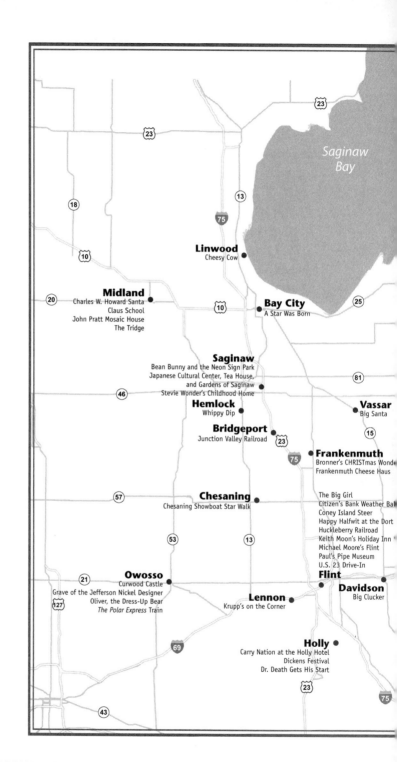

Saginaw Bay

Linwood
Cheesy Cow

Midland
Charles W. Howard Santa
Claus School
John Pratt Mosaic House
The Tridge

Bay City
A Star Was Born

Saginaw
Bean Bunny and the Neon Sign Park
Japanese Cultural Center, Tea House,
and Gardens of Saginaw
Stevie Wonder's Childhood Home

Hemlock
Whippy Dip

Vassar
Big Santa

Bridgeport
Junction Valley Railroad

Frankenmuth
Bronner's CHRISTmas Wonde
Frankenmuth Cheese Haus

Chesaning
Chesaning Showboat Star Walk

The Big Girl
Citizen's Bank Weather Ba
Coney Island Steer
Happy Halfwit at the Dort
Huckleberry Railroad
Keith Moon's Holiday Inn
Michael Moore's Flint
Paul's Pipe Museum
U.S. 23 Drive-In

Owosso
Curwood Castle
Grave of the Jefferson Nickel Designer
Oliver, the Dress-Up Bear
The Polar Express Train

Flint

Davidson
Big Clucker

Lennon
Krupp's on the Corner

Holly
Carry Nation at the Holly Hotel
Dickens Festival
Dr. Death Gets His Start

Port Austin ●
Kooky Golf

Grindstone City ●
Grindstone Memorial

N

25

142 53 142

*Lake
Huron*

81 19 25

46

Carsonville ●
Hi-Way Drive-In

53

Croswell
Be Good to Your Mother-in-Law Bridge ● 90 **Lexington** ●
Belly Bomber Hall of Fame

90

19

25

21

69 ● **Emmett**
Giant Duff Beer Can and
South Paw Left-Handed Cigarettes

● **Port Huron**
Knowlton's Ice Museum
of North America
Lightship *Huron*
Thomas Edison Depot
Museum

● **Almont**
Scared Steer

53

● **Armada**
Blake Farms Big Apple Orchard 94

24

97

CANADA

6

Detroit and Suburbs

*T*ake a close look at the flag of the City of Detroit and you'll see two Latin mottos. The first, *Speramus Meliora*, means "We hope for better things," and the second, *Resurget Cineribus*, means "It will arise from the ashes." The first could have been dreamed up by any local booster, but the second? What ashes are they talking about? Back on June 11, 1805, baker John Harvey emptied out his still-burning pipe in the wrong spot and ignited his neighbor's barn. The resulting inferno consumed all but one of Detroit's buildings, a stone fort. Luckily, nobody died.

But in reading about early Detroit traditions, it's amazing the city hasn't burned down more often. In the 1800s General Friend Palmer complained in a letter, "It was quite common then on the Fourth of July nights, and on other nights as well, during the summer season, for the boys to ignite and throw these balls [wads of cotton wicking wrapped in twine and soaked in turpentine] up and down Jefferson Avenue." Christmas was similarly raucous, according to Palmer. "It was quite the custom the night before Christmas to usher in the day with the blowing of horns and firing of guns, commencing at 12 o'clock and keeping it up until daylight."

Then, of course, came the more sinister spectacle of Devil's Night, the torching of buildings on the night before Halloween, a practice which first swept the city in the 1970s and continued until the mid-1990s. Eventually, tens of thousands of fed-up volunteers began to patrol their neighborhoods during the renamed Angel's Night to head off trouble, and finally managed to bring the weird custom under control.

None of this is to say you should expect a conflagration on your next visit to the city, particularly on a holiday . . . but you never know. Nothing last forever, not even Detroit's greatest oddball attractions—see them while you still can.

Detroit
Coney Dogs

Everywhere you go in Michigan, and particularly in Detroit, you'll see Coney Island hot dog stands. This culinary specialty did not come from New York, but from a happy accident in Detroit back in 1917. Constantine "Gust" Keros ran out of sauerkraut at his hot dog stand, so he slathered on a ladle of meat chili, some chopped sweet onions, and yellow mustard, all nestled in a steamed bun. Ta-da! The Coney Island name originally referred to the all-beef, natural casing wiener inside, but soon everyone was calling Keros's creation a Coney Island hot dog, or sometimes just a Coney dog.

Keros later renamed his shop American Coney Island. His brother William took the idea and opened Lafayette Coney Island in 1924, and the two branches of the family have been battling it out ever since, with loyal customers on both sides. American Coney Island moved its operations right next door to the Lafayette shop in 1989 when they bought the old United Shirt building downtown. If you don't want to take sides, you can have one Coney dog at American, then walk 10 feet west to Lafayette and have another. Truth be told, American does seem to have the upper hand—it's long been a must-stop for Michigan celebrities like Tim Allen, Diana Ross, Ted Nugent, Kid Rock, and Jeff Daniels, not to mention out-of-towners like Danny DeVito, Penny Marshall, and Bill Cosby. It's also the only one that's open 24 hours a day, 365 days a year.

American Coney Island, 114 W. Lafayette Blvd., Detroit, MI 48226

Phone: (586) 219-0995

Hours: Always open

Cost: $2.35/dog

Website: www.americanconeyisland.com

Directions: At the intersection of Lafayette Blvd. and Michigan Ave.

Lafayette Coney Island, 118 W. Lafayette Blvd., Detroit, MI 48226

Phone: (313) 964-8198

Hours: Sunday–Thursday 9 AM–3 AM, Friday–Saturday 8 AM–4 AM

Cost: $2.50/dog

Website: www.facebook.com/pages/Lafayette-Coney-Island/127456979952

Directions: At the intersection of Lafayette Blvd. and Michigan Ave.

ILLEGAL IN DETROIT

It might look like anything goes in Detroit, but there are several city statutes you should be aware of, lest you run afoul of the law:

⇒ You cannot tie crocodiles to city fire hydrants.

⇒ It is illegal to ogle a woman from a moving car.

⇒ On Sundays, husbands may not scowl at their wives.

⇒ You may not read a newspaper while sitting in the middle of a Detroit street.

⇒ If you plan to let your pig roam free in the city, you must put a ring in its nose.

⇒ You are allowed make out in your car, but only on your own property.

⇒ You may not play with snuff in Detroit theaters.

⇒ It is against Detroit law to decorate your car with pennants.

Detroit Diva Duo

You might not think Detroit is a city of divas, but you'd be wrong—two of America's greatest musical talents will be forever associated with the Motor City, and neither is Diana Ross. (You can read more about Miss-Ross-to-You on page 249.) No, we're talking about Aretha Franklin and Dinah Washington.

Though Aretha Franklin was born in Memphis on March 25, 1942, she has lived in Detroit since the age of five, when her father, C. L. Franklin, was named pastor of the city's New Bethel Baptist Church. Bishop Franklin was a talented orator and singer, and even had a contract with Chess Records. As a young girl, Aretha would follow her father on lecture tours and sang in the New Bethel choir. And it was in choir that she was discovered; she signed a gospel contract with J.V.B. Records at the age of 14.

When Aretha Franklin turned 18, she cut her first R&B record with Columbia, and quickly earned some R-E-S-P-E-C-T in the music industry. The "Queen of Soul" has had 20 #1 R&B singles, was inducted into the Rock and Roll Hall of Fame in 1987, and received the Presidential Medal of Freedom in 2005. But still, as famous as she's become, she has always remembered where she came from, and can still be seen from time to time at her father's former church.

New Bethel Baptist Church, 8430 Linwood St./C. L. Franklin Blvd., Detroit, MI 48206

Phone: (313) 894-5789

Hours: Services, Sunday 7:30–9:00 AM, 10:30 AM–12 PM

Cost: Donation

Website: www.nbbcdetroit.org and www.arethafranklin.net

Directions: On Linwood Blvd. (C. L. Franklin Blvd.) at Columbus St.

Dinah Washington, a diva from an earlier generation, didn't start out in the Motor City, though she ended her life here. The "Queen of the Blues" was born in Alabama in 1924, but spent most of her recording career in Chicago and New York.

Washington was married seven times. Her final spouse, footballer Dick "Night Train" Lane, brought her to Detroit's west side where the couple had a home on Buena Vista Avenue. Lane was playing for the Lions at the time. On December 13, 1963, Washington spent the day Christmas shopping in the city, then returned home where her two sons had just arrived for the holidays. Early the next morning, Lane found his wife on the bedroom floor, near death. Before Washington could be taken from the house, she expired. The coroner ruled that she was killed by a lethal (and likely accidental) combination of secobarbital, amobarbital, and booze. Washington was just 39.

A memorial service was held in Detroit on December 16 at the New Bethel Baptist Church before her body was taken to Chicago for burial. Rev. C. L. Franklin presided and daughter Aretha sang. Two days later, dressed in a yellow chiffon dress, a mink stole, and a diamond tiara, Washington was buried in the Windy City.

4002 Buena Vista Ave., Detroit, MI 48238

Private phone

Hours: Always visible; view from street

Cost: Free

Directions: Three blocks east of Livenois Ave., three blocks south of W. Davison St.

Detroit Industry, Howdy Doody, and a Shark Attack

You could almost hear millionaire art collectors licking their chops when the city of Detroit filed for bankruptcy in the summer of 2013. As the nation's fifth largest art museum, the Detroit Institute of Arts (DIA) has an outstanding permanent collection, but if rumors were true, it might not be permanent permanently. People were suggesting the museum auction off its holdings to pay the city's bills.

The DIA's best-known artwork would be the most difficult to sell, because it's part of the building itself. Diego Rivera painted *Detroit Industry* on the walls of an inner courtyard in 1932–33. The mural depicts the life of an American autoworker, from the womb to the grave, and all the assembly-line toil in between. Before it was even finished, local clergy denounced the work as vulgar and un-American for its female nudity and Christian imagery, depicting Mary and Joseph as a nurse and doctor giving the baby Jesus a vaccination. (Umm, what's wrong with *that*?) Of course, the reaction was more a response to Rivera's Marxist politics, not the work itself, as evidenced by a sign the DIA hung on the mural in the 1950s. It began: "Rivera's politics and his publicity seeking are detestable. But let's get the record straight on what he did here. He came from Mexico to Detroit, thought our mass production industries and our technology wonderful and very exciting, painted them as one of the great achievements of the twentieth century . . ."

DETROIT

➡ Bernhard Stroh established his first Detroit operation, the Lion Brewery, at 37 Catherine Street (today Madison St.) in 1850.

➡ In 1980 Saddam Hussein was given the key to the city of Detroit after he donated money to the **Sacred Heart Chaldean Catholic Parish** (310 W. Seven Mile Rd., (313) 368-6214).

➡ On September 23, 1984, a woman reported seeing a kangaroo hopping across I-94 near Detroit Metropolitan Airport. It was later spotted by sheriff's deputies.

Another popular piece in the DIA's collection is more portable—the original Howdy Doody puppet. The marionette was donated to the museum's extensive puppet collection by the late Buffalo Bob Smith, though it hasn't been on display since 2009. Maybe it will never return.

Perhaps the only appropriate artwork that could end up in an auction is John Singleton Copley's *Watson and the Shark*. The 1777 painting was commissioned by Brook Watson who, at the age of 14, lost his leg to a shark in Havana Harbor. Copley painted three versions; the original is in the National Gallery of Art, the second version is in the Museum of Fine Arts Boston, and the third version resides in the DIA. It depicts a frantic boat crew reaching out to save a young man from a slick, ravenous beast . . . not unlike the culture vultures circling the DIA.

Detroit Institute of Arts, 5200 Woodward Ave., Detroit, MI 48202

Phone: (313) 833-7900

Hours: Tuesday–Thursday 9 AM–4 PM, Friday 9 AM–10 PM, Saturday–Sunday 10 AM–5 PM

Cost: Adults $8, Seniors $6, Kids (6–17) $4

Website: www.dia.org

Directions: Two blocks north of E. Warren Ave. on M-1 (Woodward Ave.).

MOTOWN MURALS

Let's just say that a bankruptcy judge *does* hock the DIA's masterpieces. Where will you go to find art in Detroit then?

Automotive Mural

Student Center Building, Wayne State University, 5221 Gullen Mall, (313) 577-2116, http://studentcenter.wayne.edu

After you've seen *Detroit Industry*, this mural will look somewhat familiar. Painted seven years after Rivera's masterpiece, the 6-by-40-foot painting by William Gropper depicts workers on an assembly line, though there are many more workers than there are cars. Because Gropper was considered a "radical" by auto executives, he wasn't allowed to visit local plants; instead, he had to compose the painting using photos from

Life magazine. The mural was funded by the Works Progress Administration and installed in the Northwestern Branch Post Office in 1941. When that building was demolished in 1971, the artwork was relocated to Wayne State University.

Eastern Market Murals

Detroit Eastern Market, 2934 Russell St., (313) 833-9300,
www.detroiteasternmarket.com

The Eastern Market had been a part of Detroit commercial life since 1891, but by the early 1970s it had fallen on hard times (like the rest of the city). Then, in 1972, Alexander Pollack of the City Planning Department commissioned farm-themed murals to spruce the market up. Vendors and customers loved it, and today paintings cover almost every free wall in the place. A forklift driver hauls a 10-foot-tall watermelon while pulling loads of apples and pumpkins. A giant chicken guards a stall entrance. And Rat Fink–like characters are everywhere. Shop and explore!

The Cornfield

La Jalisciense Tortilla Factory, 2650 Bagley Ave., (313) 237-0008,
www.tortillamundo.com

Painted by Vito Valdez and Jim Puntigam between 1997 and 1998, *The Cornfield* depicts Mexican laborers heading into the field to sow and pick maize, and is dedicated to "the spirit of the indigenous people who cultivated the land that was once theirs." The Virgin of Guadalupe was added later, floating about the mountains in the distance.

Pope Park Mural (and Pope Statue)

Joseph Campeau & Belmont Sts., Hamtramck

Painted by Dennis Orlowski in 1982, the *Pope Park Mural* depicts street life in Kraków, the Polish city where Karol Wojtyla served as bishop, archbishop, and cardinal from 1958 to 1978. Wojtyla visited Hamtramck in 1969, nine years before he was elected pope, taking the name John Paul II. A 12-foot bronze statue of the pontiff stands on a 26-foot pedestal at one end of the park; it was created by Ferenc Varga in 1982.

Diversity Is Our Strength

Los Galanes Restaurant, 3362 Bagley St., (313) 554-4444, www.los-galanesdetroit.com

A veritable United Nations watches over the parking lot of this Mexican restaurant just a block from Detroit's Ambassador Bridge. Back in 1995, 18-year-old Arturo Cruz organized more than 70 artists to create this work honoring the efforts of Freedom House, a local refugee resettlement organization. Not only do the featured immigrants bring strength through their diversity, they appear to be 60 feet tall as they stand shoulder-to-shoulder on the painted bridge—Bunyans from every land!

The Falling Wallendas

The Flying Wallendas, perhaps the best known high-wire performers in history, earned their stage name not because they soared, but because they didn't. During a 1940s show in Akron, Ohio, four family members tumbled from the high wire but landed unhurt, and a reporter wrote, "The Wallendas fell so gracefully that it seemed as if they were flying." The odd nickname stuck.

The troupe was founded in Germany by Karl Wallenda in 1922, but they eventually made it to the States. The Ringling Brothers signed them in 1928, and they toured with the circus for many years. Yet as their fame grew, so did the pressure for more death-defying stunts, and they did away with safety nets altogether. Later, Karl developed a seven-person pyramid that became their signature stunt. And their undoing.

On January 30, 1962, the Wallendas were performing for the Shrine Circus at the Michigan State Fairgrounds when the first man on the pyramid faltered, causing the tower to collapse. Two family members were killed—Richard Faughnan and Dieter Schepp—and two more were seriously injured—Mario Wallenda was left a paraplegic, and Karl shattered his pelvis. Nevertheless, Karl performed the next day. That's a showman!

Though currently closed, the Coliseum and the fair site are expected to reopen under a future redevelopment plan.

Michigan State Fairgrounds Coliseum, 1120 W. State Fair Ave., Detroit, MI 48203

No phone

Hours: Always visible

Cost: Free

Website: www.wallenda.com

Directions: Two blocks east of Woodward Ave. (M-1), south of Eight Mile Rd.

Feather Bowling

Feather bowling is a nearly forgotten Belgian sport, even in Belgium. The sport is so rare that there is only one feather bowling venue in the entire United States: a long room adjoining the Cadieux Café on Detroit's east side. Belgian immigrants opened the two-lane clubhouse in 1929, and leagues have played here ever since. Each lane is made up of a 70-foot shallow trough lined with sawdust that has been mixed with ox blood, though

Three balls and a tickler.

rumor has it that they're currently lined with a mixture of kitty litter and peat, but no blood. Either way, I'd wash my hands after finishing a game.

The rules of feather bowling are similar to those of bocci or horseshoes. Each team has six 3¼-pound balls shaped like gouda cheese wheels—rounded on the edge, but flat on two sides. Two teams of players take turns to see who can roll their ball closest to an upright feather, the "tickler," that is inserted into the packed sawdust at the opposite end of the lane. The ball closest to the tickler gets a point, as does every ball from the same team that is closer to the tickler than the closest ball from the opposing squad. The first team to earn 10 points or more wins.

The Cadieux Café also tries to preserve Belgian culture in other ways by serving steamed mussels, rabbit, and imported beers, and playing host to pigeon-racing enthusiasts and the Cadieux Bicycle Club.

Cadieux Café, 4300 Cadieux Rd., Detroit, MI 48224

Phone: (313) 882-8560

Hours: Daily 4 PM–2 AM; League play, Tuesday 8 PM, Thursday 7 PM

Cost: Sunday–Thursday, $25/hour (per lane); Friday–Saturday, $40/hour

Website: www.cadieuxcafe.com

Directions: Six blocks east of Outer Dr. E, three blocks south of Warren Ave.

BOWL-O-RAMA

If you like bowling, feathers or not, you came to the right place—Detroit has more registered bowlers than any other city in the nation. As you drive around the metro area, you'll see that there are plenty of bowling centers to choose from, so why not visit one with something special?

Garden Bowl

4140 Woodward Ave., Detroit, (313) 833-9700, http://majesticdetroit.com/majestic-detroit-bowling/

Part of the Majestic Entertainment Center, the 16-lane Garden Bowl is the oldest bowling alley in the country, in continuous operation since 1913. Having long since disposed of Ragtime Bowling, today they host Rock 'N' Bowl and glow-in-the-dark bowling events.

Thunderbowl

4200 Allen Rd., Allen Park, (313) 928-4688, http://thunderbowl.org/

With 90 lanes, Thunderbowl is the largest bowling complex in the state, and the second largest bowling center in the nation. It is also home to the Greater Detroit Bowling Association Hall of Fame (www.mdusbc.com). If none of that excites the kids you've dragged along, Thunderbowl also has a large video arcade.

Duckpin Bowling

Bobby's Bar, Grand Hotel, 286 Grand Ave., Mackinac Island, (800) 33-GRAND, www.grandhotel.com

When you think of duckpin bowling, you probably think of New England, where it's still popular, right? As it turns out, the oldest duckpin alley in the United States is located in Bobby's Bar at the Grand Hotel on Mackinac Island. Of course, you have to stay there to play, so it might be cheaper to fly to Boston to get your fix.

Harry Houdini Death Site

The trouble began on October 19, 1926, after Harry Houdini spoke at McGill University in Montreal. After bragging about how he could withstand any blow to his washboard abs, he offered to be punched by 19-year-old Gerald Pickelman, a former high school football player, who enthusiastically obliged. Three days later, while lying on a couch in a dressing room at the Princess Theatre, he was pummeled four times by another McGill student, amateur boxer J. Gordon Whitehead, but this time, Houdini was decked before he could tense his stomach muscles to properly absorb the blow. And the following day, while reading a newspaper in the lobby of the Prince of Wales hotel, another young man walked in and clocked the magician when he wasn't prepared. "You shouldn't have done that," Houdini said, then left to grab a train to Detroit.

Days later, on Sunday, October 24, Houdini opened at the **Garrick Theater** (Griswold St. & Michigan Ave., torn down), but he barely made it through the performance and collapsed in a heap behind the final curtain. He returned to his suite at the **Hotel Statler** (1539 Washington Ave., torn down), but at 4 AM the next morning he was rushed to Grace Central Hospital. That afternoon, surgeons removed his ruptured appendix. Doctors gave him 12 hours to live, but he held on for almost a week, dying from peritonitis at 1:26 PM on October 31, 1926 . . . Halloween.

Did the pummeling Houdini endured in Montreal lead to his death? Medical experts disagree, and there was no autopsy, but the blows couldn't have helped. The hospital where he died in Room 401 was torn down in 1979, and replaced with larger buildings at the Detroit Medical Center.

Detroit Medical Center, 3663 Woodward Ave., Detroit, MI 48201

No phone

Hours: Original building torn down

Cost: Free

Website: http://houdini.org/death.html

Directions: Just north of Mack Ave. on the east side of Woodward Ave.

GO JUMP OFF A BRIDGE

In an attempt to salvage his reputation after taking too long to escape during a performance at Detroit's **Temple Theatre** (in Campus Martius, torn down), Harry Houdini announced he would jump off the 25-foot-high **Belle Isle Bridge** wearing two pair of handcuffs. On May 4, 1907, after signing a handwritten will leaving everything to his wife, Bess, he plunged into the Detroit River while thousands watched. He successfully escaped, and the Bridge Jump went on to become one of his most popular stunts. (The Belle Isle Bridge burned in 1915, and was replaced with the current MacArthur Bridge in 1923.)

The Heidelberg Project

Tyree Guyton was tired of the blight and despair he saw in his old neighborhood—the abandoned buildings, the corner drug dealers, and the crack houses, so in 1986 he decided to do something to improve it. Starting on the 3600 block of Heidelberg Street, Guyton painted and decorated five gutted buildings, some with polka dots, others with stuffed animals, toys, and other cast-off items. His father and local children helped. Guyton called it the Heidelberg Project.

Before long, the media took notice, and caravans of art lovers and the merely curious flocked to Heidelberg Street. The traffic and attention drove off the drug dealers and made Guyton a local celebrity. The city, however, didn't appreciate the focus he was bringing to its problems and mismanagement. Bulldozers showed up unannounced one morning in November 1991 and leveled four of the decorated buildings. Guyton was angry, but he used the city-sponsored vandalism as inspiration for another project, creating a new work of art using the rubble left behind by

The Heidelberg's Polka Dot House.

the demolition crews. In February 1999, the city bulldozed again, taking down three houses this time.

For the time being, every surviving structure on Heidelberg Street is privately owned, so the city cannot tear them down, even if it had the money to do so (and it doesn't). The multi-block, outdoor museum has drawn in other artists, whose works you can see in the vacant lots, porches, and trees, as well as at the **Detroit Industrial Gallery** (www.detroitindustrialgallery.com), run by artist Tim Burke. Bring your camera; it's a bit of a visual trip.

3600 Heidelberg St., Detroit, MI 48207

Contact: Heidelberg Project (Office), 42 Watson St., Detroit, MI 48201

Phone: (313) 974-6894

Hours: Daylight hours

Cost: Free

Website: www.heidelberg.org and www.tyreeguyton.com

Directions: Two blocks east of Gratiot Ave., three blocks south of Mack Ave.

OBJECT ORANGE, THE DDD PROJECT

Driving around Detroit you may notice that a number of abandoned buildings have been painted bright orange, like hunters' vests. They're actually a specific shade: Tiggerific Orange, from Behr's Disney paint line. Since 2005 a group of mysterious artists have been trying to draw attention to the city's crumbling structures by making them extremely hard to miss. Under cover of darkness, an Object Orange crew (formerly known as the DDD Project, for "Detroit. Demolition. Disneyland.") slathers every inch of a burned-out or dangerous building with paint, and the next morning city officials turn bright red. Several of the original DDD buildings have been bulldozed, but there are still plenty around.

Highway Firsts

American roads have come a long way since 1909. That was the year crews paved 1.2 miles of Woodward Avenue, between Six and Seven Mile Roads, to create the first mile of concrete highway in America. Oh sure, the town of Bellefontaine, Ohio, used concrete—artificial stone, they called it—to pave the four streets surrounding its town square in 1891, but that was just to keep the dust down. Detroit's road was different; people could actually get up a head of steam on the stretch.

The project was handled by a company named Baker & Clancy and it cost $13,492.83. It was made up of 25-foot sections of Portland cement, crushed cobblestone, sand, and limestone, and was only 24 feet wide. Drivers loved it, and by 1916, all 27 miles of Woodward Avenue, Michigan's M-1, were paved.

Woodward Avenue was also the birthplace of the three-color traffic signal, invented by police officer William L. Potts in 1920. Red and green signals had been around since before cars, first used to direct London buggies in 1868. But Potts, the police department's superintendent of signals, built a tower at Woodward and Michigan Avenue that had three lamps facing the intersection's four approaches. At first the lights were manually operated, but a year later they were made automatic, which was only possible with a yellow caution light.

Over the years, the Detroit metro area pioneered other traffic ideas as well. In 1911 the town of Trenton painted a centerline down River Road; nobody had every thought of doing that before. (Really, people?) And on

---

DETROIT

⇒ "Detroit is a simple homogeneous orgasm which has expanded to huge size." —Edmund Wilson

⇒ Creem Magazine was founded in Detroit in 1969. Its first offices stood at 3729 Cass Avenue (since torn down).

⇒ Detroit recorded the state's highest temperature ever—112° F—on July 9, 1936. The same temperature was recorded in Mio that day as well.

Thanksgiving Day 1942, the Davison Freeway (M-8) opened, the first limited-access urban expressway in the world.

And finally, where did the infamous Michigan left—a right and a U-turn, or a U-turn and a right—come from? In 1960 the first such interchange was tested on westbound Eight Mile Road to have drivers turn left onto Livernois Avenue.

Concrete Stretch, 17100–19100 Woodward Ave., Detroit, MI 48203

Phone: (313) 75-PARK-1

Hours: Always visible

Cost: Free

Website: http://peopleforpalmerpark.org

Directions: Between Six and Seven Mile Rds., on the east side of Palmer Park.

International Memorial to the Underground Railroad

Situated as it is on the US–Canadian border, Detroit was often the last station on the Underground Railroad for ex-slaves escaping north. Estimates say between 20,000 and 30,000 people seeking freedom passed through the city between 1830 and the Civil War. Thornton and Lucie Blackburn were two of the first escapees, and they busted open the doors for all who followed.

The Blackburns had escaped bondage in Kentucky in 1831, but two years later were spotted by slave catchers in Detroit. Captured and jailed, they were ordered returned to the South. But the night before they were to be taken, Lucie Blackburn was visited by two locally prominent African American women, Mrs. George French and Mrs. Madison Lightfoot. French exchanged clothing with Blackburn, who then walked out with Lightfoot. The next morning, when Thornton Blackburn was being taken to the wharf and a southbound steamer, authorities were met by a contingent of free blacks and other abolitionists bearing clubs. The sheriff was knocked out in the fracas and Blackburn was whisked away to Canada where he was reunited with his wife.

The Blackburns were later apprehended by Canadian authorities who weren't sure if the United States could demand that the couple be extradited. The Canadians finally decided that the Blackburns could stay

That-a-way.

because they had not broken any laws in Canada. Because of this ruling, the case effectively established asylum for others seeking freedom.

Today, Detroit's role in the Underground Railroad is commemorated with a sculpture in Hart Plaza. *The Gateway to Freedom* by Ed Dwight was installed in 2001. It depicts conductor George DeBaptiste, a leader in Detroit's black community, pointing a family the way to Canada, over the river. If you go to Windsor, you'll see a companion piece, *Tower of Freedom*, where a Quaker woman welcomes a runaway.

Hart Plaza, 1 Hart Plaza, Detroit, MI 48226

Phone: (313) 877-8057

Hours: Always visible

Cost: Free

Directions: Downtown at Jefferson and Woodward Aves.

DETROIT BABIES

Detroit is the birthplace of many famous people. There are actors, including Gilda Radner, George Peppard, Lily Tomlin (Mary Jean Tomlin), Robert Wagner, Ellen Burstyn (Edna Rae Gilooly), Elaine Stritch, Tom Selleck, Tom Skerritt, Harry Morgan (Harry Bratsberg), Marlo Thomas, Piper Laurie (Rosetta Jacobs), Max Gail, Sherilyn Fenn (Sheryl Ann Fenn), Pam Dawber, Martin Milner, and Kim Hunter. And there are singers and musicians, like Della Reese (Deloreese Patricia Early), Diana Ross, Jack White, Mary Wells, Salvatore "Sonny" Bono, Freda Payne, Sufjan Stevens, William "Smokey" Robinson, Jackie Wilson, Glenn Frey, Marshall Crenshaw, and Alice Cooper (Vincent Damon Furnier).

But did you know Charles Lindbergh, Judith Guest, "Judge" Greg Mathis, Jeffrey Eugenides, John Mitchell, and Francis Ford Coppola were born here? How about Ed McMahon, Ralph Bunche, John DeLorean, Sugar Ray Robinson (Walker Smith Jr.), Nelson Algren, William Boeing, Mitt Romney, and Kemal Amin "Casey" Kasem? Detroit babies, each and every one!

Joe Louis's Big Fist

He was the World Heavyweight Champion for 12 years, but when Detroit erected a monument to Joe Louis in 1986, it raised a few eyebrows. Why? Some fussbudgets felt the 28-foot bronze mega-fist, the size of an 18-wheeler, was too violent for a town that was reeling with violence. Others thought it had something to do with the long-since-dissolved Black Panther Party.

Newsflash, gang: he was a *boxer*. Louis successfully defended the heavyweight title 25 times, starting in 1937. Best of all, one of those bouts was a rematch against Germany's Max Schmeling. Hitler had attributed Schmeling's 1936 victory to "Aryan superiority," but the second fight between the pair on June 22, 1938, lasted only one round—two minutes and four seconds, to be exact—during which Schmeling was knocked off his feet three times. His trainer threw in the towel.

Joe Louis Barrow was born in Lafayette, Alabama, but his family moved to Detroit in 1926 when he was 12 years old. The Barrows lived at **2700 Catherine Street** (today Madison Street); the Big Fist is walking distance from where the home once stood. The city's monument was created by Robert Graham and financed by *Sports Illustrated*, and today is one of the most popular artworks in the city.

Hart Plaza, 1 Hart Plaza, Detroit, MI 48226

Phone: (313) 877-8057

Hours: Always visible

Cost: Free

Website: www.robertgraham-artist.com/civic_monuments/joe_louis.html

Directions: Downtown at Jefferson and Woodward Aves.

Motown Museum

Next to the automobile industry, no other Detroit institution has had as great an impact on American culture as Motown Records. Originally billed as "The Sound of Young America," it became a big part of the soundtrack for the 1960s and '70s, introducing the world to artists such as Smokey Robinson and the Miracles, Diana Ross and the Supremes, Martha and the Vandellas, the Temptations, Mary Wells, the Four Tops, Marvin Gaye, Stevie Wonder (see page 222), Rick James, Lionel Richie, and the Jackson Five.

Motown's founder, Berry Gordy, had been trying to break into the music industry as a songwriter for a couple of years with marginal success, but after he bought a home on Grand Avenue in 1959 with wife-to-be Raynoma Liles, things really took off. The couple lived upstairs, but the ground floor became Motown's offices—what Gordy proclaimed as Hitsville, USA on a sign out front. The home's garage was converted into Studio A, known by performers and producers as the "Snake Pit." The first song recorded at the Motown studio was "Money (That's What I Want)."

The Snake Pit's garage location turned out to be both a curse and a blessing. On the one hand, engineers had to turn off the air-conditioning and place a guard by the bathroom to avoid having hums or flushes on the

The place they did the things they did.

tracks whenever they were recording. On the other hand, the building's unique (and flawed) acoustics created an echo, which became part of the signature Motown Sound. Also, before any Motown song was released, Gordy ran it through a mocked-up cheap car radio to hear how it would sound to most listeners, an idea he came up with during a short, unhappy stint on a Lincoln-Mercury assembly line.

Motown moved its office downtown to the **Donovan Building** (2457 Woodward Ave., torn down) in 1968, though it continued to record at the Snake Pit until the whole operation moved to Los Angeles in 1972. Gordy's older sister, Ester Gordy Edwards, saved the original studio and archives, and later turned it into a museum. Here you'll see a great collection of

---

DETROIT
➡ Two African lions have been found in separate incidents at abandoned Detroit crack houses.

Gordy artifacts, including a Michael Jackson sequined glove and black hat, three 32-pound spangled Supremes dresses, Stevie Wonder's favorite candy machine, and Studio A, just as it looked when Motown went west. The studio's famous piano was recently refurbished, a project paid for by Paul McCartney.

2648 W. Grand Blvd., Detroit, MI 48208

Phone: (313) 875-2264

Hours: September–June, Tuesday–Saturday 10 AM–6 PM; July–August, Monday–Friday 10 AM–6 PM, Saturday 10 AM–8 PM

Cost: Adults $10, Seniors (62+) $8, Kids (5–12) $8

Website: www.motownmuseum.com

Directions: Five blocks west of the John C. Lodge Freeway (M-10) on Grand Blvd.

MOTOWN MANIA!

Of course, not all of the Motown magic occurred at 2648 W. Grand Boulevard. The city is filled with historic music sites . . . or at least the vacant lots where those sites once stood.

Berry Gordy's Childhood Home

Farnsworth & St. Antoine Sts., Detroit (torn down)

The Gordy Family was a tight-knit family, to put it mildly. Berry was the seventh of eight children born to Bertha and Berry "Pops" Gordy, owners of the adjacent Booker T. Washington Grocery Store. Berry Junior was born at home on November 28, 1929. The Gordys had an improvement fund, named the Ber-Berry Fund, from which family members could borrow if every member approved. It was an $800 family loan that young Berry used to establish Motown. Yet it came with strings attached, namely, many of the Gordy family were involved in business operations of the record label.

Berry Gordy Discovers the Miracles

Flame Show Bar, 4264 John R St., Detroit (gone)

Berry Gordy's musical career began at the Flame Show Bar. Gordy's sisters Gwen and Anna ran the club's cigarette and photo concessions, and Berry loved to hang out and listen to the acts. The Flame Show's owner, Al Green (not the one you're thinking of), was also Jackie Wilson's manager, and it was Green who bought Gordy's first song: "Reet Petite." Wilson recorded it, and it reached #11 on Billboard's R&B chart. Gordy would later write other Wilson hits, including "That Is Why (I Love You So)" and "Lonely Teardrops."

One day in 1957, hanging out in the Flame Show's offices before the club opened, Gordy met the Matadors, a high school group that had come in for an audition. Green's successor, Nat Tarnopol (Green had died), turned them away, but Gordy asked their 17-year-old leader, William "Smokey" Robinson if he wanted to write songs with him, and in exchange Gordy would help the Matadors make a few recordings. In 1958, Gordy produced their first singles, "Get a Job" and "My Mama Done Told Me," released under the group's new name: the Miracles.

Berry Gordy Meets the Temptations

St. Stephen's Community Center, 4329 Central Ave., Detroit, (313) 841-0783

In 1959, while Berry Gordy was managing the Miracles, but before he founded Motown, he brought the group to a show at St. Stephen's Community Center. The Miracles were supposed to close the show, but the screaming crowds wouldn't let another act, the Distants, leave the stage. Yet one member, Otis Williams, was able to sneak off to the bathroom where he found himself side-by-side with Gordy at the urinals. Gordy told them he liked their act, and suggested the Distants join his yet-established label. Two years later the group signed on with Miracle Records, a Motown subsidiary, as the Temptations.

Berry Gordy Discovers Mary Wells

20 Grand, 14th St. & W. Warren Ave., Detroit

It wouldn't be fair to say Berry Gordy discovered Mary Wells; more accurately, she thrust her talent upon him. In 1960 Wells approached Gordy as he left the 20 Grand, a popular Detroit nightclub. The 17-year-old had a song that she thought would be good for Jackie Wilson, "Bye, Bye, Baby," and wanted a chance to stop by Motown's offices. Gordy asked her to sing it a cappella, out on the street. She did, and he told her to come to Hitsville the next day, where he soon signed her up.

Berry Gordy and the Supremes

Brewster-Douglass Housing Projects, 2700 St. Antoine St., Detroit (torn down)

In the summer of 1960, four young women from the Brewster-Douglass housing projects showed up at Hitsville. Florence Ballard had formed the Primettes by inviting Mary Wilson, Diane Ross, and Betty McGlown to join her. Gordy passed them in the studio's waiting area while they were auditioning for Motown's Robert Bateman, and Gordy told them to come back after they graduated high school, though they didn't wait that long. McGlown dropped out before the others signed contracts in 1961; they started by singing backup vocals on other performers' tracks. Ballard came up with the group's new name, the Supremes, but Ross quickly elbowed her way into a leadership roll, mostly by wrapping Gordy around her finger. She also started referring to herself as Diana, and irritated most Motown performers, who called her Miss-Ross-to-You behind her back. It was nothing new. "When she was poor, living with her parents, she was just as snotty as she is now," an acquaintance later observed, "So her fame didn't make her snotty."

Motown Discovers Stevie Wonder

2701 Hastings St., Detroit (torn down)

After leaving Saginaw (see page 222), the Judkins family moved into an apartment near the Brewster-Douglass housing project. Here young Steveland Judkins's musical talents blossomed with each new instrument he was given, first a harmonica, then drums, and finally a thirdhand piano. When he wasn't singing in the choir at the **White Stone Baptist Church** (today the New White Stone Missionary Baptist Church, 13343 Fenkell St., (313) 491-7850), he was usually on the front porch of the family's apartment, wailing away. A member of his congregation passed by the home one day and saw him playing the bongos, which got him tossed from the choir, but Steveland was also here when he was spotted by his cousin Ronnie White (of the Miracles), who thought Berry Gordy should meet him. In 1961, after hearing Steveland play, Gordy put the 11-year-old under contract as Stephen Hardaway Judkins, soon to be known as Little Stevie Wonder.

Berry Gordy Discovers the Marvelettes

Inkster High School, 3250 Middlebelt Rd., Inkster, (734) 326-8519, http://inksterhs.sharpschool.net/

The Marvelettes got their start in 1960 through the glee club at Inkster High School in suburban Detroit. At first the quintet called themselves the Casinyets, as in Can't Sing Yets, but later changed their name to the Marvels. In 1961 they finished fourth in the school's talent show. Gordy liked their sound, and asked them to audition at Motown with a song they wrote themselves: "Please, Mr. Postman." Impressed, Gordy signed the group as the Marvelettes; a reworked version of that song became the studio's first #1 pop hit.

Motown Discovers Martha and the Vandellas

20 Grand, 14th St. & W. Warren Ave., Detroit

The same nightclub where Berry Gordy first met Mary Wells also brought Martha and the Vandellas to Motown. After a set at the 20 Grand in 1962, Martha Lavaille (later Reeves) was invited by Motown's Mickey Stevenson to audition for the label.

She showed up on the wrong day and was offered a reception-ist's job instead. But Lavaille's talent was unmistakable, and when Mary Wells failed to show up for a session one day, she was given a chance to record with her new group, the Del-Phis. Gordy signed them up as the Vandellas, a combination of Van Dyke Avenue and Della Reese.

Gordy Mansion

918 W. Boston Blvd., Detroit

Once the cash really started rolling in, Berry Gordy upgraded his living arrangements by buying a three-story mansion in Detroit's Boston-Edison neighborhood in 1969. It had an Olym-pic-size swimming pool, a two-lane bowling alley, an English pub, and even a secret tunnel. Aware of his authoritarian repu-tation around Motown, Gordy commissioned a painting of him-self as Napoleon Bonaparte to hang in the ballroom. When the Jackson Five visited, they had the run of the top floor. Gordy kept this home even after moving to Los Angeles, but eventu-ally sold it in 2002.

Florence Ballard's Tragic End

Detroit Memorial Park East, 4280 E. 13 Mile Rd., Warren, (877) 751-1313, www.detroitmemorialpark.com

After being unceremoniously forced out of the Supremes by Diana Ross and Berry Gordy in 1967, Florence Ballard slid downhill fast. Her solo career never took off, and she ended up broke and sick in a home at **17701 Shaftsbury Street** in Detroit. On February 21, 1976, she entered **Mt. Carmel Mercy Hospital** with numbness in her extremities. She died of a heart attack the next day at the age of 32. Ballard's funeral was held at the New Bethel Baptist Church (see page 230); when Diana Ross showed up for the service, the assembled mourners booed and hissed. But at least she showed up; Gordy didn't even attend, though he paid for Ballard's funeral.

Nancy Kerrigan Gets Clubbed

"Why? Whyyyyy? Whyyyyyyy?" cried Nancy Kerrigan as she grasped her right knee, having just been struck by a baton-wielding goon following a practice session at Detroit's Cobo Arena. The assault on January 6, 1994, forced Kerrigan to withdraw from the National Figure Skating Championships, and two days later Tonya Harding was holding a gold medal and an invitation to the upcoming Winter Olympics in Lillehammer, Norway.

Mean Girl Harding was an obvious suspect from the beginning. (She once said of competing in the Olympics, "To be perfectly honest, what I'm thinking about are dollar signs.") The attacker, Shane Stant, and getaway driver Derrick Smith were soon linked back to Jeff Gillooly, Harding's ex-husband, and Shane Eckhardt, her no-neck bodyguard. The final planning had taken place at a Detroit-area Super 8 motel. Though Gillooly copped a plea before the Olympics to testify against Harding, the wheels of justice didn't turn fast enough to prevent Harding from competing. Her threatened lawsuit certainly helped persuade Olympic officials to back off as well.

Kerrigan went on to win a silver medal in Lillehammer, bested by Ukraine's Oksana Baiul. Harding blamed a shoelace malfunction for her poor showing. All three men involved in Kerrigan's attack served prison time; Harding was given three years' probation and 500 hours of community service for impeding an investigation, fined $160,000, and ordered to undergo a psychiatric examination. She was also barred for life from any events sponsored by the US Figure Skating Association. For a while she took up boxing, and pounded Paula Jones in a 2002 bout broadcast on Fox TV's *Celebrity Boxing*.

Cobo Arena, 1 Washington Blvd., Detroit, MI 48226

Phone: (313) 877-8777

Hours: Always visible; check website for events

Cost: Free

Website: www.cobocenter.com

Directions: Above the tunnel on the John C. Lodge Fwy. (Rte. 10), where it meets the river.

Detroit Super 8, Metro Airport, Room 122, 9863 Middlebelt Rd., Romulus, MI 48174

Phone: (734) 946-8808

Hours: Always visible

Cost: Free; Rooms, check website

Website: www.super8.com

Directions: North of Goddard Rd. on the east side of the airport.

ALSO AT COBO

The attack on Nancy Kerrigan is not the only pop culture happening to take place at Cobo Arena. Of course, today it is home to the annual **North American International Auto Show** (www.naias.com), which most people just call the Detroit Auto Show. But two popular rock albums were also recorded here. Anyone in the Kiss Army (www.kissonline.com) knows that the band's first live album **Alive!** was recorded in part at the venue in 1975. Later the same year, Bob Seger & The Silver Bullet Band (www.bobseger.com) recorded **'Live' Bullet** during two September shows at the arena. The bestselling album was released in 1976. Cobo Hall is also where **Martha Reeves and the Vandellas** parted ways, following a concert on December 21, 1971.

Orsel and Minnie McGhee House

Ossian and Gladys Sweet are often credited with integrating Detroit housing (see next entry), but their courageous stance was mainly a victory over the criminal charges stemming from the shootout that transpired after their arrival. Not until 1944 did a black family, Orsel and Minnie McGhee and their two children, achieve a victory over the city's restrictive local covenants.

Shortly after the McGhee family moved into an all-white community in 1944, they were sued by their next-door neighbors, Benjamin and Anna Sipes. The Sipeses got a judge to nullify their home sale and order the McGhees to move out, but the McGhees refused. Thurgood Marshall argued the McGhees' case all the way to the US Supreme Court where, in its 1948 *Sipes v. McGhee* decision, the justices ruled that restrictive covenants violated the Constitution's Fourteenth Amendment.

4626 Seebaldt Ave., Detroit, MI 48204

No phone

Hours: Always visible

Cost: Free

Website: http://detroit1701.org/McGheeHome.html

Directions: Two blocks north of Tireman Ave., two blocks west of I-96.

Ossian and Gladys Sweet House

It is important to remember that the desegregation of American society was achieved not through government action but through the determination of people willing to put their lives at risk by challenging restrictive covenants. In Detroit, Ossian and Gladys Sweet, and Orsel and Minnie McGhee (see previous entry) paid the price, and won the victories, that eventually ended institutionalized racism in housing.

In 1925, Ossian Sweet, a prominent Detroit doctor, and his wife, Gladys, purchased a home on the city's east side for $18,500. The Sweets' new neighbors, who were white, met at the **Howe School** (2600 Garland St.) on July 14, where they formed the Waterworks Park Improvement Association. Its stated goal was to keep the neighborhood segregated, and its members threatened to dynamite the Sweets' home if they dared move in.

Yet the Sweets did just that on September 8, assisted by nine armed friends and the police. The next evening a mob attacked the house, hurling rocks and bottles through the family's windows. When they rushed the front porch, shots from inside the house killed one member of the mob who stood across the street, and injured another.

Ossian Sweet and ten others were charged with first-degree murder, but only Sweet and his brother Henry went to trial. They were defended in court by Clarence Darrow, who had been hired by the local NAACP chapter. (The case led to the creation of the NAACP Legal Defense Fund.) The doctor's trial ended in a hung jury, and his brother was found innocent by a second jury, which ruled that he had the right to defend his brother and

The Ossian and Gladys Sweet house.

sister-in-law against violence. After being reunited, Ossian and Gladys Sweet lived in their Garland Avenue home until 1944.

2905 Garland St., Detroit, MI 48214

No phone

Hours: Always visible

Cost: Free

Website: http://detroit1701.org/SweetHome.htm

Directions: Three blocks east of Cadillac Ave., at Charlevoix Ave.

Point of Origin?

Everyone and everything has to start somewhere. Visitors to Detroit can be forgiven for thinking that the bronze plaque outside the Fountain Bistro in Campus Martius Park labeled "Point of Origin" would be that spot. But upon closer inspection, you'll see that it just marks the point from where Augustus Brevoort Woodward started laying out the *new* Detroit in 1806, following the Great Fire of 1805. The city was actually founded on July 24, 1701, by Antoine Laumet de la Mothe, sieur du Cadillac, who the French governor of Acadia described as "the most uncooperative person in the world . . . a scatterbrain who has been driven out of France for who knows what crimes." But that's another story.

Woodward was inspired by Pierre L'Enfant's plan for the nation's capital, with avenues radiating like spokes connecting circular plazas. But Woodward was not given the authority to compel landowners to divide their land according to his new map, which is why Detroit has such a strange tangle of streets downtown, but a grid everywhere else. Thanks a lot, Augustus.

Campus Martius Park, 800 Woodward Ave., Detroit, MI 48226
Phone: (313) 962-0101
Hours: Daily 7 AM–10 PM
Cost: Free
Website: www.campusmartiuspark.com
Directions: At the intersection of Woodward Ave., Monroe St., and Michigan Ave.

Tomb of the Boy Governor

Talk about an overachiever! Democrat Stevens T. Mason was just 19 years old in 1831 when he was appointed secretary of the Michigan Territory by President Andrew Jackson. Mason then became acting governor in 1834 when his boss, Governor George Porter, perished in an Asiatic fever epidemic that wiped out 1 in 7 Michigan citizens. At the same time as voters approved the state's constitution in 1835, Mason was elected the first governor, though he wasn't officially recognized in Washington until the state joined the Union on January 26, 1837. He commissioned the state's first flag—today known as the Brady Guard flag—which had his portrait on one side; it was never adopted by the legislature. Mason was reelected later that year, but after an economic downturn he decided not to run in 1839.

After leaving office, Mason left the state entirely to set up a law practice in New York City. It was there, following a New Year's Eve bash, that he succumbed to pneumonia and died on January 4, 1843. He was just 31 years old. Though a "funeral" was held in Detroit, minus Mason's body, he was buried in Marble Cemetery in New York's East Village. In 1905, when it looked like that graveyard would be redeveloped, the Mason family decided to move his body back to Detroit.

In June 1905, a second funeral was held for the Boy Governor, and this time he was in attendance. His body was reburied downtown at the site of the state's first capitol building (1828–1847), which had burned down in 1893. Three years later a statue of Mason by Albert Weinert, cast in bronze that was melted down from the cannons of Fort Michilimackinac, was placed over his grave. In 1955 the triangular Capitol Park was redeveloped into a transit center, and it looked as if Mason's grave would be moved again, this time to Lansing. The city quickly relocated the body, covered it with a stone pedestal, and put the statue on top. He had to be dug up one more time, in 2010, when the park was again refurbished. That's where you'll find him today, housed in an aboveground vault.

Capitol Park, Shelby & Griswold Sts., Detroit, MI 48226

No phone

Hours: Always visible

Cost: Free

Website: http://boyguv.com/

Directions: Just north of State St., one block north of Michigan Ave., one block west of Woodward Ave.

SUBURBS

Allen Park
World's Largest Tire

It looms 86 feet tall alongside I-94, east of the airport—the World's Largest Tire. More than just a promotional gimmick, it was a working Ferris wheel in the US Rubber Pavilion at the 1964–65 New York World's Fair, transporting such luminaries as Jackie Kennedy and the Shah of Iran. But when the fair was finished, the tire was disassembled and rebuilt in this Motor City suburb, its 24 gondolas removed and replaced with an all-weather tread.

Able to withstand 11-foot nails.

In 1994, the 12-ton whitewall got a new hubcap and neon lighting. And in 1998, when Uniroyal wanted to advertise its Tiger Paw NailGard feature, it ordered a 250-pound, 11-foot nail and jammed it into the structure. And it didn't go flat!

In 2003 the tire was refurbished once again. The whitewall was painted black, the hole patched, and the nail was auctioned off on eBay, earning $3,000 for the local historical society. The nail was purchased by Allen Park businessman Ralph Roberts, who has kept it in the community; you can still see it making appearances at local events.

Enterprise Dr., Allen Park, MI 48101

No phone

Hours: Always visible; best viewed from eastbound I-94

Cost: Free

Website: www.uniroyaltires.com/about/gianttire.html

Directions: On the south side of I-94, just east of the Southfield Rd. interchange.

Bloomfield Hills
Jimmy Hoffa Disappears

It's the same story every few years: the feds cordon off a vacant lot or suburban backyard, fire up the backhoe, and start digging while news outlets speculate, "Has Jimmy Hoffa been found at last?" So far, the answer to that question has always been the same: nope.

The last time anyone saw the labor leader alive was on July 30, 1975, at around 2:30 PM. Hoffa had gone to the Machus Red Fox Restaurant in Bloomfield Hills to meet with Anthony "Tony Jack" Giacalone and Anthony "Tony Pro" Provenzano. Hoffa called home from a nearby hardware store, asking why Tony (not saying which Tony) hadn't shown up yet. Soon it was Hoffa who was missing.

There was no evidence that Hoffa was forcibly taken from the restaurant. Investigators believe he left with someone he mistakenly trusted, probably Charles "Chuckie" O'Brien, who drove a maroon Mercury sedan that some witnesses spotted in the area. The Hoffas had raised Chuckie since the age of three following the death of his father, but he was also a friend of Giacalone. Tony Jack and Tony Pro were incredibly, publicly visible that day—a sure clue that they were somehow involved. O'Brien offered cops a cockamamie alibi, something about taking his Mercury to a carwash because a coho salmon he had delivered to an associate had bled all over the backseat, and he needed the upholstery scrubbed. *Riiiiight.*

So where did Hoffa go? The FBI's best theory was that he was "taken for a ride" by Salvatore "Sally Bugs" Briguglio and Frank "The Irishman" Sheeran. Author Charles Brandt (*I Heard You Paint Houses: Frank "The Irishman" Sheeran and Closing the Case on Jimmy Hoffa*, 2004) claims that Sheeran confessed in a deathbed letter to taking Hoffa to **17841 Beaverland Street** in Detroit, shooting him, and incinerating his body. Sheeran's daughter insists the letter is a forgery.

And that's just one story. Maybe Donald "Tony the Greek" Frankos shot Hoffa at a Detroit home, chopped up his body, stuck it in a basement freezer, and later transferred it to an oil drum that was buried in the end zone of New Jersey's Giants Stadium. Or perhaps he was executed, rolled in a rug, and buried in Bay City. Or beneath a garage in Cadillac, or a barn in Milford. Or bulldozed into a Highland gravel pit. Or fried in a vat of liquid zinc. Or chipped in an industrial tire shredder. Maybe he was flattened in a Hamtramck car compactor, entombed in a block of concrete off Key West, or dumped in the Pine Barrens of New Jersey. Perhaps he was stabbed in the head by Richard "The Ice Man" Kuklinski, sealed in a drum, sold as scrap to a Japanese auto manufacturer, and made into a car bumper. And some people think he never left Bloomfield Hills, and remains buried beneath a mansion's swimming pool near Turtle Lake. *These are all theories that have been taken seriously by the FBI.*

Whatever the case, Hoffa was declared dead on July 30, 1982. Does knowing why really matter at this point?

Joe Vicari's Andiamo Italian Steakhouse (former Machus Red Fox Restaurant), 6676 Telegraph Rd., Bloomfield Hills, MI 48301

Phone: (248) 865-9300

Hours: Monday–Thursday 11:30 AM–10 PM, Friday 11:30 AM–11 PM, Saturday 4–11 PM, Sunday 4–9 PM

Cost: Free; Lunch, $10–25; Dinner, $15–50

Website: www.andiamoitalia.com/michigan-locations/bloomfield-township

Directions: On Rte. 24 (Telegraph Rd.), one block south of Maple Rd.

Chesterfield and New Baltimore
Avenue of the Giants

You might suspect there's something strange in the water as you drive northeast on I-94 out of Detroit. Growth hormones, perhaps? As you pass Exit 237 in Mt. Clemens, it's hard to miss the four-story English dandy in a bow tie and bowler standing beside the highway, a sign for the **Gibraltar Trade Center** (237 N. River Rd., (586) 465-6440, www.gilbraltartrade .com). Then you exit at 23 Mile Road eastbound in Chesterfield, and pass a **Big Boy** (29300 23 Mile Rd., (586) 949-1700, www.bigboy.com) hoisting a burger high over his head. Still, nothing particularly weird—Big Boys are everywhere in Michigan.

But then a few blocks later you spot a huge, fiberglass, great white shark hanging on the façade of **Captain's Car Wash** (29600 23 Mile Rd., (586) 948-4500). What's going on here? A couple miles after that, you see a 25-foot-tall stucco golfer in a green cap at the **RiverBend Driving Range** (33190 23 Mile Rd., (586) 725-8987, http://riverbenddrivingrange.weebly .com) on the south side of the highway. His stance says he's ready to tee off, but he has no club in his hands.

And finally you pass into New Baltimore and see where all this enormity originates from: a miniature golf course run by **World's Finest Frozen Custard**, its holes surrounded by dozens of mismatched, oversized commercial statues. An old steakhouse Angus steer, a patriotically painted huge Holstein, a pink hippo, a pinker elephant, a colossal chicken, a big buffalo, a large lion, a huge A&W "Teen" holding a soft-serve ice cream cone, and several swan boats from Boblo Island's Tunnel of Love. And watching over it all from a stone pedestal, a 15-foot Muffler Man in a wide-brimmed white hat and green shirt they've named Greg E. Normous, master of it all.

World's Finest Frozen Custard & Mini Golf, 33538 23 Mile Rd., New Baltimore, MI 48047

Phone: (586) 725-1315

Hours: Always visible; Store, March–October, daily 11 AM–9 PM

Cost: Free; Custard, $2.75 and up; Crazy Golf, $4/person

Website: www.worldsfinestfrozencustard.com

Directions: Two blocks west of Baker Rd. on Rte. 29 (23 Mile Rd.).

Commerce
Backyard Breeder Reactor

From an early age, David Hahn loved chemistry and physics. Neighborhood kids called him a mad scientist since he was always showing up with some new chemistry trick to try and impress them. After Hahn's parents divorced in 1985, when he was nine, his father convinced him to join the Boy Scouts, Clinton Township Troop 371, which met at the VFW Hall in Mt. Clemons. Hahn soon focused on earning one badge in particular: the Atomic Energy merit badge.

Ever since he'd read about Marie and Pierre Curie in *The Golden Book of Chemistry Experiments*, Hahn had wanted to be like them, so he created his own backyard laboratory. He believed that nuclear power might ease his parents' problems paying their gas and electric bills. So, like any good Boy Scout, he took the initiative. He would solve the world's energy crisis *and* earn that merit badge—he would build a breeder reactor!

After conducting a fair amount of research, the 17-year-old Hahn uncovered where to locate all the radioactive elements necessary to build his own device: americium-241 pellets from a smoke detector, thorium dioxide from gas-lantern mantles, radium scraped off the numbers of old glow-in-the-dark clocks, and tritium from a night vision gun site. He found pitchblende (uranium ore) by simply wandering around northern Michigan with a Geiger counter. And as a Boy Scout, he was able to talk a local civil defense agency out of a lead suit —"for a demonstration," he told them. He never returned it.

Though Hahn spent weekdays at his father's home in Clinton Township, where he attended **Chippewa Valley High School** (18300 19 Mile Rd.), on weekends he stayed with his mother in the Golf Manors subdivision in suburban Commerce Township. Most of his processing and refining work took place in a potting shed behind his mother's home, on which he had painted a red "radioactive hazard" symbol—safety first!—not that anyone noticed. He often worked late into the night, burning, mixing, and reacting materials to get the components he needed.

In a lucky accident, the Clinton Township police busted Hahn by mistake on August 31, 1994, while responding to reports of a tire thief. Asked to open his car's trunk, they found a toolbox filled with strange, wrapped materials. Worried that it might be a nuclear device, they had the car towed to the police station. Investigators soon realized what a hazardous mess they had on their hands, yet it wasn't until the following spring that the EPA figured out that they had a second radioactive hot spot in the Golf Manor shed. On June 26, 1995, workers in hazmat suits hauled away the shed in a scene out of *E.T.* Neighbors were left to guess why.

Strangely enough, Hahn hadn't broken any laws, which is not to say he didn't get in trouble; his dad grounded him for two weeks and took away his car keys. The Boy Scouts still offer the Atomic Energy merit badge, though today it is called the Nuclear Science merit badge.

Golf Manors, Pinto Dr., Commerce, MI 48382

Private phone

Hours: Always visible; view from street

Cost: Free

Directions: North off Commerce Rd., four blocks west of Union Lake Rd.

CLAWSON CITY
➡ You may legally sleep with your chickens, cows, goats, and goats in Clawson City.

DEARBORN
➡ Rocker Bob Seger was born in Dearborn on May 6, 1945.

"WE ALMOST LOST DETROIT"

Detroit has been in far more danger of radioactive destruction than when it faced a reckless kid with a talent for chemistry. Back on October 5, 1966, the **Enrico Fermi Nuclear Generating Station** (www.dteenergy.com/nuclear/) in Newport, southwest of the city, had a partial meltdown. A spigot in the Fermi 1 reactor clogged, causing the core temperature to pass 700°F and melting several fuel rods. Never heard of this accident? Then some PR firm earned its commission . . .

The Fermi plant is still operating its Fermi 2 reactor. On August 8, 2008, three weeks before announcing Sara Palin as his running mate, presidential candidate John McCain visited the facility to push for more nuclear plants in the United States, including a Fermi 3 reactor. He sure could pick 'em!

Dearborn

The Henry Ford/Greenfield Village

Next to the Smithsonian, there's no better museum to find America's pop culture junk, the *good stuff,* than the Henry Ford and its sister institution, Greenfield Village. The front entrance to the Henry Ford was designed to resemble Independence Hall, but the interior is a wide-open space reminiscent of a 1920s Ford assembly factory, and it's BIG. The building was dedicated October 21, 1929, on the 50th anniversary of the creation of the lightbulb. Among the guests in attendance were Marie Curie, Orville Wright, President Herbert Hoover, and Will Rogers. Albert Einstein was patched in via radio from Germany.

Ford's collection started with mostly industrial junk, but has grown to include so much more, including:

⇒ the Montgomery city bus on which Rosa Parks was arrested

⇒ Mahatma Gandhi's spinning wheel

- Edison's "last breath" in a test tube, one of eight that rested on a table next to his death bed (Edison believed in reincarnation, and that his soul would depart on his last breath)
- an Oscar Mayer Wienermobile
- the first Blue Bird school bus
- George Washington's folding camp bed
- Abraham Lincoln's bloodstained rocking chair from Ford's Theatre
- John Kennedy's death-limo, a 1961 Lincoln
- Ronald Reagan's near-death-limo, a 1972 Lincoln
- Alexander Graham Bell's patent model for the telephone
- a working replica of *The Spirit of St. Louis* from the 1957 Jimmy Stewart film
- Buckminster Fuller's Dymaxion House
- the largest steam locomotive ever built
- an original Holiday Inn room
- Charles Kuralt's 1975 "On the Road" Ford Motor Coach
- a 1934 letter from Clyde Barrow thanking Ford for his quality V-8 getaway cars

Even at a brisk pace it'll take you half a day to get through it all. When you're ready for a break, have a bite at the Michigan Café—all the food comes from the Great Lakes State. Once you're done, it's off to Greenfield Village. Henry Ford tried to re-create an idyllic town from his youth, but populate it with homes and businesses of the famous. (He even tried to buy the Eiffel Tower, but the French turned him down.) You'll see:

- a replica of Thomas Edison's Menlo Park lab
- a replica of Thomas Edison's Menlo Park machine shop
- a replica of Thomas Edison's Menlo Park office and library

- Thomas Edison's Fort Myers lab
- Thomas Edison's grandparents' Canadian homestead
- the Wright brothers' Dayton bicycle shop and home
- Orville Wright's 1871 Ohio birthplace
- Robert Frost's Ann Arbor home
- the Logan County Courthouse from Postville, Illinois, where Lincoln practiced law
- Noah Webster's Connecticut home where he wrote his *American Dictionary of the English Language*
- Harvey S. Firestone's Ohio birthplace (and livestock)
- a replica of George Washington Carver's Missouri birthplace
- H. J. Heinz's Pennsylvania home where he developed his horseradish sauce
- Luther Burbank's garden office (from California) behind his Massachusetts birthplace
- Henry Ford's birthplace, moved here from nearby Greenfield in 1944
- a replica of Ford's first auto plant

And if you still can walk, come back the next day to take the Ford Rouge Factory Tour. Busses to the plant leave from the Henry Ford. You'll watch the entire assembly line from an 80-foot-high observation deck, as well as get a look at the complex's 10.4-acre living roof.

20900 Oakwood Blvd., Dearborn, MI 48124
Phone: (800) 835-5237 or (313) 982-6001
Hours: Museum, daily 9:30 AM–5 PM; Village, April–October, 9:30 AM–5 PM, November, Friday–Sunday 9:30 AM–5 PM
Cost: Museum, Adults $17, Seniors (62+) $15, Kids (5–12) $12.50; Village, Adults $24, Seniors $22, Kids $17.50; Combo, Adults $35, Seniors $30, Kids $25.50; Factory Tour, Adults $15, Seniors $14, Kids $11
Website: www.hfmgv.org
Directions: North 2.5 miles on Oakwood Blvd. from I-94.

ROSA PARKS IN MICHIGAN

The 1950s city bus at the Henry Ford isn't the only legacy from the Montgomery Bus Boycott that ended up in Michigan—so did Rosa Parks herself. Unable to find work in Alabama, Parks and her husband, Raymond, moved to Hampton, Virginia, in 1957, and then to Detroit later that year. Parks continued to work as a seamstress until 1965 when she was hired to be the receptionist at the office of Congressman John Conyers. She lived out of the public eye until her husband died in 1977, then returned to assist the civil rights movement into the 1980s. In 1987 she established the **Rosa and Raymond Parks Institute for Self Development** (www.rosaparks.org) with her friend Elaine Eason Steele. The Michigan-based foundation teaches schoolchildren about the Underground Railroad and the civil rights movement, and it also supports jobs programs and community development. Parks received the Congressional Medal of Honor in 1999, and died in Detroit on October 24, 2005. She and her family have been entombed in the **Rosa L. Parks Freedom Chapel** at Woodlawn Cemetery (19975 Woodward Ave., (313) 368-0100, http://woodlawncemeterydetroit.com) in northwest Detroit.

Farmington Hills
Marvin's Marvelous Mechanical Museum

There aren't many museums where you're allowed to touch everything, but then Marvin's Marvelous Mechanical Museum isn't just any museum—it's an amusement parlor, too! Of course, it'll cost you. There's no entrance fee, but you're going to be dropping a lot of quarters before you leave.

Marvin Yagoda opened his collection of coin-operated games and amusements to the public in 1990, though today it is run by his son Jeremy. Every square inch of floor space is jammed with pinball machines, love meters, dancing robotic animals, space simulators, jukeboxes, flip movie projectors, and the oldest gypsy fortuneteller in existence (1923).

Fun and educational!

You'll certainly believe the Yagodas' claim: "Over 1,000 electrical outlets, all used." The best pieces in the collection are the antique mechanical shows where a morality play or goofy visual joke plays out before you. A hooded criminal drops from the gallows in front of a French prison. A band of six monkeys plays a happy tune. The Spanish Inquisition tortures infidels in a dungeon. No, this isn't all kid stuff.

When you run out of quarters, there's still plenty to see. Over your head, 50 airplane models circle the room on a moving track. Carnival banners, movie posters, magicians' playbills, and neon signs cover the very tall walls. And funky artifacts are jammed in everywhere, including an original spotlight from Alcatraz and a 15-foot-tall fake Cardiff Giant made for P. T. Barnum.

31005 Orchard Lake Rd., Farmington Hills, MI 48334

Phone: (248) 626-5020

Hours: Monday–Thursday 10 AM–9 PM, Friday–Saturday 10 AM–11 PM, Sunday 11 AM–9 PM.

Cost: Free

Website: http://marvin3m.com

Directions: Three blocks south of 14 Mile Rd. and Northwestern Hwy.

Garden City

Garden City Firsts

Anywhere you go in the United States, you're likely to run into a corporate institution that started in the modest Detroit suburb of Garden City. Why? Because both Kmart and Little Caesars Pizza were born here.

Technically, Kmart grew out of another retail chain; Sebastian Kresge bought two five-and-dime stores in 1897, one on Detroit's Woodward Avenue, which he renamed S. S. Kresge. (How original!) The company expanded operations up through the start of the Great Depression, but then contracted as shoppers had fewer nickels and dimes to spend. By the 1950s, it became clear that its old-fashioned retail approach was on the way out, so S. S. Kresge reinvented itself, launching the first Kmart in Garden City on March 1, 1962. Before the end of the year, 17 more stores had opened.

Four and a half years after the launch of the first Kmart, Sebastian Kresge died at the age of 99. Stores across the nation dimmed their blue lights and closed for one hour in his honor, but then it was back to business. Though it has gone through changes in recent years, namely becoming part of the Sears retail empire, the chain's original store is still open for business in Garden City.

Big K, 29600 Ford Rd., Garden City, MI 48135

Phone: (734) 425-2450

Hours: Daily 8 AM–10 PM

Cost: Free

Website: www.kmart.com

Directions: One block west of Middlebelt Rd. on M-153 (Ford Rd.).

Three years *before* the first Kmart opened in town, Garden City also saw the first Little Caesars Pizza open in a local strip mall on May 8, 1959. Owners Mike and Marian Ilitch called it Little Caesar's Pizza Treat at first because Marian thought Mike acted like a little Caesar.

The chain eventually started offering two pizzas for the price of one under its current catchphrase, "Pizza! Pizza!" however, the long side-by-side pizza boxes are long gone. Like the first Kmart, the first Little Caesars is still standing strong and serving customers in Garden City.

32594 Cherry Hill Rd., Garden City, MI 48135

Phone: (734) 427-2820

Hours: Monday–Thursday 11 AM–11 PM, Friday–Saturday 11 AM–midnight, Sunday noon–10 PM

Cost: Free; Pizza, $5 and up

Website: www.littlecaesars.com

Directions: One block east of Venoy Rd.

Hamtramck
Disneyland North

Years ago, Dmytro Szylak immigrated to the United States from Ukraine, settled in Hamtramck, and then worked for General Motors for 32 years. When he finally retired in 1992, he didn't know what to do with his time, but he had to do *something*. Szylak decided to honor both his homeland and his adopted home, and came up with Disneyland North (sometimes called Hamtramck Disneyland).

Michigan's Mickey. Photo by author, courtesy Dmytro Szylak

No, the two-story artwork Szylak built on his garage is in no way affiliated with the Walt Disney Company, its shareholders, or affiliates. It is
instead a ramshackle tower of wood scraps, appliance fans, mannequins,
Christmas lights, plywood cutouts of soldiers, rocking horses, airplane
models, and blow-mold Santas, all slathered in buckets of bright paint—
mostly yellow and blue, the Ukrainian national colors. The city wasn't too
keen on the project at first, especially because it teetered inches from the
alley's power and telephone lines. But the more positive attention Szylak
brought to Hamtramck, the less they cared . . . as long as he disconnected
the lights on the towers.

Disneyland North can really only be appreciated from the alley, and
if you're lucky, Szylak will be in the backyard to allow you in for a closer
look. It'll cost you a "donation," but your financial contribution will go
toward maintaining this incredible, unique artwork.

12087 Klinger St., Hamtramck, MI 48212

Private phone

Hours: Daylight hours

Cost: Free; donations strongly encouraged

Directions: South of Carpenter St., two blocks west of Conant St.

Livonia
Chin's Chop Suey

Chin Tiki (2121 Cass Ave.) was a Detroit institution for almost 20 years.
It was designed by Marvin Chin to be a Polynesian paradise: thatched
hut booths, blowfish lamps, totem heads, lava rock walls covered in fake
orchids, and an indoor waterfall with a bamboo bridge on each of its two
floors—the top floor was a banquet hall with a stage that featured hula
dancers and fire breathers. The waitresses wore floral print sarongs and
the waiters wore bright Hawaiian shirts. But Chin Tiki was in the wrong
place at the wrong time: 1970s Detroit. The restaurant closed its doors in
the early 1980s, though it was used for a scene in *8 Mile* in 2002; unfortunately, the crew looted the place after filming wrapped, and dreams of
reopening never materialized. Chin died in 2006, and the building was
torn down in 2009.

A sad story, indeed, were it not that Chin also owned another South Seas establishment in suburban Livonia. Today run by Marvin's descendants, Chin's Chop Suey looks more like a standard Chinese/Polynesian restaurant—no hula dancers or scantily clad servers—but it does have plenty of tiki statues, thatched hut booths, black light murals, plastic palms, and rattan furniture to satisfy the average tikiphile. There's even an enormous clam near the register, its mouth opened wide to reveal a basketball-sized red pearl.

Towering tikis.

28205 Plymouth Rd., Livonia, MI 48150

Phone: (734) 421-1627

Hours: Monday–Thursday 11 AM–9:30 PM, Friday 11 AM–10:30 PM, Saturday 11 AM–9:30 PM, Sunday 12:30–9:30 PM

Cost: Meals, $7–12

Directions: One block east of Harrison Rd., five blocks west of Inkster Rd.

TINIER TIKIS

If you're a hip cat who digs tiki culture, there are two other Polynesian-themed establishments you can visit in southeast Michigan, though neither is a holdover from the 1950s, and together they wouldn't make a Chin's Chop Suey. But you're in the upper Midwest, so what do you expect, a Polynesian wonderland?

Waves

24223 Jefferson Ave., St. Clair Shores, (586) 773-3840, www.waveschill-lgrill.com

The two Moai heads flanking the entrance to Waves look promising, but the interior is a bit disappointing unless you snag one of the restaurant's few booths. Each blue vinyl banquette is topped with a thatched hut roof with a translucent shell pendant lamp. Fake palms, fake masks, and fake miniature outrigger canoes finish off the decorating theme, but it's a half-hula effort at best.

Mai Kai Lounge

Tecumseh Inn & Suites, 1445 W. Chicago Blvd., Tecumseh, (517) 423-7401, www.tecumsehinnsuites.com

The Mai Kai Lounge was once a drinking establishment off the lobby at the Tecumseh Inn. Five c-shaped booths, each upholstered in a different bright color, and a couple swinging rattan chairs jam the limited floor space. Green Astroturf and palm tree murals cover the walls, and the tables are painted with South Seas patterns. Today the lounge is used for serving the motel's continental breakfast, so you either have to book a room to see it, or sweet talk the front desk clerk for a peek inside.

Plymouth
United Memorial Gardens

You certainly don't have to be dead to enjoy all there is to offer at United Memorial Gardens. How many cemeteries that you know of have a full-scale replica of the Tabernacle of Moses, complete with the Ark of the Covenant? Or a gazebo with 76 "Facts of Life" etched in stone for kids to read and contemplate? Or a Gateway to Animal Heaven section, where you'll find a Pet Rest Chapel, a birdhouse-shaped mausoleum, and a large granite doghouse? United Memorial Gardens has all of these!

Best of all, however, is its strange celebration of Michigan tourist attractions in the northeast corner of the cemetery. Thirty-seven granite monuments are arranged in the shape of the state. Each one honors a different destination, with a cartoon and description carved onto each upturned slab—three boxes of cereal from Battle Creek, the salt mines of Detroit, a shopping bag from a Michigan mall, Jackson's Cascade Falls, a dune buggy on Sleeping Bear Dunes, and much, much more.

4800 Curtis Rd., Plymouth, MI 48170

Phone: (734) 454-9448

Hours: Daylight hours

Cost: Free

Website: http://unitedmemorialgardenscemetery.com

Directions: Just north of M-14 (Warren Rd.) on Curtis Rd.

Pontiac and Rochester

Madonna-rama

Though she was born in Bay City (see page 192), Madonna Louise Ciccone's family lived at **443 Thors Street** in suburban Pontiac when she greeted the world in 1958. The Ciccones would later build a home at **2036 Oklahoma Avenue** in what is today Rochester Hills, where Madonna lived until she left for the University of Michigan on a dance scholarship.

Growing up in Rochester Hills, Madonna received her first kiss at **Holy Family Regional School** (1240 Inglewood Ave.) when she was ten. Two years later she created her first on-stage scandal, dancing to the Who's "Baba O'Riley" in a skimpy dress during a performance at **St. Andrews Church** (1400 Inglewood Ave.), the same church where she would take her confirmation name, Veronica. She attended **West Middle School** (500 Old Perch Rd.) and **Rochester Adams High School** (3200 W. Tienken Rd.), where she got straight As, joined the Thespian Society, and was a cheerleader and baton twirler.

Madonna's father and stepmother lived in Rochester Hills until 2001, when they sold their home to local investors. The home was put up on eBay later that year, and joke bidding got up to a ridiculous $999 million before the bottom fell out on September 11. It was later sold at auction, and twice more, before it was gutted by a suspicious fire in 2008. The damaged house was purchased in 2012, but its future remains uncertain.

2036 Oklahoma Ave., Rochester Hills, MI 48307

Private phone

Hours: Always visible; view from street

Cost: Free

Website: www.madonna.com

Directions: Two blocks north of Walton Blvd., then two blocks east of Brewster Rd. on Oklahoma Ave. to where it turns south and becomes Texas Ave.

Redford
Silvio's Italian-American Historical Artistic Museum

From the outside it looks like any other urban storefront—clutter in the windows, a little run-down, and hard to tell if it's even open. But inside, wow: statues and dolls, postcards and photos, hand-lettered signs and portraits of popes, flags and dozens of 10-foot-tall concrete grottos encrusted with bisque figurines, broken dishware, shells, coins, plastic flowers, you name it, and it's all in honor of Italy. Italy! ITALY!!! You have just entered the fertile, creative mind of Silvio Barile, baker, artist, and cultural evangelist for all things Italian.

Barile was born in the village of Ausonia, Italy, and was just a young boy during the Nazi occupation. His family lived in a labor camp, and his father was forced to rebuild bridges and roads destroyed by Allied bombers. Silvio would sing to soldiers for extra food. Ten years after the war was over, he immigrated to the United States where, in 1961, he opened this Redford bakery and pizzeria. Troubled by media images of Italians in the 1970s, he began a one-man quest to educate America about the greatest culture in the history of humankind. (That would be Italian culture.)

In time, Barile's museum would expand to an adjoining storefront, then out into a back courtyard, and eventually across the alley to a sculpture park he calls Silvio's American Forum. There you'll find dozens of enormous concrete artworks, some 15 feet tall, each with a different theme: Emperor Constantine, the Vatican, Columbus sailing to the New World, Santa Maria, Julius Caesar, the Coliseum, the Leaning Tower of Detroit, and (in brief departures from all the Italiana) the Statue of Liberty and the Three Stooges.

The best way to experience the museum is to get a personal tour from Silvio, who will quiz you on your understanding of Italian history, break into song, and reminisce about what people today have lost sight of. He's usually here, but if not, walk around to the alley—most of his American Forum is clearly visible through the fence.

The Leaning Tower of Detroit.

26417 Plymouth Rd., Redford, MI 48269

Phone: (313) 937-2288

Hours: Call ahead, or take your chances

Cost: Free

Directions: One block west of Fordson Hwy., one block east of Southwestern Hwy.

Southfield
Bo Schembechler Death Site

It was a day Michigan Wolverines fans would just as soon forget. It shouldn't have come as any surprise—Bo Schembechler was no stranger to heart attacks. The longtime football coach had his first coronary on the last day of 1969, on the eve of the 1970 Rose Bowl, when his squad faced the USC Trojans (and ultimately lost). He had a quadruple bypass in 1976, followed by another heart attack in 1987, and another quadruple bypass.

Schembechler retired from coaching the Wolverines in 1990, with a 194–48–5 school record. But his heart, such as it was, remained in Ann Arbor. For years he cohosted a popular college pregame show with sportscaster Don Shane called *Big Ten Ticket*. After taping an episode in October 2006, he collapsed at the studio; doctors outfitted him with a pacemaker and he returned to the broadcast. Then on November 17, 2006, just before taping, Schembechler collapsed in the bathroom at station WXYZ-TV. He was rushed to **Providence Hospital** (16001 W. Nine Mile Rd.) in Southfield where he was pronounced dead. Four days later he was buried in **Forest Hill Cemetery** (415 S. Observatory St., (734) 663-5018, http://foresthillcemeteryaa.org/) in Ann Arbor, where you can find him today.

WXYZ-TV, 20777 W. 10 Mile Rd., Southfield, MI 48075

Phone: (248) 827-7777

Hours: Always visible

Cost: Free

Website: www.wxyz.com

Directions: One block west of the John C. Lodge Fwy. (M-10).

Sterling Heights

Michael Dukakis, Tank Commander

On September 13, 1988, Democratic presidential candidate Michael Dukakis came to Michigan to visit General Dynamics Land Systems and unveil his plan to purchase more tanks for the Pentagon, should he be elected. In what seemed like a slam-dunk photo-op—it had worked for Margaret Thatcher just a few years earlier—he put on a uniform and took a ride in an M1 Abrams tank.

The shots of Dukakis in an enormous helmet, tooling around a field while pointing at nothing in particular, were just what the George H. W. Bush campaign wanted. Campaign ad man Greg Stevens, under the direction of Lee Atwater, used the tank footage behind a rolling scroll of demonstrably false claims that Dukakis wanted to gut the defense budget, and TV viewers laughed, and laughed, and laughed. Never mind that Dukakis, who had served in the US Army, was being unfairly smeared by two men who never put on a uniform.

WYANDOTTE

➡ Lee Majors, the Six Million Dollar Man, was born Harvey Lee Yeary in Wyandotte on April 23, 1939.

The tank ad, along with the race-baiting Willie Horton ads, likely cost Dukakis the election, and became a blueprint for modern big-money campaigns. Don't worry about substance. Don't worry about issues. Look for the best way to mock and demonize your opponent—in the end, voters will reward your candidate.

General Dynamics Land Systems, 38500 Mound Rd., Sterling Heights, MI 48310

Phone: (586) 825-4000

Hours: Always visible

Cost: Free

Website: www.gdls.com

Directions: South of 17 Mile Rd., west of Van Dyke Ave. (M-53).

Taylor
Giant Paint Can

There are four ways you can paint a house. First, with a brush, but that's slow. A roller is faster, but you still need a brush to get into all the tight corners. Faster still is a sprayer, but who has one of those? No, what you need to get the job done pronto is a giant can that you can dip the whole building into. Where could you find one of them?

Care for a dip?

In Taylor! Looming over the intersection of Van Born and Beech Daly roads, hanging off the front corner of a local paint store, is the biggest bucket of acrylic enamel you ever did see. You might not be able to dunk a house in it, but it's certainly larger than a hot tub. Most furniture would take just a few seconds.

Model Wallpaper & Paint Co., 25757 Van Born Rd., Taylor, MI 48180

Phone: (313) 291-8800

Hours: Always visible; Store, Monday–Friday 9 AM–4:30 PM, Saturday 9–11:30 AM

Cost: Free

Directions: At Beech Daly Rd., north of I-94.

7

CHRISTMAS TOUR

There are many ways to appreciate all the strange destinations Michigan has to offer—you can even come up with your own Oddball themed tour. Given the variety of locations found in this book, you could map out a Paul Bunyan Tour, or Big and Little Bridge Tour, or Colossal Cow Tour. So to show how it's done, this chapter is devoted to the state's passion for strange yuletide sites and traditions, starting at Thanksgiving and ending on Christmas day.

Now Bill O'Reilly might claim that there's a "War on Christmas." In 2005 he reported the city of Saginaw had banned its employees from wearing green and red together. The story was fact-checked and turned out to be a complete fabrication. What *is* true is that it's illegal to sell liquor in Michigan on Christmas Day, but that's hardly an attack on any holiday tradition. You just have to buy your booze a little earlier, like Santa and Mr. O'Reilly do.

No, as will soon become clear, Michigan *lovvvvvves* Christmas. So fill up the sleigh—we're off to celebrate the season, Oddball style.

Marshall
Turkeyville U.S.A.

In the years before American retailers officially moved it to mid-September, the Christmas season always began the day after Thanksgiving, the same day you scarfed down cold turkey sandwiches and leftover onion dip. Today, thanks to Turkeyville U.S.A., you can feast on buttered turkey sandwiches any time you want. Or turkey salad sandwiches. Or turkey club sandwiches. Or barbequed turkey. Or turkey with noodles. Or turkey soup. Or turkey tacos. Or turkey . . . well, you get the idea.

The first egg in the Turkeyville U.S.A. story was laid in the early 1960s. Grandpa Wayne and Grandma Marjorie Cornwell had been raising turkeys on their farm for two decades, but then they started selling sandwiches at the Calhoun County Fair. They were so popular the Cornwells decided to open a one-room restaurant. Before long, the couple was gobbling up more land for their operation, adding an ice cream parlor (famous for Turkey Trax—peanut butter ice cream with chocolate chips and Reese's peanut butter cups), a bakery, an enormous gift shop, and a dinner theater. Today, loyal customers devour the equivalent of 15,000 30-pound turkeys a year.

And there's more! Outside you'll find a miniature railroad. Almost a mile of ⅛-scale track winds through the Camp Turkeyville RV Resort, through tunnels and over trestles, before returning to the Hawkins Junction Station. The live steam, diesel, and electric engines are maintained by the Mid-Michigan Railroad Club (http://midmichrr.com); rides are free, but donations are greatly appreciated. Come during one of Turkeyville U.S.A.'s many events—flea markets, craft shows, Civil War reenactments, Plow Days, BBQ cook-offs, or Corvette Celebrations—and stay a while.

18935 15½ Mile Rd., Marshall, MI 49068

Phone: (800) 228-4315 or (269) 781-4293

Hours: Restaurant, daily 11 AM–8 PM; Train, May–October, check website

Cost: Free; Turkey sandwiches, $3.99 and up

Website: www.turkeyville.com

Directions: West of I-69 at the Turkeyville Rd./N-Drive exit.

HAM IT UP

If turkey isn't your thing, perhaps a ham will do. The spiral-sliced ham was invented in Detroit by Harry J. Hoenselaar, who patented the process in 1949. In 1957 he opened the first **HoneyBaked Ham Co.** store in Detroit, though its corporate offices are now located in Ohio (www.honeybaked.com).

Southfield
Michigan's First Mall

After eating your fill of cold Thanksgiving turkey, it's off to the mall to shop, shop, shop! Why not go to Michigan's first mall: Northland Center?

Though strip malls began appearing in the 1920s as more Americans bought cars, it wasn't until after World War II that the first modern suburban malls went up. Financed by Hudson's and designed by Victor Guen, crews broke ground on Northland Center in 1952. Doors finally opened to the public on March 22, 1954. A four-story Hudson's sat at the center of the complex, surrounded by smaller retailers. Only semi-enclosed, it had a post office, landscaping with fountains and sculptures, and, if you ran out of gas, a helpful parking lot crew would give you a free gallon to get you home.

Northland Center was to be the first of four malls in the Detroit suburbs, followed by Eastland Center in Harper Woods (1957), Westland Center in Westland (1965), and Southland Center in Taylor (1970). Most were expanded and enclosed in the 1970s, and today look nothing like their original configurations. And you can forget the free gas.

Northland Center, 21500 Northwestern Hwy., Southfield, MI 48075
Phone: (248) 569-6272
Hours: Monday–Saturday 10 AM–9 PM, Sunday noon–5 PM
Cost: Free
Website: www.shopatnorthland.com
Directions: At the intersection of Northwestern Hwy./John C. Lodge Fwy. and Greenfield Rd.

Midland
Charles W. Howard Santa Claus School

If you venture into any mall during the holiday season, you'll no doubt run into a long line of frazzled parents and mostly excited (but sometimes terrified) children waiting to see the fat guy in red, the bringer of the goodies, Santa H. Claus. And there's a good possibility this jolly old elf was trained at the Charles W. Howard Santa Claus School in Midland.

Wait . . . *trained*? Don't worry, wide-eyed readers, these are just "helper Santas"—the *real* Santa is still at the North Pole.

This Kris Kringle college was established in 1937 by Charles W. Howard of Albion, New York. From 1948 to 1965, Howard rode the sleigh every year in the Macy's Thanksgiving Day Parade. As a Santa expert, he felt the overall quality of department store Santas could be improved, and developed a curriculum for St. Nicholas wannabes.

The school moved to Michigan in 1984, where today it is run by "Dean" Thomas Valent. Classes cover topics such as clothing and makeup, ho-ho-ho-ing, Santa sign language, Christmas history and traditions, live reindeer habits, and "Practice Santa Flight Lessons." They are all conducted at the recently refurbished and very merry Santa Claus House in downtown Midland. Eleven months of the year it looks like a simple cottage, but in December, when it is open to the kiddies, it's decked out like a North Pole track home.

Contact: 2408 Pinehurst Ct., Midland, MI 48640

Phone: (989) 631-0587

Hours: Courses held in October; check website

Cost: Three-day course, $425; Mr. & Mrs. Claus combo, $835

Website: www.santaclausschool.com

Santa Claus House, 379 W. Main St., Midland, MI 48640

Phone: (989) 839-9661

Hours: First Tuesday after Thanksgiving–December 23; check website for times

Cost: Free

Website: www.midlandfoundation.org/santa-house

Directions: On the southern corner of Main St. and Jerome St. (M-20).

Christmas
Christmas Town

If a single Santa House leaves you wanting more, head up to the UP where an entire town is named for the holiday. The town of Christmas was incorporated in 1939, the same year Julius Thorson opened an ornament factory here. Unfortunately, that business burned down a year later and was never rebuilt. Still, the town's name remained, as did streets like Tinsel Drive, Reindeer Run, Sleigh Way, Mistletoe Lane, and Scrooge's Alley.

In the 1960s Francis Mercer opened Santa's Workshop, which is more of a gift shop than an elf-filled factory. Anyone walking in will *feel* like an elf, however, because of the 35-foot Santa sign looming over the front entrance. Behind the building you'll also find a concrete snowman and two plywood cartoon cutouts of nursery rhymes. The first is of the old

Kris Kringlezilla.

woman in the shoe; you can pretend to be an unruly child hanging out of the front door at the heel. The second is of Peter, Peter, pumpkin eater who sits smirking as his wife stares out from her pumpkin prison. Windows are cut out so you can pose in solidarity with her, a prisoner of a sexist patriarchy.

Counting the package-shaped sign in front of the Christmas Motel (E7621 W. M-28, (906) 387-7100, www.christmasmotel.net), that's about all there is to see of a yuletide nature in Christmas. These days the residents seem more interested in drawing suckers to the town's Kewadin Casino. The only jingling you'll hear here are the ding-a-lings of hundreds of slot machines.

Santa's Workshop, E8035 St. Nicholas Ave., Christmas, MI 49862

Phone: (906) 387-2929

Hours: May–December, Monday–Friday 9:30 AM–9 PM, Sunday noon–5 PM

Cost: Free

Website: www.santas-workshop-christmas.com

Directions: On Rte. 28, two blocks east of the Kewadin Casinos.

OTHER CHRISTMASY TOWNS

Other Michigan communities also have Christmasy sounding names:

Antlers	Green	St. Nicholas
Balsam	Holly	Snow
Evergreen Acres	North Star	Spruce
Frost	Piney Woods	Star

Frankenmuth
Bronner's CHRISTmas Wonderland

Far larger than the town of Christmas is the 27-acre yuletide megastore known as Bronner's CHRISTmas Wonderland in Frankenmuth. The closer you get to this Bavarian-themed burg, the more Santa-themed billboards you'll see. And when you get closer . . . the *lights*! Bronner's mall-sized parking lot is festooned with hundreds—*hundreds*—of illuminated fiberglass and blow-mold figures, from snowmen to wise men to gingerbread men, along with jumbo tree ornaments, candy canes, toy soldiers, and oversized twinkling snowflakes festooning the traffic islands, trees, lawns, flower beds, hills, and ditches. Bronner's says its daily electric bill tops $1,250.

And wait until you step inside! Every square inch of this barnlike structure—the World's Largest Christmas Store—is filled with themed artificial trees, stockings, nativity scenes, strings of lights, and animated elves and reindeer. Step into the Nutcracker Suite, where thousands of models, big and small, stand wide-eyed, mouths agape, poised to crack your nuts. Or visit the Hummel Room where Bronner's has every doughy-faced statuette ever created. Christmas villages? They fill a whole wing of the complex. And if you're looking for a unique ornament, you'll have more than 6,000 different styles to choose from. Forget the angels, snowmen, and colored balls—why not decorate your tree with glittery glass replicas of sushi rolls, left-handed electric guitars, Egyptian pyramids, or Bud Light six-packs?

Lest you think this is all about the merchandise, expect to find a Christian tract inserted into your shopping bag—everyone gets one. And in 1992 Bronner's built an exact replica of the *Silent Night* Memorial Chapel from Oberndorf, Austria, the church where the iconic song was first performed in 1818. It's their way of keeping Christ in CHRISTmas, in case you missed their not-too-subtle over-CAPITALIZED name.

25 Christmas Ln., PO Box 176, Frankenmuth, MI 48734

Phone: (800) ALL-YEAR or (989) 652-9931

Hours: June–December, Monday–Saturday 9 AM–9 PM, Sunday noon–7 PM; January–May,
    Monday–Thursday & Saturday, 9 AM–5:30 PM, Friday 9 AM–9 PM, Sunday noon–5:30 PM

Cost: Free

Website: www.bronners.com

Directions: East of Main St./Gera Rd. (M-83) north of Townline Rd.

Vassar

Big Santa

Now that you've got your presents and ornaments, you need a tree. There are many Christmas tree farms in Michigan—it's a major agricultural industry—but one farm stands out for its 16-foot supersized Santa welcoming you to the place. What's more, it's not very far from Bronner's, so you can make a day of it. Cut your own tree or select one from Pennywick's precut yard. Come on the weekend between Thanksgiving and December 24 and

A jolly big elf.

the little ones can visit with a flesh-and-blood Santa, though he's regular sized.

Pennywick Tree Farm, 3295 W. Sanilac Rd., Vassar, MI 48768
Phone: (989) 823-3306
Hours: Always visible
Cost: Free
Website: www.facebook.com/pages/Pennywick-Tree-Farm/280616318642175
Directions: West of Washburn Rd. on Rte. M-46 (Sanilac Rd.).

Berrien Springs
Christmas Pickle Capital of the World

Do you hang a Christmas pickle on your tree? According to tradition, a single pickle is hung on the tree and the child who finds it gets a special present.

But do you know how this weird practice originated? Back in medieval Europe, two Spanish brothers were heading home for the holidays and stopped at a lonely inn. The innkeeper murdered the two boys, stole their belongings, and stuffed their bodies into a pickle barrel. Yet as luck would have it, St. Nicholas stopped by the same establishment that evening, struck the barrel with his mighty staff, and both kids came back to life—a Christmas pickle miracle! (Another tale of its origin goes back to a Civil War POW who begs for a pickle on his deathbed, then is revived by the pickle. Not very Christmasy. Or believable.)

Today, the pickle-producing community of Berrien Springs honors this quirky tradition with a Christmas Pickle Festival in December. It starts with a parade led by the Grand Dillmeister who hands out gherkins to good little boys and girls. St. Pickolous rides along in a sleigh pulled by Rudolph the Red-Nosed Pickle.

All Over Town, Berrien Springs, MI 49103
Phone: (269) 471-1202
Hours: First Sunday in December
Cost: Free
Directions: Just east of US Rte. 31 on Snow Rd.

YES, VIRGINIA, THERE IS A POTTERVILLE

If George Bailey had never been born and old man Potter ruled Bedford Falls, he might have come up with a place like Potterville . . . Michigan. Back in 2002, 35 tank cars on a Canadian National train derailed as they passed the police station (319 N. Nelson St.); the town was evacuated for five days because of the propane spill. Back in 1994, Potterville was also the epicenter for a 3.4 magnitude earthquake, just two months after 22 residents were injured in Fox Park by a single lightning bolt. And did you hear about the pallet factory fire of 2008? It burned for four *days*. Two years later, another fire leveled a good part of downtown. About the only thing still left to attract holiday visitors is its famous eatery: Joe's Gizzard City (see page 183).

Muskegon
The Singing Christmas Tree

Let's face it: as nice as your tree is, at most it's eight or nine feet tall, and it sure doesn't sing. For that you have to go to Muskegon, home of the Singing Christmas Tree since 1985. Its conical frame stands 67 feet tall, is wrapped in a mile of greenery, and is decorated with 25,000 lights and 240 singing teenagers. That's right, members of the Mona Shores Choir Association, a high school choir, are the baubles in the branches.

You have to get your tickets early if you want to attend one of the four performances of this popular local tradition. Before the show starts, it takes about six to eight minutes to load the kids into the interior risers. Hundreds more gather around the base. The spot at the very peak is reserved for a singer who has had a personal challenge in the previous year, like climbing a 67-foot scaffold in the dark.

Performing on the tree is not always a merry affair—with all the lights and sweaty bodies it can get hot, and choir members have been known to pass out. Luckily there are parent volunteers, known as Tree Monkeys, hiding below the boughs to drag the fallen to safety. The Christmas show must go on!

Frauenthal Center for the Performing Arts, 425 W. Western Ave., Muskegon, MI 49440

Phone: (231) 722-2890

Hours: Check website for schedule

Cost: Check website

Website: http://frauenthal.org/

Directions: One block southeast of Shoreline Dr. (Rte. 31), between Third and Fourth Sts.

Gaylord
Gaylord Ice Tree

The kids in the Singing Christmas Tree wouldn't have to worry about heat exhaustion if they performed on the Gaylord Ice Tree. Then again, they could just as easily injure themselves by slipping off and cracking their skulls.

Every winter for more than 70 years, a tower of metal pipes in front of the Gaylord City County Building has (purposely) spewed water mist into the air, and as it falls it forms a 20-foot-tall, 250-ton iceberg. A sign by the tree describes it as

By May, the Ice Tree is more like an Ice Shrub.

CENTRAL LOWER NORTHERN MICHIGAN'S LARGEST ICE TREE, but as far as I've determined, it's Michigan's *only* ice tree—northern, southern, upper, lower, eastern, western, or anywhere in between.

The ultimate size and shape of the Ice Tree, as well as the number of months it's around, depends on the weather; the photo above was taken in *May*. If you can't make it to see the tree in person, there's always the city's webcam (www.otsegocountymi.gov/web-cam-162/).

Gaylord City County Building, 225 W. Main St., Gaylord, MI 49735

Phone: (989) 731-7520

Hours: Cold months

Cost: Free

Website: www.gaylordmichigan.net/ice-tree--22/

Directions: On M-32 (Main St.) at Chicago Ave. six blocks east of I-75.

Mason
Santa's Giant Mailbox

Omigosh, omigosh, omigosh . . . with all this shopping and decorating and singing, you've forgotten to get your Christmas wish list in the mail to Santa! If you've been more nice than naughty, be sure to tell him what you want because, by gum, You've Got It Coming!

There's no better way to send your letter than to mail it from the Ingham County Courthouse lawn, where every year the city erects an enormous Santa's Mailbox, along with a fiberglass Santa. You have to climb a flight of nine stairs to get to the top—still not bad considering what that 1,700-year-old St. Nick has to go through to bring you, and everyone else, your mountains of gifts.

Ingham County Courthouse, 315 S. Jefferson St., Mason, MI 48854

No phone

Hours: Thanksgiving–Christmas Eve

Cost: Free

Website: www.mason.mi.us

Directions: At the intersection of Ash (M-36) and Jefferson Sts.

Plymouth
"You'll Shoot Your Eye Out"

And what did you ask Santa to bring you for Christmas? An Official Red Ryder Carbine-Action Two-Hundred-Shot Range Model Air Rifle? C'mon, kid, everyone knows, *You'll shoot your eye out!*

The classic Daisy Air Rifle, the only thing Ralphie Parker ever wanted for Christmas, was originally a giveaway from Michigan's Plymouth Iron Windmill Company. Starting in 1886, farmers received an air-pump BB gun with the purchase of a windmill; the guns were strong enough to kill birds that landed on the towers, yet not powerful enough to damage the metalwork. The rifle got its popular name from the company's general manager, Lewis Cass Hough, who proclaimed, "It's a daisy!" on firing a new model.

Soon, with fewer and fewer sales for bullet-ridden parts, yet more and more people asking for the guns, Plymouth dumped the windmill business and later adopted the Daisy name.

Daisy left Plymouth for Rogers, Arkansas, in 1958, but folks here have never forgotten the company. The local history museum has a room devoted to early patents, models, and advertisements. It also has an impressive Abraham Lincoln collection, including the 16th president's personal dictionary, a scrap of bloody fabric from Ford's Theatre, and a lock of hair cut from his head wound by Surgeon General Joseph K. Barnes.

Plymouth Historical Museum, 155 S. Main St., Plymouth, MI 48170
Phone: (734) 455-8940
Hours: Wednesday & Friday–Sunday 1–4 PM
Cost: Adults $5, Kids (6–17) $2
Website: www.plymouthhistory.org
Directions: Three blocks north of Ann Arbor Tr. in downtown Plymouth.

Westland
Wayne County Lightfest

Since Santa hasn't yet brought you an Official Red Ryder Carbine-Action Two-Hundred-Shot Range Model Air Rifle, you still have two eyeballs to appreciate all the beautiful holiday decorations. Why not get one last look at the longest drive-thru Christmas light display in the Midwest, the Wayne County Lightfest?

This popular annual display starts one week before Thanksgiving and runs through New Years Eve. On your 4½-mile drive you'll see animated yuletide scenes, tunnels of flashing bulbs, decked-out buildings, and bright outlines of crèches, candles, American flags, toy soldiers, dinosaurs, dragons, and at least one menorah.

7651 Merriman Rd., Westland, MI 48185
Phone: (734) 261-1990

Hours: Mid-November–December, 7–10 PM

Cost: $5/car

Website: www.co.wayne.mi.us/events/2731.htm

Directions: Enter off Merriman Rd. between Warren Rd. and Ann Arbor Tr.

'TIS THE SEASON

The Wayne County Lightfest isn't the only holiday festival in the state. Here are a few more annual events to help you ring in the season.

Dutch Winterfest

Holland Convention & Visitors Bureau, 78 E. Eighth St., Holland, (800) 506-1299 or (616) 394-0000, www.holland.org/winterfest/

As with everything else in this town, Holland's Christmas celebration is Dutch themed. Santa Claus in a sleigh pulled by reindeer? Nope. Instead, Sinterklaas rides into Centennial Park on a white horse, led by his "helper" Zwarte Piet, during the town's Parade of Lights. According to tradition, Zwarte Piet—Dutch for Black Pete—was a Moorish slave freed by Sinterklaas who then devoted his life to serving the bearded fellow . . . a sort of modified slavery. Thankfully, Zwarte Piet is not played in blackface here, as he often is at celebrations in the Netherlands. Dutch Winterfest also includes an open-air Kerstmarkt and an ice-sculpting competition.

Dickens Festival

Village of Holly, Holly, (248) 215-7099, www.hollychamber.com/events/Holly-Dickens-Festival-Days

Unless you're an unrepentant Scrooge, Holly's Dickens Festival is sure to get you in the spirit. Local volunteers wander the streets in Victorian garb, greeting you with cockney accents and singing century-old carols. Smell the aroma of roasted chestnuts as you go a-wassailing through the quaint downtown. Dickens fans can also enjoy a local production of *A Christmas Carol* put on by the Blue Heron Theatre Company (www.blueherontheatre.org).

The Big, Bright Light Show

Main St., Rochester, (248) 656-0060, www.downtownrochestermi.com /events/big-bright-light-show/

If the manger in Bethlehem were decked out like the main drag in Rochester, the wise men wouldn't have needed a star to guide them—the 1.5 million lights would have done the trick. Every holiday season the retailers in this Detroit suburb cover their businesses in lights as thick as paint. Each building along Main Street from the South Bridge to Romeo Road, and Fourth Street from Walnut to Water, gets a unique color so that you can tell them apart.

Elk Viewing Sleigh Ride Dinner

Thunder Bay Resort, 27800 M-32, Hillman, (800) 729-9375, www.thunderbayresort.com

This 45-minute horse-drawn sleigh ride (a wheeled carriage, actually) will take you over the Thunder Bay River and through the Northwoods to view newborn elk calves on the way to a "cabin," where you will enjoy a wine tasting and a five-course gourmet dinner. All liquored up, its time to snuggle for the 45-minute trip back. The sleigh ride is only offered March through May, after the elk have given birth, but many theologians claim Jesus was born in the spring anyway.

Winter Carnival

1400 Townsend Dr., Houghton, (906) 487-1885, www.mtu.edu/carnival/

Another post-Christmas wintery celebration not to be missed is held in early February on the campus of Michigan Tech. Since

1922, students have competed in curling, broomball, ice fishing, and human dogsled races, but it is the snow sculptures that bring out the crowds. Dorms, sororities, fraternities, and campus departments use the region's most prevalent natural resource to carve elaborate creations and win valuable prizes. Each year's snow-sculpting theme is unique, such as 2013's "Heroes and Villains Find Their Powers in These Frozen Winter Hours."

Owosso

The Polar Express Train

The big day is getting even closer! Maybe you want to confirm that Santa got the list you mailed. *How do you get to the real North Pole?* you wonder. Any kid will tell you, "Aboard the *Polar Express*." Author and illustrator Chris Van Allsburg (www.chrisvanallsburg.com) wrote about the train in his 1986 picture book of the same name. In it, a young Allsburg rides the train to Santa's Workshop and receives the first gift of Christmas, a shiny jingle bell from the sleigh.

When the book was made into a CGI movie in 2004, the filmmakers needed authentic steam locomotive sounds, so they came to Owosso and the Steam Railroading Institute. This working museum had restored the Pere Marquette No. 1225 engine in 1988, and it could chug and hiss and toot all they needed.

The train is also rechristened the *North Pole Express* each December and takes riders on a four-hour excursion to see Santa at his house at the Saginaw County Fairgrounds. You have to wonder how much fake snow they need to pile up to pull that one off.

Steam Railroading Institute, 405 S. Washington St., PO Box 665, Owosso, MI 48867

Phone: (989) 725-9464

Hours: June–August, Wednesday–Sunday 10 AM–4 PM; September–May, Friday–Sunday 10 AM–4 PM

Cost: Museum, $5/person; North Pole Express, $50–70/person

Website: http://michigansteamtrain.com/north-pole-express/

Directions: On Rte. M-71 (Washington St.), just south of the river.

Royal Oak
Arctic Ring of Life

For all you geography-obsessed killjoys who claim that a train couldn't possibly make it to the North Pole because of, you know, *the Arctic Ocean*, perhaps you should go to the Detroit Zoo instead. The park's Arctic Ring of Life habitat is North America's largest polar bear exhibit. Visitors walk through a 70-foot clear underwater tunnel as bears swim overhead, licking their chops. These carnivorous creatures share the tank with a pod of harbor seals, though they are all kept safely apart by a clear barrier—no "survival of the fittest" show is included in your ticket. The tunnel dumps out in the chilly ice cave where you'll find even more animals, including snowy owls, arctic foxes, and Harp seals.

8450 W. 10 Mile Rd., Royal Oak, MI 48067

Phone: (248) 541-5717

Hours: April–August, daily 9 AM–5 PM; September–October, daily 10 AM–5 PM; November–March daily 10 AM–4 PM

Cost: Adults $14, Seniors (62+) $10, Kids (2–14) $10

Website: www.detroitzoo.org

Directions: North of I-696, west of Woodward Ave.

Muskegon
Birthplace of Snowboarding

Ah, finally . . . Christmas Day! Mom and dad have been hitting the eggnog and grandpa's passed out on the couch. It's a great day for lounging and relaxing, or playing in the boxes your gifts came in.

But not everyone wants to be unproductive on the 25th. Back in 1965, on Christmas Day, Muskegon parent Sherman Poppen invented the snowboard to get his daughters out of the house. Poppen took two old wooden skis and screwed them together, side-by-side, to be used as a sort of surfboard on the snow-covered dunes in the area. His wife, Nancy, came up with a name for the contraption: the Snurfer.

The Brunswick Corporation licensed the idea from Poppen a year later, and marketed it under its silly name until the 1980s. By then people were calling them snowboards. One of the few places you still see them

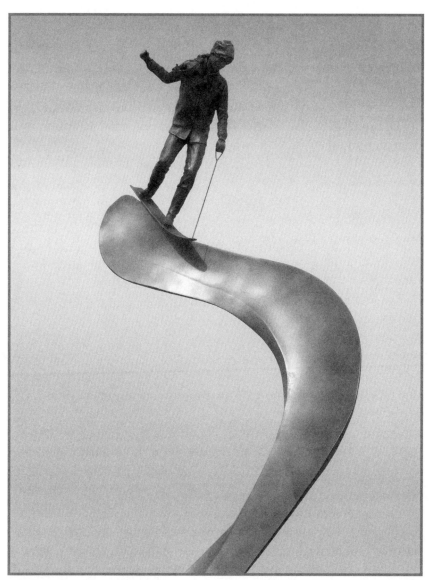

Wendy Poppen snurfs into history.

called Snurfers is in Muskegon where a sculpture has been erected in the Poppens' honor. *The Turning Point* by Jason Dreweck and Teresa Hansen shows a 10-year-old Wendy Poppen taking her first trip down a slope, a long silver ribbon of snow ahead of her. Another Snurfer, a modern adult man, is at the bottom. A nearby plaque says, "A special thanks to you Sun, Wind, and Rain." But oddly, Snow gets no mention.

477 W. Western Ave., Muskegon, MI 49440

No phone

Hours: Always visible

Cost: Free

Directions: One block east of Shoreline Dr. (Rte. 31), between Fourth and Fifth Sts.

EPILOGUE

*L*ast summer, while writing this book, I came across a hidden gem called Totem Village west of St. Ignace. At first, it looked like a typical tourist trading post—birch bark wallpaper, endless racks of T-shirts, and shelves filled with Indian dolls, rubber tomahawks, and dream catchers. I shelled out $5 to see the "museum." I entered a cluttered hallway past a diorama of a French trapper buying pelts from a pair of Indians, a cask of firewater on the table. Maps, bearskins, documents, and crude paintings of Native American life covered the walls—nothing all that remarkable. But then I came to a large, two-story shed at the end of the hall, my eyes adjusted to the dim light, and I rocked back on my heels at the sight before me.

Ten elaborate totems stood at the center of the cavernous room, some almost banging the ceiling, surrounded by a fence made of aspen branches. The ground was bare dirt covered in needles, soft to the step like a woodland floor. Around the perimeter were hand-carved, life-sized figures and scenes of Native Americans with tepees and canoes, all nestled in a forest of aromatic but long-dead junipers. Cutouts on some walls offered views into smaller illuminated dioramas of Ft. Mackinac, sweat lodges, logging camps, and Lake Michigan schooners. It was like stepping through a portal into the 1950s—no glossy educational signage or humidity-controlled display cases, just tons of Northwoods kitsch. I was in Yooper heaven.

Three months later I called Totem Village to confirm my notes, and asked the owner what the hours would be next season, when my book came out. "The museum is gone," she said. "It's being auctioned off in Ann Arbor in August."

Gone. Kaput. Sayonara. I'd say, *You had your chance*, but you didn't even have that. The same goes for Prehistoric Forest in the Irish Hills—

They don't make museums like this anymore.

its volcano now permanently dormant, its stucco dinosaurs as extinct at the real ones. The world's largest hairball, once found in the corridor of MSU's Anthony Hall, has been flushed away. Rosie's Diner in Rockford? Closed. The Weird Michigan Wax Museum in St. Ignace? Melted. And the world's largest stove at the Michigan State Fairgrounds? It burned up in 2011. Well, perhaps they shouldn't have made it out of wood.

The point I'm trying to make, if it isn't clear, is that should get out and see these weird sites while you still can, while they're still around, while gas is still under $5/gallon. They won't last forever.

Now—get moving!

ACKNOWLEDGMENTS

his book would not have been possible without the assistance, patience, and good humor of many individuals. My thanks go out to the following people for allowing me to interview them about their roadside attractions: Silvio Barile (Silvio's Italian-American Historical Artistic Museum), Ritch Branstrom (Adhoc Workshop), Karen Ann Brzys (Gitche Gumee Agate and History Museum), James Draper (Gerald R. Ford Museum), Harriet Fiorani (Iron County Historical Museum), Hillary Fisher (Blueberry Store), Gerald Ganske (Moran Iron Works), Tyree Guyton (The Heidelberg Project), Richard C. Hess (Waldenburg Heirloom Furniture), George Kutlenios (Holly Hotel), Tom Lakenen (Lakenenland), Kevin Milligan (Cairnscape), Ed Moody (Pumpkin Ed), Michael Moore, Tom Moran (Big Busts), Dean Oswald (Oswald's Bear Ranch), Julie Rinke (Doherty Hotel), Reb Roberts (Sanctuary Folk Art), Mike Schragg (US Postal Service Museum), Paul Spaniola (Paul's Pipe Museum), Bob Sutherland (Cherry Republic), Dmytro Szylak (Disneyland North), Thomas Valent (Charles W. Howard Santa Claus School), Janis Vollmer (Call of the Wild), and Jeremy Yagoda (Marvin's Marvelous Mechanical Museum).

To the anonymous and always informed tour guides I met at many Michigan museums, my sincere thanks, particularly those I met at the American Museum of Magic, the Amway World Headquarters and Welcome Center, the Bottle House, the Bug House, Curwood Castle, the Detroit Institute of Arts, the Dr. Beaumont Museum, the Fort de Buade Museum, the Fort St. Joseph Museum, the Great Lakes Shipwreck Historical Museum, Historic Adventist Village, the Holland Museum, the Iron Mountain Iron Mine, the Kelsey Museum of Archaeology, the Kimball House Museum, the Lenawee County Historical Museum, the Monroe County Historical Museum, the Motown Museum, the Museum Ship

Valley Camp, the Muskegon Museum of Art, the Music House Museum, Mystery Hill, the Mystery Spot, the Plymouth Historical Museum, the Shrine of the Pines, the Teenie Weenie Pickle Barrel Cottage, the Thomas Edison Depot Museum, and all the historic buildings at Greenfield Village.

For research assistance, I am indebted to librarians and tourist bureaus in the communities of Adrian, Ann Arbor, Atlanta, Bath, Battle Creek, Bay City, Benton Harbor, Berrien Springs, Cadillac, Calumet, Charlevoix, Chelsea, Chesaning, Clare, Coldwater, Colon, Croswell, Crystal Falls, Dearborn, Detroit, Elk Rapids, Flint, Frankenmuth, Garden City, Gaylord, Grand Haven, Grand Marais, Grand Rapids, Hamtramck, Hancock, Holland, Holly, Ironwood, Ishpeming, Jackson, Kalamazoo, Kaleva, Kalkaska, Lansing, Laurium, Manistee, Manistique, Marquette, Marshall, Mason, Midland, Mio, Montague, Muskegon, Niles, Norway, Oscoda, Ossineke, Owosso, Petoskey, Plymouth, Pontiac, Portage, Port Huron, Rochester, Saginaw, St. Ignace, St. Louis, Saugatuck, South Haven, Tawas City, Tecumseh, Traverse City, and Ypsilanti.

I met many friendly servers at strange and interesting restaurants around the state, including American Coney Island in Detroit, Andiamo Bloomfield Township in Bloomfield Hills, the Antlers Bar in Sault Ste. Marie, the Burger King in Kalamazoo, the Cadieux Café in Detroit, Chin's Chop Suey in Livonia, Cops & Doughnuts in Clare, the Corner Bar in Rockford, Crane's Pie Pantry Restaurant & Bakery in Fennville, the Dogpatch Restaurant in Munising, the Grand Hotel on Mackinac Island, the Hilltop Family Restaurant in L'Anse, the Holly Hotel in Holly, Jilbert Dairy in Marquette, Joe's Gizzard City in Potterville, the Keyhole Bar & Grill in Mackinaw City, Lafayette Coney Island in Detroit, Legs Inn in Cross Village, the Mio Pizza Shop in Mio, Railside Bar & Grill in Elmira, Robinette's Apple Haus & Winery in Grand Rapids, Screams Ice Creamatory in Hell, Sleder's Family Tavern in Traverse City, Stafford's Weathervane Restaurant in Charlevoix, Turkeyville U.S.A. in Marshall, Wimpy's Place in Lexington, and the World's Finest Frozen Custard in New Baltimore.

To Eugene Marceron and Dmytro Szylak, thank you both for being models. To my Michigan family and friends—Joey and Claudia, Zak, Samantha, Lee and Rob, Lisa, Scott, the Navins, and all the Wilkinses—I hope I did your state proud. Thank you Amelia Estrich and Jon Hahn for turning this manuscript into a book, and to my longtime editor Cynthia Sherry for championing the Oddball series for the last decade and a half. Finally, to Jim Frost, I wouldn't want to be on this strange journey with anyone else.

RECOMMENDED SOURCES

*I*f you'd like to learn more about the places and individuals in this book, the following are excellent sources.

Introduction

General Michigan Guides: *Off the Beaten Path Michigan, Tenth Edition* by Jim DuFresne (Globe Pequot, 2010); *Michigan Curiosities: Quirky Characters, Roadside Oddities & Other Offbeat Stuff, Second Edition* by Colleen Burcar and Gene Taylor (Globe Pequot, 2007); *Weird Michigan: Your Travel Guide to Michigan's Local Legends and Best Kept Secrets* by Linda S. Godfrey (Sterling, 2006); *Strange Michigan: More Wolverine Weirdness* by Linda S. Godfrey and Lisa A. Shiel (Trails Books, 2008); *Backroads and Byways of Michigan: Drives, Day Trips & Weekend Excursions* by Matt Forster (Countryman Press, 2009); *Uncle John's Bathroom Reader—Plunges into Michigan* by the Bathroom Readers' Hysterical Society (Portable Press, 2005); *Bathroom Book of Michigan Trivia: Weird, Wacky and Wild* by Brian Hudson and Andrew Fleming (Blue Bike Books, 2007); *It Happened in Michigan: Remarkable Events That Shaped History* by Colleen Burcar (Globe Pequot Press, 2011); *Ultimate Michigan Adventures: 98 One of a Kind Destinations & Diversions* by Gary W. Barfknecht (Friede Publications, 1994); *Awesome Almanac: Michigan* by Annette Newcomb and Jean F. Blashfield (B&B Publishing, 1993); *Michigan Trivia* by Ernie and Jill Couch (Rutledge Hill Press, 1995)

1. The Upper Peninsula

The Toledo War: *The Toledo War: The First Michigan–Ohio Rivalry* by Don Faber (University of Michigan Press, 2008)

Anatomy of a Murder: *Anatomy of a Murder* by Robert Traver (St. Martin's Griffin, 2005)

Italian Hall Stampede: *Death's Door: The Truth Behind Michigan's Largest Mass Murder* by Steve Lehto (Momentum Books, 2006)

Bishop Frederic Baraga: *Shepherd of the Wilderness* by Bernard J. Lambert (Franciscan Herald Press, 1974); *The Diary of Bishop Frederic Baraga: First Bishop of Marquette, Michigan* by Regis M. Walling and N. Daniel Rupp, eds. (Wayne State University Press, 2001)

George Gipp: *The Gipper: George Kipp, Knute Rockne, and the Dramatic Rise of Notre Dame Football* by Jack Cavanaugh (Skyhorse Publishing, 2010)

Dr. Beaumont: *Frontier Doctor: William Beaumont, America's First Great Medical Scientist* by Reginald Horsman (University of Missouri Press, 1996)

Grand Hotel: *Grand Hotel: Mackinac Island* by John McCabe (Wayne State University Press, 1987)

SS *Edmund Fitzgerald*: *29 Missing: The True and Tragic Story of the Disappearance of the SS* Edmund Fitzgerald by Andrew Kantar (Michigan State University Press, 1998); *Mighty Fitz: The Sinking of the Edmund Fitzgerald* by Michael Schumacher (University of Minnesota Press, 2012)

2. Northern Michigan

Music House Museum: *Music House Museum* by MHM (Music House Museum, 2001)

Shrine of the Pines: *Shrine of the Pines* by Marie Moore (Paul Bunyan Press, 1982)

King Jesse Strang: *Assassination of a King: The Life of James Jesse Strang* by Roger Van Noord (University of Michigan Press, 1997)

Mushroom Buildings: *Mushroom Houses of Charlevoix* by Mike Barton (Boulder Press, 2009)

Cross in the Woods: *The Cross in the Woods* by Adith Conroy, Mary Gilson, and Bro. Thom Smith (Cross in the Woods, Date unknown)

Mackinac Bridge: *Mackinac Bridge* by Robert Sweeney, Tim Burke, and Sara Gross (Penrod/Hiawatha, Date unknown); *Mackinac Bridge* by Mike Fornes (Arcadia, 2007)

Robert Wadlow: *Boy Giant: The Story of Robert Wadlow The World's Tallest Man* by Dan Brannan (Alton Museum of History and Art, 2003)

3. Western Michigan

House of David: *The House of David* by Christopher Siriano (Arcadia, 2007)

Gerald R. Ford: *Gerald R. Ford: The American Presidents Series: The 38th President, 1974–1977* by Douglas Brinkley (Times Books, 2007); *Gerald R. Ford: An Honorable Life* by James Cannon (University of Michigan Press, 2013)

Holland, Michigan: *Holland: The Tulip Town* by Randall P. Vande Water (Arcadia, 2002)

Buster Keaton: *Buster Keaton: Tempest in a Flat Hat* by Edward McPherson (Newmarket Press, 2007)

Jonathan Walker: *Jonathan Walker, the Man with the Branded Hand* by Alvin F. Oickle (Lorelli Slater, 1998)

USS *Silversides*: *The War Below: The Story of Three Submarines That Battled Japan* by James Scott (Simon & Schuster, 2013)

4. Central Michigan

Laura Smith Haviland: *A Woman's Life Work: Labors and Experiences* by Laura Smith Haviland (Forgotten Books, 2008)

US Peace Corps: *When the World Calls: The Inside Story of the Peace Corps and Its First Fifty Years* by Stanley Meisler (Beacon Press, 2011)

Bath School Bombing: *Bath Massacre: America's First School Bombing* by Arnie Berstein (University of Michigan Press, 2009)

Sojourner Truth: *Sojourner Truth: A Life, A Symbol* by Nell Irvin Painter (W. W. Norton, 1996); *Narrative of Sojourner Truth* by Sojourner Truth (Dover, 1997)

Wellville: *The Road to Wellville* by T. C. Boyle (Penguin, 1993); *The Great American Cereal Book: How Breakfast Got Its Crunch* by Martin Gitlin and Topher Ellis (Abrams Image, 2012)

"JIFFY" Mix: *"Jiffy": A Family Tradition, Mixing Business and Old-Fashioned Values* by Cynthia Furlong Reynolds (Chelsea Milling Company, 2008)

Magic Johnson: *My Life* by Earvin Magic Johnson with William Novak (Fawcett, 1993)

Republican Party: *Grand Old Party: A History of the Republicans* by Lewis Gould (Random House, 2003)

Malcolm X: *The Autobiography of Malcolm X* by Malcolm X and Alex Haley (Penguin, 2001); *Malcolm X: A Life of Reinvention* by Manning Marable (Penguin, 2011)

Moon Tree: *A Walking Tour of Capitol Square* by Michigan Capitol Committee (Capitol Tour Guide Services, 1994)

George Armstrong Custer: *Custer: The Controversial Life of George Armstrong Custer* by Jeffry D. Wert (Simon and Schuster, 1996)

Iggy Pop: *Iggy Pop: Open Up and Bleed* by Paul Trynka (Three Rivers, 2008); *The Stooges: The Authorized and Illustrated Story* by Robert Matheu (Abrams, 2009)

5. Eastern Michigan

Madonna: *Madonna: Like an Icon* by Lucy O'Brien (It Books, 2008)

Michael Moore: *Michael Moore: A Biography* by Emily Schultz (ECW Press, 2005); *Citizen Moore: The Life and Times of an American Iconoclast* by Roger Rapoport (RDR Books, 2007); *Here Comes Trouble: Stories from My Life* by Michael Moore (Grand Central Publishing, 2011)

Carry Nation: *Carry A. Nation: Retelling the Life* by Fran Grace (Indiana University Press, 2001)

Dr. Jack Kevorkian: *Prescription Medicide: The Goodness of Planned Death* by Dr. Jack Kevorkian (Prometheus Books, 1991)

Thomas Edison: *The Wizard of Menlo Park: How Thomas Alva Edison Invented the Modern World* by Randall E. Stross (Broadway Books, 2008)

Stevie Wonder: *Signed, Sealed, and Delivered: The Soulful Journey of Stevie Wonder* by Mark Ribowsky (Wiley, 2010)

6. Detroit and Suburbs

General Detroit: *The Detroit Almanac: 300 Years of Life in the Motor City* by Peter Gavrilovich and Bill McGraw, eds. (Detroit Free Press, 2000); *Hidden History of Detroit* by Amy Elliott Bragg (History Press, 2011); *Detroit: A Motor City History* by David Lee Poremba (Arcadia, 2001); *Art in Detroit Public Spaces, Third Edition* by Dennis Alan Nawrocki (Wayne State University Press, 2008)

Aretha Franklin: *Aretha Franklin: The Queen of Soul* by Mark Bego (Skyhorse, 2012)

Dinah Washington: *Queen: The Life and Music of Dinah Washington* by Nadine Cohodas (Pantheon, 2004)

Harry Houdini: *The Secret Life of Harry Houdini: The Making of America's First Superhero* by William Kalush and Larry Sloman (Atria, 2007); *The Life and Many Deaths of Harry Houdini* by Ruth Brandon (Random House, 1993)

Heidelberg Project: *Connecting the Dots: Tyree Guyton's Heidelberg Project* by Heidelberg Project (Wayne State University Press, 2007)

Underground Railroad: *The Underground Railroad in Michigan* by Carol E. Mull (McFarland, 2010)

Joe Louis: *Joe Louis: Hard Times Man* by Randy Roberts (Yale University Press, 2012)

Motown: *Motown: Music, Money, Sex, and Power* by Gerald Posner (Random House, 2002); *To Be Loved: The Music, The Magic, The Memories of Motown: An Autobiography* by Berry Gordy (Warner Books, 1994); *The Birth of the Detroit Sound: 1940–1964* by Marilyn Bond and S. R. Boland (Arcadia, 2002); *Motor City Rock and Roll: The 1960's and 1970's* by Bob Harris and John Douglas Peters (Arcadia, 2008); *Temptations* by Otis Williams with Patricia Romanowski (Cooper Square, 2002); *The Lost Supreme: The Life of Dreamgirl Florence Ballard* by Peter Benjaminson (Lawrence Hill Books, 2008)

Nancy Kerrigan Gets Clubbed: *Women on Ice: Feminist Responses to the Tonya Harding/ Nancy Kerrigan Spectacle* by Cynthia Baughman (Routledge, 1995)

Ossian and Gladys Sweet: *Arc of Justice: A Saga of Race, Civil Rights, and Murder in the Jazz Age* by Kevin Boyle (Picador, 2004)

Boy Governor Stevens T. Mason: *The Boy Governor: Stevens T. Mason and the Birth of Michigan Politics* by Don Faber (University of Michigan Press, 2012)

Jimmy Hoffa: *"I Heard You Paint Houses": Frank "The Irishman" Sheeran and the Inside Story of the Mafia, Teamsters, and the Final Ride of Jimmy Hoffa* by Charles Brandt (Steerforth Press, 2005); *The Death of Jimmy Hoffa* by Terence F. McShane (CreateSpace, 2011); *Digging for the Truth: The Final Resting Place of Jimmy Hoffa* by Jeffry Scott Hansen (Spectre Publishing, 2009)

Backyard Breeder Reactor: *The Radioactive Boy Scout: The True Story of a Boy and His Backyard Nuclear Reactor* by Ken Silverstein (Random House, 2004)

Fermi 1 Meltdown: *We Almost Lost Detroit* by John G. Fuller (Ballantine, 1976)

The Henry Ford Museum: *Henry's Attic: Some Fascinating Gifts to Henry Ford and His Museum* by Ford R. Bryan (Wayne State University Press, 1996)

Rosa Parks: *The Rebellious Life of Mrs. Rosa Parks* by Jeanne Theoharis (Beacon Press, 2013); *Rosa Parks: My Story* by Rosa Parks with Jim Haskins (Puffin, 1999)

Tiki Culture: *Tiki Road Trip: A Guide to Tiki Culture in North America, Second Ed.* By James Teitelbaum (Santa Monica Press, 2007)

Silvio's Italian-American Historical Artistic Museum: *Silvio's Galleria Delle Belle Arti and Historical Sculpture Garden* by Detroit Artist Market (Detroit Artists Market, 1992)

7. The Christmas Tour

Daisy Air Rifles: *Daisy Air Rifles!* by Cass S. Hough (Daisy Division, 1976)

City Index

Andiamo Italian Steakhouse),
258–260

Bridgeport
Junction Valley Railroad, 193–194

Brooklyn
St. Joseph Stations of the Cross
Shrine (St. Joseph's Church),
155–156

Buchanan
Bear Cave, 106

Burton
Michigan Voice's Former Headquarters, 203

Buttersville
Fr. Jacques Marquette Death Site, 39

Cadillac
Cadillac Sound Garden, 58

Calumet
George Gipp High School and Grave,
22
International Frisbee Hall of Fame
(The Colosseum), 5
Italian Hall Stampede, 5–6
Keweenaw National Historic Park
Headquarters, 5–6

Camden
Tristate Corner (Hillsdale County
Historical Society), 156–157

Carney
Rolling Cow (Carney Roundup
Rodeo), 164

Carsonville
Hi-Way Drive-In, 72

Caspian
Monigal Logging Miniatures (Iron
County Historical Museum), 6–7

Charlevoix
Beat-Up Bunyan on a Buckboard
(Smith's Little Acres), 87
Charlevoix Chamber of Commerce,
59
Cherry Republic Outpost, 69
Lodge at Charlevoix, 59
Mushroom Buildings, 59
Stafford's Weathervane Restaurant, 59
World's Largest Cherry Pie Oven
(Fire Department #2), 60–61

Cheboygan
Sea Shell City, 61–62

Chelsea
Birthplace of "JIFFY" Baking Mixes
(Chelsea Milling Company), 157

Chesaning
Chesaning Showboat Star Walk
(Chesaning Chamber of Commerce), 196

Chesterfield
Avenue of the Giants, 260–261
Big Boy, 260
Captain's Car Wash, 260
Riverbend Driving Range, 260

Christmas
Christmas Motel, 283
Christmas Town, 282
Santa's Workshop, 282–283

Clare
Big Chicken (Bob's Lounge), 171
Cops & Doughnuts, 62
Leprechauns at the Tap Room
(Doherty Hotel), 63–64

Clinton
Southern Michigan Railroad, 195

World's Largest Stormy Kromer Cap
(Stormy Kromer Mercantile), 15–16

Site Index